True Revival

True Revival

Reviving the Church in

Every Generation

Larry G. Johnson

Published by Anvil House Publishers, LLC Owasso, Oklahoma
www.anvilhousebooks.com

Printed in the United States of America.
Cover: Whitley Graphics

The website addresses recommended throughout this book are offered as a resource to you. Except for the articles posted by the author on culturewarrior.net, these websites are not intended in any way to be or imply an endorsement on the part of Larry G. Johnson or Anvil House Publishers, nor do we vouch for their content.

Scripture quotations marked CEB are taken from the Holy Bible, Common English Bible, CEB. Copyright © 2011 Common English Bible, Nashville, Tennessee. Scripture quotations marked KJV are taken from the Holy Bible, King James Version. Scripture quotations marked NIV are taken from the Holy Bible, New International Version, NIV. Copyright © 1973, 1978, 1984 Biblica, Inc. Used by permission of Zondervan. All rights reserved worldwide. www.zondervan.com.

ISBN: 978-0-9839716-6-5

Library of Congress Control Number: 2018911605

To my wonderful daughters-in-law:

Lindsey Farthing Johnson
(Curtis 12-20-2003)

Rachel Bruce Johnson
(Philip 12-22-2006)

Contents

Book I

True Revival – Reviving the Church in Every Generation

Contents

Book II

History of Evangelical Revivals and Awakenings

Preface

An evangelical revival or awakening is an outpouring of the Holy Spirit in the body of Christ (the Church) which brings about a *revival of New Testament Christianity*. The large number of evangelical churches that have departed from New Testament Christianity is not the reason for the disappearance of revival but just the opposite. The disappearance of true revival among evangelical denominations and their local churches is the reason for the precipitous spiritual decline of the power and influence of those churches and consequently the moral decline of the nation. Evangelicalism was born in revival and cannot be sustained without revival in every generation. It is a reciprocal relationship.

The revival of 1905 and its derivative, the Pentecostal revival that began in 1906, brought the last general awakening of America. However, revivals at the local level continued to be the most important factor in sustaining the passion for New Testament Christianity in evangelical churches into the 1970s and early 1980s. However, even during the bountiful evangelical harvest throughout the two decades following the end of World War II, there were hints of spiritual decay in the church and society that were evident to many discerning individuals. But their warnings fell on deaf ears and hardened hearts, and that autumnal season of evangelicalism foreshadowed the coming spiritual barrenness of a wintry landscape devoid of revival in the church. Following the 1970s and 1980s, revival as it had been known since the early 1700s was a thing of the past in the vast majority of evangelical churches.

The general theme of *True Revival* is that America is lost without the church and the church is lost without revival. The purpose of *True Revival* (Book I) is to call the leadership and laity of America's evangelical churches to teach, preach, and seek revival in their churches. *True Revival* is a companion book to the author's *Evangelical Winter – Restoring New Testament Christianity* that documents the decline of the evangelical church in the twentieth century and thereafter and exhorts the church to seek revival.

Knowledge and experience of special outpourings of the Holy Spirit (revival) among evangelical pastors and lay men and women have substantially disappeared over the last two generations. Many people speak of praying for and seeking revival, but it is a safe guess that most do not really know that for which what they are asking or wanting. Therefore, *True Revival* is intended to be instructive as to: the great need for revival of the evangelical church; the purpose, nature, and general characteristics of revival; the general outworking of revival;

manifestations; and Satan's efforts and schemes to defeat true revival through false teachers, false manifestations, and false revivals.

Book II is an instructive history of evangelical revivals and awakenings since the early 1700s and will give testimony of the importance of revivals throughout the history of the church. Revivals are hindered when the church has no knowledge or understanding of past revivals and history of the church.

The spiritual ancestors of the evangelicals were the Pilgrims and Puritans who left Europe to establish "a pure and stainless church" beginning with the arrival of the Pilgrims in 1720 and the Puritans a decade later. Historian Sherwood Eddy called those early years of colonial Puritanism "...the finest expression of spiritual life that Britain or America or Continental Europe had at that time."* After forty years this excellent spiritual life established by the once persecuted and hardy pioneers began to decline among the more lukewarm and worldly second and third generations. In the 1670s several pastors began preaching the need for revival among pastors and congregations. The church was stirred and revivals came as a result of prayer and the special outpourings of the Holy Spirit during the late 1600s and early 1700s. Out of these early stirrings came a renewal movement called *evangelicalism* that fundamentally changed many churches and denominations and helped birth the First Great Awakening that began in the 1720s. As evangelicalism flourished in the churches, so did revival flourish and sustain each succeeding generation of evangelicals down to the twentieth century.

---

* Sherwood Eddy, *The Kingdom of God and the American Dream*, (New York: Harper & Brothers Publishers, 1941), pp. 48, 56.

Acknowledgements

We haven't received the world's spirit but God's Spirit so that we can know the things given to us by God. These are the things we are talking about—not with words taught by human wisdom but with words taught by the Spirit—we are interpreting spiritual things to spiritual people. [1 Corinthians 2:12-13. CEB]

The Holy Spirit is the agent of empowerment for Christian service. Those followers of Christ who were gathered together on the day of Pentecost received this enduement of power promised by Christ by being baptized in the Holy Spirit. From that day forward, individual believers that are baptized in the Holy Spirit receive the power of God's Spirit and a personal boldness so they can serve His purposes, and the primary purpose is to effectively communicate the message of Jesus to others.

Christians who wish to communicate God's message either in the spoken or written word must seek the same anointing (an empowering and personal commissioning for His purposes). It is the same anointing that came upon Christ and the disciples in the first century in order to communicate spiritual things to spiritual people. That is what this author has attempted to do in *True Revival*. And whatever success has been achieved in communicating spiritual things, all glory belongs to the Holy Spirit who gives the anointing.

I must also express my deepest appreciation to my wife Sherryl for her untiring work of proof reading my books. Her comments, questions, and recommendations were substantially incorporated into the finished work. Without her continual encouragement and faithful efforts this book would not have been completed.

Special appreciation must be expressed to four men whose books laid the foundations upon which *True Revival* rests: Dr. Martin Lloyd-Jones (1899-1981), Dr. J. Edwin Orr (1912-1987), Dr. Thomas S. Kidd, and Mathew Backholer.

Books by Larry G. Johnson

Tar Creek – A History of the Quapaw Indians, the World's Largest Lead and Zinc Discovery, and the Tar Creek Superfund Site. ©2008
[Finalist - Oklahoma Book Award Non-fiction Book of the Year 2010 by the Oklahoma Center for the Book, the state affiliate of the Center for the Book in the Library of Congress.]

Ye shall be as gods – Humanism and Christianity – The Battle for Supremacy in the American Cultural Vision. ©2011 (Study Guide available: Student and Teacher Editions)

Evangelical Winter – Restoring New Testament Christianity. ©2016

Culture Wars – Dispatches from the Front. ©2016

True Revival – Reviving the Church in Every Generation. ©2018

Book I

True Revival

Reviving the Church in Every Generation

1

The Only Hope for the Church and America

Dr. Martyn Lloyd-Jones was one of the most gifted preachers of the twentieth century. In addition to pastoring Westminster Chapel in London for twenty-five years, he preached extensively in Europe and the United States. In 1959, Dr. Lloyd-Jones preached a series of sermons commemorating the one hundredth anniversary of the Welsh Revival of 1859 which had a powerful and profound impact on Wales, England, the United States, and other parts of the world as well. He did so because he saw the appalling condition of the church of his day and the need for revival as exceedingly urgent. These sermons eventually became a widely acclaimed book titled *Revival*.[1]

Dr. Jones saw a profound and perilous difference between the conditions of the church in 1959 England and America than that which existed one hundred years earlier. The problems in 1859 were not ones of general denial of the Christian truth but of apathy toward Christ and the church. Correction was a matter of awakening and arousing the church from their lethargy. The kinds of problems facing the church in 1959 were far deeper and more desperate. The moral and spiritual landscape had dramatically changed. Dr. Lloyd-Jones saw the modern-day problems as not just apathy but a "complete unawareness, even a denial of the spiritual altogether…the whole notion of the spiritual has gone. The very belief in God has virtually gone."[2]

It has been fifty-nine years since Lloyd-Jones preached those sermons at a time when the Christian nations and individual Christians were far more sensitive, agreeable, and desirous of a divine move of the Holy Spirit in their midst, that is, a quickening divine visitation. Now, the church is in far more serious condition than that of Dr. Lloyd-Jones' day. Many church leaders and their congregants are oblivious to their great spiritual sickness and disastrous departures from biblical truth, doctrines, and holy lifestyles. The church has become acclimatized to the rising tide of secularism and humanism that has inundated the Western world.

As the spirit of the world invaded the church over the last six decades, there has been a corresponding displacement of the irreplaceable power and presence of the Holy Spirit within the church. Without the centrality of the Holy Spirit, the efforts, actions, and programs of the church are merely a form of godliness but which deny the power thereof. Rev. Pierre Bynum has stated that because of the rebellion of the church, America is ripe for destruction.

> The Evangelical Movement in this country is characterized by an arrogance that is almost beyond belief. The neglect of prayer, the involvement in Philistine methodology, the moral evils, the doctrinal corruptions that characterize the Movement are sufficient to cause the people of Sodom to wonder at God's justice in destroying their city while sparing the United States.[3]

Pride has hardened the hearts of many in the American church just as the hearts of the Israelites were hardened except for a remnant. Paul described the condition of the hard-hearted Israelites. "…God gave them a spirit of stupor, eyes so that they could not see and ears so that they could not hear, to this very day." [Romans 11:8. NIV] Is this not an appropriate description of the cluelessness and naiveté of many of the leaders and laity in the American evangelical church of the twenty first century?

Conditions that demand revival of the church

Revival is the *only event* that can avert spiritual disaster for the church and turn a nation back to God. But God always sends men and women to warn of these approaching disasters. These modern-day watchmen on the wall are godly leaders and faithful intercessors who recognize the signs of the times and are calling attention to the woeful condition of both the church and the nation. They have sounded the alarm since the end of World War II to the present day. Here we quote just a few of these valiant watchmen and their warnings that span the last seven decades.

> …without revival in the church there is really no hope for the Western world at all.[4] [J. I. Packer summarizing the thrust of Dr. Martyn Lloyd-Jones in his series of sermons in 1959 marking the 100th anniversary of the Welsh revival of 1859.]

> Jesus Christ has today almost no authority at all among the groups that call themselves by His name. By these I

mean not the Roman Catholics nor the liberals, nor the various quasi-Christian cults. I do mean Protestant churches generally, and I include those that protest the loudest that they are in spiritual descent from our Lord and His apostles, namely the evangelicals.[5] [A. W. Tozer, *The Waning Authority of Christ in the Churches*, 1963.]

However much opinions of the realities involved may differ, no one can deny that there is widespread discussion of the decline of Western culture.[6] [Richard M. Weaver, *Visions of Order – The Cultural Crisis of Our Time*, 1964.]

Imperceptibly, through decades of gradual erosion, the meaning of life in the West has ceased to be seen as anything more lofty than the "pursuit of happiness... the West's own historical evolution has been such that today it too is experiencing a drying up of religious consciousness...Here again we witness the single outcome of a worldwide process, with East and West yielding the same results, and once again for the same reason: Men have forgotten God.[7] [Nobel laureate, Orthodox Christian author, and Russian dissident Alexandr Solzhenitsyn in his address, given when he received the Templeton Prize for Progress in Religion in May of 1983, in which he explained the process of alienation of the people of God and traditional Christian morality and beliefs through secularism and humanism.]

Truth demands confrontation. It must be loving confrontation, but there must be confrontation nevertheless...Here is the great evangelical disaster—the failure of the evangelical world to stand for truth as truth. There is only one word for this—namely *accommodation*: the evangelical church has accommodated to the world spirit of the age.[8] [Francis A. Schaeffer, *The Great Evangelical Disaster*, 1984.] [emphasis in original]

5

Conformity to the spirit of the times appears to characterize the clergy as well as the laity...religion is declining because those identified with it do not actually believe in it...It is difficult to say that religion even exists if it keeps giving up its tenets to appease its members and critics...The first question, then, is why belief evaporated, why the West has become so rapidly secularized.[9] [Robert H. Bork, *Slouching Toward Gomorrah*, 1996.]

After two hundred years of earnest dedication to reinventing the faith and the church and to being more relevant in the world, we are confronted by an embarrassing fact: Never have Christians pursued relevance more strenuously; never have Christians been more irrelevant.[10] [Os Guinness, *Prophetic Untimeliness*, 2003.]

Western civilization is over. Everybody knows it...Following centuries of pride, schism, compromise, synthesis with humanism, and general hard-heartedness, God may be withdrawing His grace from the Western nations—at least for the time being. Nevertheless, there is always mercy for those who seek and those who are humbled before the almighty God. (Romans 11:20).[11] [Kevin Swanson, *Apostate – The Men who Destroyed the Christian West*, 2013.]

Rebellion, decline, and renewal of God's people in the Bible

The pattern of sin and falling away from God followed by repentance, revival, and restoration of His people is a recurrent theme in the history of God's dealings with the Israelites. In the Old Testament there were at least twelve instances of revival,[12] and seven of these cycles are found in the first sixteen chapters of Judges. Preceding each of these revivals there were at least four common elements present:

- A spiritual decline among God's people.
- A righteous judgement from God – While varying from revival to revival, God's judgement led to prayer, brokenness, repentance, and a desperate seeking of God's

face. Sometimes God's judgement led to the deaths of the wicked.

- The raising up of an immensely burdened leader or leaders who had a heavy burden of the moral and spiritual needs of God's people and the nation.
- Extraordinary actions were taken, the most common of which was a call for a Solemn Assembly of the people who humbled themselves, sought the Lord, wept, fasted, mourned, prayed, confessed and repented of their individual and national sins, and who committed themselves to leading a godly life and separation from all unrighteousness of the nations.[13]

Revival – The only hope for the church and America

Revivals have been the sustaining lifeblood of the Protestant evangelical churches since they emerged just prior to and during America's First Great Awakening in the early 1700s. The quest for revival was discarded by the liberal churches more than one hundred years ago, and revival most certainly was never sought after or tolerated in the Roman Catholic Church or Eastern Orthodox churches. Nevertheless, revivals remained the central source of renewal and power of evangelical churches through the early 1960s and for some churches into the 1980s.

Beginning in the 1960s, the leadership in evangelical churches, seminaries, and other Christian organizations increasingly appear to have ignored the lessons of the Israelites' rebellion, decline, and renewal in the Old Testament and have relegated revival to the dusty and forgotten shelves of church history. America's pulpits became noticeably silent on matters of revival, and revivals virtually disappeared from the evangelical landscape along with the itinerant evangelists that held one and two-week revival meetings (longer if the Holy Spirit was moving upon the hearts and lives of those attending). As a result many pastors and most of the laity under the age of fifty have little remembrance of revival meetings or have never experienced an extraordinary powerful outpouring of the Holy Spirit in a local church.

Revival – Two opinions

One of the reasons for the absence of revivals is that they are controversial. Revivals are a supernatural work of the Spirit of God, and this supernatural aspect instills fear in the hearts of many Christians. Some claim revivals are "of the devil" or a form of mass hysteria. Others fear the supernatural manifestations of revival. Still others are opposed to revivals because they fear loss of control over church life. That occurs because revivals are a supernatural work of the Holy Spirit and cannot be controlled or directed by men. Revivals always challenge the status quo, upset the comfortable forms of godliness, and shine the light of God's Word into the dark corners of the church where the spirit of the world often resides.

Others dismiss talk of revival and revival meetings as not being relevant to the needs of the church or compatible with the popular methods and techniques of doing church in these modern times. For most American evangelical pastors, revival is passé, out-of-date, archaic, unfashionable, obsolete, and an inconvenience in our fast-paced modern lives. It would be safe to say that the vast majority of evangelical churches haven't sought revival or held a revival meeting in a quarter of a century. Revivals have been replaced by new ways of doing church. We are told that the modern Christian does not have the patience, time, or inclination to attend revival meetings. As previously stated, the subject of revival is missing from the preaching of most evangelical pastors in America. The focus has switched from revival to building the church through Church Growth methods and techniques that are seeker-friendly.

But there is another group. They are the contrite and lowly in spirit. It is to them that God said, "I live in a high and holy place, but also with him who is contrite and lowly in spirit, to *revive* the spirit of the lowly and to *revive* the heart of the contrite." [Isaiah 57:15. NIV] [emphasis added] These Christians are in great sorrow as a result of the vapid fare that now passes for Christianity in many churches. They are distraught by the casualness and carelessness with which many Christians approach church life and the things of God. They are crushed by the reality of a spiritually bankrupted nation that is being sucked into the vortex of a moral cesspool that threatens to engulf their children, friends, neighbors, and co-workers. They are the spiritually hungry and know that God has more for them than what they are receiving from the great majority of evangelical churches today. They want more than just programs, entertainment, activities, and playing church. They hunger for more of God—a life-changing, soul-drenching deluge of the manifest presence of God. What they seek is God's promise of revival!

———

The purpose of Book I is to call the leadership of America's evangelical churches to teach, preach, and seek revival in their churches. Lay men and women are called to pray unceasingly for a divine manifestation of God's presence in their midst. Given the significant ignorance of revivals and matters pertaining thereto among both pastors and the laity, many aspects of revival will be examined and considered in this book. These include:

- Need for revival
- Meaning of revival
- Purposes of revival
- Prerequisites for revival
- Characteristics and happenings in revival
- Hindrances to revival
- False revival
- Seeking revival

In Book II a history of evangelical revivals and awakenings since the early 1700s is presented.

It has been over one hundred years since the last significant, widespread revival of the American evangelical church followed by a general moral and spiritual awakening in America. The condition of the Western church is vastly more spiritually barren and destitute than any time since immediately before the Reformation. As a consequence, a large part of the American evangelical church is sick, and without a course correction very soon it may be a sickness unto death. The symptoms are many—powerlessness, apathy, worldliness, biblical ignorance, false teachers, false doctrine, rebellion, and apostasy to name just a few. Yet, the majority of its pastors and congregations are oblivious to their spiritual condition and imminent peril.

America's only hope is the church, and the only hope for the church is revival. But before revival will come, the church must recognize its spiritual barrenness, its great need of revival, and embrace the necessary prerequisites that make revival possible.

2

The General Purpose and Nature of Revivals and Awakenings

What is revival?

An evangelical revival or awakening is an outpouring of the Holy Spirit in the body of Christ (the Church) which brings about a *revival of New Testament Christianity.* All authentic revivals and awakenings have a common theme or pattern which "is always the repetition of the phenomena of the Acts of the Apostles..."[1] As the Holy Spirit is the central agent in all revivals of the church, Christians must have knowledge of the truth with regard to these phenomena. One of the chief concerns of the apostle Paul in his writings to the first century church was an explanation and instruction regarding the manifestations of the spiritual gifts necessary for building up of the church. There was no thought of stopping or limiting these manifestations. Rather, Paul laid out a solid base of spiritual knowledge to counter the dangers of intemperate, reckless, and unwise spiritual manifestations. Paul's concern for truth and proper instruction regarding spiritual gifts also applies when seeking periodic revivals of the church over the centuries. That is the purpose of this book—to bring a greater understanding of revival based on the foundation of New Testament Christianity and the history of evangelical revivals in the church since the late 1600s.

The truth of God's word is more important than the experience of revival

The student of revival must first understand that seeking and experiencing a special outpouring of the presence of the Holy Spirit is not the ultimate goal for individual Christians or the church in this world. Obedience to the *truth and authority of God's inerrant Word* must always take precedence over *experience.* "Heaven and earth shall pass away, but my words shall not pass away." [Matthew 24:35. KJV] In our obedience to His Word we glorify God. Therefore, Christians must not seek to experience His presence in any manner that is not consistent with the truth of the Word of God. In other words, the truth of God's Word must always be the final authority by which all spiritual experiences are judged and that includes those experiences that occur in special outpourings of the Holy Spirit which we call revival. The final measure of the genuineness of any revival, various manifestations occurring during revival, and other spiritual experiences must always be the truth found in the unadulterated and inerrant Word of God.

To understand how the church has been revived periodically since its creation, the Christian must understand the work and operation of the Holy Spirit in the body of Christ in both individuals and the church. From time to time there are unusual and powerful outpourings of the Holy Spirit on members of the body of Christ. These outpourings are essential and central to the revival and continued survival of the church *in every generation.*

Here we must make clear that those special *seasons of outpouring* of the Holy Spirit to revive the body of Christ are separate and distinct from the *on-going work* of the Holy Spirit as it relates to the individual Christian. First, the Holy Spirit was sent by the Father to bring sinners into a personal relationship with Jesus. Among His many other roles, the Holy Spirit was sent to abide within and comfort Christians after Jesus returned to the Father. This role of the Holy Spirit is confirmed in Romans 8:10-11 which tells us that the Holy Spirit is living in every born-again Christian. Through the abiding presence of the Holy Spirit within each born-again Christian, he or she can experience and live a spiritually transformed and renewed life.[2]

Second, the baptism in the Holy Spirit is a distinct and separate work of the Holy Spirit apart from spiritual birth (i.e., conviction, repentance, and salvation or being born-again) and the abiding or indwelling presence of the Holy Spirit. Jesus did not begin his public ministry until he had been "anointed...with the Holy Spirit and power." [Acts 10:38. KJV] Likewise, after the resurrection but before his return to heaven, Jesus instructed His disciples to wait until they were baptized in the Holy Spirit before they began their ministry of sharing his message to the world. "But you will receive power when the Holy Spirit comes on you; and you will be my witnesses in Jerusalem, and in all Judea and Samaria, and to the ends of the earth." [Acts 1:8. NIV] In other words, the purpose of being baptized in the Holy Spirit is to be "set apart, commissioned and empowered for service."[3]

The special seasons of outpouring of the Holy Spirit lead to revival of New Testament Christianity within the church. As a consequence of revival, there will be subsequent individual instances of salvation (the abiding presence) and the empowerment of believers through the baptism of the Holy Spirit. But as the church departs from

New Testament Christianity, it will inevitably depart from those seasons of the special outpouring of the Holy Spirit and true revival.

Purpose of revivals and awakenings

In its most elemental form, an evangelical revival or awakening is an outpouring of the Holy Spirit in the body of Christ (the Church) which brings about a *revival of New Testament Christianity*. The revival or awakening may be an outpouring of the Holy Spirit to a single individual; two or three gathered in His name; a congregation; a city, district, country, or continent; or a larger group of believers throughout the world.[4]

Revivals come in various ways and last for varying lengths of time—some linger for only a brief time and some have an ongoing influence that may last a lifetime. It must be repeated that all authentic revivals and awakenings are "…always the repetition of the phenomena of the Acts of the Apostles…" The wondrous New Testament narrative of the establishment of the church, the conversion of sinners, and the periodic revival of believers within the church may be said to be the pristine pattern for all who follow the way of the Cross. When the New Testament pattern is followed, revivals and awakenings always result in the revitalization of the lives of Christians and the apprehension of wayward nominal Christians and non-Christians when they have a saving encounter with Christ through the operation of the Holy Spirit.[5] Thus, the purpose of evangelical revivals and awakenings must always be seen as a *restoration and revitalization of New Testament Christianity* within the body of Christ. Revivals that do not faithfully adhere to the truth of God's Word and do not restore and revitalize New Testament Christianity within those churches may be said to be revivals in name only or false revivals. Such revivals are not of divine origin.

Two conditions in the Church that require revival

The word "revival" indicates that something has changed. When the church's adherence to New Testament Christianity begins to diminish, it must be revived. We can easily identify the conditions of the church that require revival: powerlessness and a loss of the fear of God.

First, the church has become or is rapidly becoming *powerless*. This powerlessness occurs for several reasons and includes the following. The church no longer gives central place to the Holy Spirit in their gathering together and worship. One of the consequences is that the operation of the gifts of the Spirit in the body of believers is not evident as they once were. There is a marked decline in the number of sinners being converted and Christians being filled with the baptism of the Holy Spirit. Church attendance becomes intermittent for most of the congregation. Enthusiasm for God or the things of God has been replaced by the quest for entertainment and activities. The Bible is no longer the central source for preaching and teaching because it has been replaced with man's wisdom, ideas, and social concerns.

The second sign that a church is in need of revival is a noticeable *decline in the fear of God*. A. W. Tozer wrote that, "No one can know the true grace of God who has not first known the fear of God."[6] But fear is a negative concept in our modern society. To the modern world the concept that God's children must fear him is abhorrent because they do not understand the biblical meaning of the fear of God. Even though Christians have an intimate, loving relationship with their heavenly father, there must be an awe and respect for His majesty. It is a *filial* fear similar to that of a child for his or her father. For Christians, it is a fear of offending or displeasing the heavenly father who is our loving creator and provider. The world wrongly sees a Christian's fear of God as a *servile* fear of a cruel master. And the evangelical church that presents only the soft side of religion agrees with the culture's assessment of fearing God. As a result many in the church downplay the importance of a Christian's filial fear of God. This fear has been largely replaced by a flippant, casual, and cavalier attitude toward God in an effort to soothe the sinner's fear of God's judgement.[7] It is also a safe assumption that the loss of reverence for God and the things of God among a large segment of the body of Christ is a direct result of their loss of the fear of God.

God's reasons for sending revival

Dr. Lloyd-Jones listed four reasons why God sends revival. First, God sends revival and blessings upon the church *for the glory of God*. He does this so that all people of the earth may know the hand of the Lord is mighty. His miraculous blessings attract the attention of the saint and sinner alike. We see this in the Old Testament when Joshua and the Israelites crossed the Jordan on dry ground. The Israelites alone represented God, and all other nations were pagan. He did this miracle in order that those unbelievers on the outside who scoff and deride God's kingdom and His people may be astonished, apprehended, and chastened.[8] However, many who seek revival do so for their own personal blessings. But personal blessings are a byproduct of revival. It must be reiterated that God sends revival to bless his people for His glory.

A second reason that God sends revival is *to restore a healthy fear of God in the body of Christ* (the church). When a season of revival has run its course, people have been wonderfully reminded that the living God in all of His power and glory dwells among them. But over time these special visitations of God tend to be forgotten by many in the body of Christ as the effects of revival wear away. Christians begin to see the church as nothing more than an institution or organization. Such a view leads Christians toward an attitude of casualness in their relationship with Him, with casualness comes loss of the fear of the Lord, and with loss of fear comes disobedience. This disobedience stems from less reliance on God and greater self-reliance through scholarship and learning, organizing skills, activities, and busy-ness.[9] When God is no longer feared, the church also loses its reverence for His majesty, power, and holiness. With loss of fear of the Lord, His nature becomes merely a utilitarian tool, a part of the furniture of the church that is summoned into service as needed. The loss of fear of the Lord is a particularly distinguishing trait of the modern American church. In other words, they have lost their consciousness of God who dwells among them.

The third reason God sends revival is that when Christians dwell in the full power and presence of God, they are *no longer fearful of men*. Revival takes the fear of men away from God's children. They no longer fear the giants in the land when they realize that the living God resides among them. Lloyd-Jones described the church's fear of man in a 1959 sermon, also recorded in his book *Revival*.

> The church is so afraid. She is afraid of organized sin, and her argument is, "We must be doing something because look at the world. It is attracting the young people, it gives them a happy pleasant Saturday night, entertains them, teaches them how to sing and do this and that. Well now we must do the same thing..." The church is so afraid they are going to lose their young people they feel they must do the same. Oh, what a tragedy, what a departure from God's way...So we trim and modify our gospel, because we are afraid of learning and of knowledge and of science...

There is no need to be afraid of any of these powers...There is nothing new about all of this. The Christian Church has always had to fight the world and the flesh and the devil...And the church has often quaked and feared, but never when there has been revival, because then they know that the living God is among them...[10]

Fifty-eight years after Lloyd-Jones preached this message, we still see the same fear of man gripping the church, but we have substituted today's seeker for yesterday's youth of six decades ago. The church now says, "We must be doing something because look at the world. It is attracting the seekers, it gives them a happy pleasant Saturday night, entertains them, teaches them how to sing and do this and that. Well now we must do the same thing..." To avoid offense, the seeker-friendly church offers an ever changing array of attractions and activities for seekers to sample until they find something they like. This is done in lieu of a forthright presentation of the uncompromised Word of the living God and reliance on the convicting power of the Holy Spirit in reaching the lost and hell-bound seeker-sinners in the church's midst.

The fourth reason God sends revival is that it *delivers us from our enemies*. And in every revival that has ever been, deliverance always means praise, adoration, worship, and thanksgiving to God, and an enjoyment of God's riches by His people.[11]

Revivals in the Old and New Testaments

As described in Chapter 1, the pattern of sin and falling away from God followed by repentance, revival, and restoration of His people is a recurrent theme in the history of God's dealings with the Israelites in the Old Testament. This pattern is illustrated in Psalm 80 and 85 as the author pleads with God to once again *revive* and *restore* His chosen people.

Return to us, O God Almighty! Look down from heaven and see! Watch over this vine, the root your right hand has planted, the son you have raised up for yourself. Your vine is cut down, it is burned with fire; at your rebuke your people perish. Let your hand rest on the man at your right hand, the son of man you have raised up for yourself. Then we will not turn away from you;

revive us, and we will call on your name. *Restore us*, O
Lord God Almighty; make your face shine upon us, that
we may be saved. [Psalm 80:14-19. NIV] [emphasis
added]

Will you not *revive us again*, that your people may
rejoice in you? Show us your unfailing love, LORD, and
grant us your salvation. I will listen to what God the
LORD says; he promises peace to his people, his faithful
servants—but let them not turn to folly. Surely his
salvation is near those who fear him, that his glory may
dwell in our land. [Psalm: 85:6-9. NIV] [emphasis
added]

Revival historian Mathew Backholer points out in his book
Revival Fires and Awakenings that both the Old and New Testaments do
not use the term "revival" to describe a spiritual renewal. However, a
special visitation of the Holy Spirit that leads to a spiritual renewal can
clearly be defined as a revival through "inspired inference" in the light of
numerous instances of rebellion, decline, and renewal clearly presented
by the events and lives of many individuals and groups in the Bible."[12]
    The Holy Spirit was active in communicating God's message to
His people in the Old Testament, but until the church was established in
the first century, the Holy Spirit came upon (e.g., empower, influence,
work through) only a few people. Generally, these were the faithful
individuals, judges, and various leaders of God's Old Testament people
who were energized, empowered, or influenced to accomplish a special
task or purpose or to speak out as a messenger from God. However, there
was not a general or widespread outpouring of the Holy Spirit on the
people, but those that were specially touched by the Holy Spirit often led
the people into seasons of revival and renewal within the nation of Israel
through mass repentance and turning from their wicked ways.[13]
    In the Old Testament, the occurrence of revival was shown by
God's glory coming down such as when King Solomon dedicated the
temple (1 Kings 8:10-11 and 2 Chronicles 5:13-14). Old Testament
revivals were characterized by mass repentance under God's conviction
and the leading of the Spirit. Backholer listed eight examples of revivals
in the Old Testament, all recorded in the books of Genesis, 1st and 2nd
Kings and 2nd Chronicles. These revivals were generally led by various
leaders, prophets, or kings under the influence and direction of the Holy
Spirit. In the New Testament the Holy Spirit fell en masse on His people

beginning on the day of Pentecost. Backholer recorded twenty examples of New Testament revivals.[14]

Revivals and awakenings in Church history

One of the great failings of the church during the last one hundred years is its tendency to view the swelling tides of moral and cultural decline in the twentieth and twenty-first centuries as something quite new and unique in the history of the church. But as mentioned above, this view occurs because of the church's fear of organized sin. This fear has led the church to believe that it must develop new techniques and methods, soften the gospel's message, make certain accommodations for the sinner, and employ modern business practices to meet the world's challenge on its own terms. But in the words of Martyn Lloyd-Jones, "...the man who experiments in the midst of crisis is a fool."[15]

As a result of this misguided thinking, these modern churchmen ignore the rich history of the church's past which they believe has nothing to teach them in the modern age. Worse yet, they even ignore the basic teachings of the Bible in their quest to redefine the church and employ the latest and greatest solutions to win the lost. This is self-reliance spoken of above and is the mother of disobedience.

In American history we can count five revivals that rise to the level of awakenings that spread over many parts of the nation and to other parts of the World. Here we must briefly clarify the difference between a revival and an awakening. Revivals tend to be localized events (church, village, town, or city). An awakening affects a much larger area (district, county, or country), can last for years or decades, and significantly affect the moral standards of a society. Some awakenings continue to be called revivals such as the Businessmen's Revival of 1857-58, the Welsh Revival of 1904-1905, and the Pentecostal revival of 1906-1909, but they still are considered to be broad awakenings.[16] Since the early twentieth century, there have been no revivals or awakenings of the magnitude of the revivals previously mentioned. After one hundred years, the church is in desperate need of revival, and the nation is in desperate need of a general spiritual awakening which can only come through a revived church.

Given the importance of the church's history of revivals and awakenings during the last three hundred years, that history is explored in Book II in the last half of this book. Although the focus will be on the history of recorded revivals and awakenings, it is important to remember that many thousands of other revivals and lesser awakenings that came, ran their course, and wonderfully infused life into the affected churches and their congregations for years afterward. The vast majority of these revivals may have been mostly forgotten and have never been recorded in the history books of men, but their eternal consequences have been faithfully written in the annals of heaven.

3

What is True Revival?

Ask twenty Christian lay men and women under the age of fifty to describe what a revival is and you will likely get twenty different answers, and most will be incorrect. The same may be said of many in the clergy. Very simply put, revival means to bring the church back to life. Noah Webster's dictionary of 1828 lists four definitions that are helpful in understanding revival in the biblical sense.

1. Return, recall or recovery to life from death or apparent death; as the revival of a drowned person.
2. Return or recall to activity from a state of languor; as the revival of spirits.
3. Return, recall or recovery from a state of neglect, oblivion, obscurity or depression; as the revival of the letters or learning.
4. Renewed and more active attention to religion; an awakening of men to their spiritual concerns.[1]

Here we see that revival is actually being defined as the *opposites* of death or apparent spiritual death, languor, neglect, oblivion, obscurity, and depression. Put another way in a spiritual or religious context, revival is spiritual life instead of death, vigor instead of languor, attention instead of neglect, awareness instead of oblivion, prominence instead of obscurity, and joy instead of depression. A return to spiritual life in these areas is the *result* or *outcome* of true revival, but the terms still do not define the true meaning or essence of revival.

The difficulty of defining true revival is that much of the modern evangelical church has never experienced or has forgotten what true revival is, how it occurs, and why it is important. As a consequence, many in the church attempt to artificially stimulate the opposites of spiritual decline which results in a form of godliness that does not rely on the true source of revival—the Holy Spirit. In other words, the church is using the world's methods to achieve an imitation of the fruits of revival while remaining oblivious to the true source, nature, and purpose of revival. Jim Cymbala called this "icing, but no cake."

The exaltation of church growth formulas or denominational names over the power of the Holy Spirit is deeply distressing, and we are no better than the Babylonians making sacrifices to the tools of our trade.

Here is the critical question: What if the things sold to us as solutions over the past two decades—"we've got the answer" conferences, leadership books, high-profile pastors with big personalities, and new models of doing church—are really the *problem* and not the answer?

First, many of the techniques are not found in Scripture. We don't need more technicians; we simply need more of God.

It is likely that we are seeing a fulfillment of those perilous times that Paul told Timothy about when men would have a form of godliness, but deny the power.

That's why our churches are so often powerless and Christianity is in decline. God's answers for us have been replaced by human intelligence, leaving us as dim lights in an increasingly dark world.

The only answer to a lukewarm church or struggling Christian is the same as ever—the fire of the Holy Spirit![2] [emphasis in original]

What is true revival?

The Holy Spirit is the source of true revival. But how does true revival occur? Dr. J. Edwin Orr said, "The key factor in revival is the outpouring of the Holy Spirit. The outpouring of the Holy Spirit results in the revival of the church."[3] Revival is an amazing, unusual, and extraordinary *visitation of the Spirit within the church,* and these special visitations of God have been provided by His divine providence over the course of the history of His church. But it is also important to understand that individual Christians, apart from a group or church setting, may experience the blessings of revival from an outpouring of the Holy Spirit.[4]

What happens when the there is a visitation of the Spirit in the church or an individual's life? For an answer we look to the words of Dr. Martyn Lloyd-Jones from his book *Revival*. Lloyd-Jones described the extraordinary happenings that occurred in a revival held by the great eighteenth century evangelist George Whitefield.

> God came down. Oh yes, they had been enjoying the presence and blessing of God before, but not like this, something wonderful had happened. God was in the very midst, God came down. That is exactly what happens during revival.
>
> What does this mean? Well, we can describe it like this. It is a consciousness of the presence of God the Holy Spirit literally in the midst of the people. Probably most of us who are here have never known that, but that is exactly what is meant by a visitation of God's Spirit. It is all above and beyond the highest experiences in the normal life and working of the Church. Suddenly those present in the meeting become aware that someone has come amongst them, they are aware of a glory, they are aware of a presence. They can not define it, they can not describe it, they can not put it into words, they just know that they have never known anything like this before. Sometimes they describe it as 'days of heaven on earth.' They really feel that they are in heaven – they have forgotten time, they are beyond that, time has no longer any meaning for them, nor any real existence, they are in a spiritual realm. God has come down amongst them and has filled the place and the people with a sense of his glorious presence.
>
> And, always, of course,…it is also a manifestation of the power of God, not only the glory and the radiance of God's presence, but especially his power…[5]

We can now define true revival as a sovereign act of God which brings life back to the body of Christ through an extraordinary visitation of the Spirit of God among His people. Simply put, it is God in the midst of His people. More generally, revival can be said to be an awakening of the evangelical religion. Sometimes the word "revival" is also "…used to explain the amazing results of an outpouring of the Spirit of God, a visitation of the Holy Spirit, when Christians are revived, sinners are saved, and communities are changed and become God-fearing."[6]

Dr. Lloyd-Jones' description of revival is indeed beautiful and thrilling; however, he also calls revival a process. His description above dwells on but *one moment* during the "revival process" of bearing the burden, praying for revival, conviction of sin, confession, repentance, forgiveness, revival, restoration, and blessing.

Stages in the process of true revival

A process always has a beginning and an end. It is the same with the process or pattern of revival. Here we are not saying that man merely follows a recipe and in a matter of time a revival is ready to be taken from the oven fully baked. That revival is a process or sequence of events is confirmed by Dr. Lloyd-Jones.

> There are, generally speaking, stages, and steps, in the coming of revival. You will hardly ever find, in all of the histories of revival, that the Church suddenly, in one move, as it were, or in one step, passes from her condition of lifelessness and an almost moribund state into a condition of mighty power and revival and influence. No, there are generally particular steps and stages.[7]

When we speak of revival and spiritual awakening, it is in the context of something that happens at one and the same time to a number of individuals in the church. However, the stages of revival can and do have the same application and effect on individuals not part of a general revival or awakening in the church.

Revivals follow the pattern of the early church as found in the first two chapters of the Acts of the Apostles. First the one hundred twenty gathered in the upper room in prayer and petition, then the three thousand that gladly received the word and were baptized. In the early stages of revival such as burden bearing and prayer, the number involved may be relatively small. As the outpouring of the Holy Spirit occurs in response to the prayers of the intercessors, conviction, confession, and repentance becomes evident and spreads throughout the church and the lives of many unbelievers who come to see God's power at work. As the mighty presence of the Holy Spirit spreads over the church, hearts are arrested and sin exposed. Many will continue to be drawn by the arresting power of the Holy Spirit, but others will flee.

Stages of Revival – The cross before the crown

The cross of Christ stands at the center of all creation, the fall, and redemption of mankind; so too must the cross stand at the center of revival. Christ said, "Whoever wants to be my disciple must deny themselves and take up their cross and follow me. For whoever wants to save their life will lose it, but whoever loses their life for me will find it. [Matthew 16:24-25. NIV] This is the only path from the prodigal's pig wallow to the foot of the cross and eternal fellowship with the Son of God. Carrying the burden of sin for a lukewarm church, intercession, conviction, repentance, and confession are the painful elements of revival that lead us to the foot of the cross. We cannot find true revival and restoration without first experiencing the pain of death to self at the cross.

- Burden of sin - The realization of one's desperate position

The pattern of revival never varies in that it begins with a realization of one's distant position in relation to Christ. It is a realization of the hopelessness of the situation apart from hope in a loving God and the promises of His Word. There is an unrelenting feeling of emptiness within, a deep hunger or yearning, which can be satisfied only by a return of the presence of God. This hunger or yearning flows from an anguished heart that senses there is not a fullness in his or her relationship with Christ. They have become estranged from their first love or have become completely backslidden. This anguish of heart does not pass but continually weighs on the heart of the distraught Christian or backslider. There can be no hope for revival apart from this indisputable realization. As this realization lingers, it becomes a *burden* for some which is the first step in the process of revival. Revival will never come until people lay their pride, rebellion, and lethargy on the altar and recognize their desperate spiritual condition and/or that of the church.

It is only when the church critically examines itself, both individually and corporately, that the realization of its desperate state will occur and the burden for revival will grow. Why has it been so long since the church has experienced the divine outpouring of the Holy Spirit? Why is the church so powerless and counts for so little in combatting the escalating moral decline in families, schools, communities, the nation, and culture at large? Why is there widespread casualness in the acceptance of the world in the church? Why is there such a growing ignorance of God's Word? Why is there a rush to unity with apostate churches? Only when the church asks the tough questions and considers its obvious failures in a serious manner will the burden for revival grow and revival come.

- Prayer – "Soul Travail"

A heavy burden for the demise of the church and a hunger for a return of God's presence lead to *prayer* which is the second step necessary in seeking revival, both personally and corporately. Prayer for revival is an incessant and desperate plea for mercy and a casting of one's complete trust and dependence on God. Dr. A. T. Pierson once said, "There has never been a spiritual awakening in any country or locality that did not begin in united prayer."[8]

Prayer for revival will be of no avail unless there is recognition of the great spiritual need for revival and a heart-felt intercession for the church. Such prayers are not a casual, intermittent recitation of the awfulness of the one's situation and a request for a bandage to treat the abrasions caused by one's encounters with a fallen world so that one may get back to more pressing matters of the moment. That type of prayer will never lead to revival and restoration.

- Conviction of sin

Intense, sustained intercession coupled with the influence of pungent preaching leads to the presence and convicting power of the Holy Spirit. The sign that revival has come is that men and women will be profoundly and deeply convicted of sin. *Conviction* of sin is the third step in the revival process. The presence of the Holy Spirit brings *conviction* of sin upon many in the church as well as sinners who have come under the broad sweep of intercessory prayer and anointed preaching. In his *True and False Revival*, Andrew Strom describes the power of conviction.

> When Moses came down from the mountain, he carried the holy presence and glory of God with him. The people wanted to run and hide! That is what true revival has always been like. It is an invasion of the awesome holy presence of God—which is why the pattern

26

(process) of what happens in revivals often repeats itself. Men's hearts are essentially the same in each generation—so God's holy presence has the same effect. Some get convicted, some want to run and hide, many cry loudly in repentance.[9]

- Deep repentance

The early stages of true revival are always first a "cleansing, purging process" in which self is slain at the foot of the cross and leads to the fourth step of *deep repentance*. Thus, true revival, as Jim Cymbala has said, comes from the fire of the Holy Spirit. As has been noted, the fire that brings about conviction and repentance is a painful process, but he who endures will receive the assurance of God's forgiveness. Some may be so overcome with distress at the magnitude of their conviction of sin by the Holy Spirit that they may be unable to do anything but lie face-down while crying out unto God for mercy and forgiveness. But those that persevere will reap the fruit of revival.[10]

But conviction must not be confused with remorse. Two men under the convicting power of the Holy Spirit may have different responses to the sorrow caused by their spiritual conditions. One may have a godly sorrow unto repentance while the other may be sorry about his condition but not sorry enough to rectify the cause of that condition. The apostle Paul in his second letter to the Corinthians described the consequence of following the path of true repentance or that of mere remorse. "Godly sorrow brings repentance that leads to salvation and leaves no regret, but worldly sorrow brings death." [2 Corinthians 7:10. NIV]

- Confession of sin

The Holy Spirit brings conviction of sin in one's life, and *confession* of sin is the sinner's response to that conviction. Specific sins should be confessed and repented of by name. Sometimes, under the prompting of the Holy Spirit, there will be confession of sin privately to other brothers and sisters who may have been wronged. In some cases the Holy Spirit may prompt public confession. Both confessions assist in the joyful realization that those sins have been covered by the blood of Christ. However, there are certain situations in which some sins should not be confessed publicly. To do so may cause harm to those sinned against, may cause others to sin because of the lurid details disclosed, or that will re-ignite heart-break, humiliation, or grief to those who have suffered similar wrongs in the past. Lastly, once sins have been confessed publicly or privately, the repentant sinner should leave the confession under the blood along with the sin itself, never to see the light of day again.[11]

Stages of Revival – The crown

The early stages of the revival process are painful. During these stages God has led from the realization of the church's need and burden for revival, through conviction of sin, repentance, and possibly confession. The convicted sinner arrives at a point where he must respond by either repenting or rejecting the free gift of Christ. Those that reject Christ will face judgement and eternal death, but for those that repent, God continues the revival process as he *forgives*, *revives* (brings to life that which was dead), *restores* relationship with the Father, and *blesses* His children. This is the crown that follows the cross, and nothing better describes this joyful conclusion of the revival process than the Word of God.

- Forgiveness

    In him we have redemption through his blood, the forgiveness of sins, in accordance with the riches of God's grace. [Ephesians 1:7. NIV]

    For he has rescued us from the dominion of darkness and brought us into the kingdom of the Son he loves, in whom we have redemption, the forgiveness of sins. [Colossians 1:13-14. NIV]

    If we confess our sins, he is faithful and just and will forgive us our sins and purify us from all unrighteousness. [1 John 1:9. NIV]

- Revival

    Therefore if anyone is in Christ, he is a new creature; the old things passed away; behold, new things have come. [2 Corinthians 5:17. NIV]

28

But because of his great love for us, God, who is rich in mercy, made us alive with Christ even when we were dead in transgressions—it is by grace you have been saved. And God raised us up with Christ and seated us with him in the heavenly realms in Christ Jesus, in order that in the coming ages he might show the incomparable riches of his grace, expressed in his kindness to us in Christ Jesus. [Ephesians 2:4-8. NIV]

- Restoration

For I am convinced that neither death nor life, neither angels nor demons, neither the present nor the future, nor any powers, neither height nor depth, nor anything else in all creation, will be able to separate us from the love of God that is in Christ Jesus our Lord. [Romans 8:38-39. NIV]

Dear friends, now we are children of God, and what we will be has not yet been made known. But we know that when Christ appears, we shall be like him, for we shall see him as he is. All who have this hope in him purify themselves, just as he is pure. [1 John 3:2-3. NIV]

- Blessing

But blessed is the one who trusts in the Lord, whose confidence is in him. They will be like a tree planted by the water that sends out its roots by the stream. It does not fear when heat comes; its leaves are always green. It has no worries in a year of drought and never fails to bear fruit. [Jeremiah 17:7-8. NIV]

And God is able to bless you abundantly, so that in all things at all times, having all that you need, you will abound in every good work. [2 Corinthians 9:8. NIV]

Every good and perfect gift is from above, coming down from the Father of the heavenly lights, who does not change like shifting shadows. [James 1:17. NIV]

Revival – Process or methods?

Before we close this chapter, we must make a careful distinction between the *process, steps, or stages* that occur in revival and those who propose the use of certain *methods* to assure revival comes. To be blunt, there are no methods by which men can bring revival. Methods are of men's making, but those seeking revival must understand that revival is entirely a work of the Holy Spirit. Evangelistic campaigns can be produced by men, but men have never produced revival for revival is a *sovereign* work of God but subject to the freewill of men. But some will point to the claims of the great revivalist Charles Finney during the first half of the nineteenth century who seems to imply that there are methods to be followed which can produce revival.

> I [Finney] said that a revival is the result of the right use of the appropriate means. The means which God has enjoined [ordered] for the production of a revival, doubtless have a natural tendency to produce a revival. Otherwise God would not have enjoined them. *But means will not produce a revival, we all know, without the blessing of God.* No more will grain, when it is sown, produce a crop without the blessing of God. It is impossible for us to say that there is not as direct an influence or agency from God, to produce a crop of grain, as there is to produce a revival.[12] [emphasis added]

Although Finney believed the Spirit works through natural means and human agency,[13] the intent and true meaning of his position on the origins of revival were often misunderstood or misapplied by many. As a result, Finney's words created a great chasm between those supporting the sovereignty of God as opposed to the blessing of God when no such breach exists when speaking of the origin of revival. We cannot separate the blessing of God from the sovereignty of God regarding the special outpouring of the Holy Spirit on God's people. However, less spiritual promoters have taken Finney's words and wrongly used them to justify promotional evangelism abounding with large measures of ungodly commercialism and sensationalism.[14]

Mathew Backholer summarizes three differing views as to how revivals originate:

1. It is a totally sovereign work of God, whilst man makes application of God's promises. Jonathan Edwards, Duncan Campbell, and Dr. Martyn Lloyd-Jones held this view and they saw revival.
2. Anybody can have revival at any time as long as the conditions and promises have been appropriated. Charles Finney, Jonathan Goforth, and Edwin Orr held this view and they saw revival.
3. Just preach the pure gospel. George Whitefield, John Wesley, and Howell Harris held this view and they saw revival.[15]

Backholer points to the common denominator among the three views as "the work of the Holy Spirit as God comes down and convicts of sin." In spite of which one of these views one may hold, it must be recognized that there are those people in the church who have such an anointing on their lives that revival occurs. Backholer concludes that the three views of how revival originates "…are all part of the same swing of God's revival pendulum; it just depends at which end you are viewing the marvelous work of God."[16]

———

The discussion in this chapter has been little more than a bare-bones, non-dynamic overview of the process or steps in the general outworking of revival in the individual and the local church. In the next chapter we shall attempt flesh out these bones and give life to the process of revival in order to gain an understanding of the general course of events that occur when there is a special outpouring of the Holy Spirit and the church experiences a season of true revival.

4

The General Course of Events in Revival

The discussion in the last chapter gave the student of revival a foundational understanding of the elements of revival, but it was little more than a linear, non-dynamic overview of the process or stages in the general outworking of revival. In this chapter we shall examine the compelling, life-giving properties of Holy Spirit-led revivals that infuse vitality into the church, sweeps away the rubbish of man-centered religion, and grips the hearts and minds of His people and sinners alike for the glory of God.

To describe revival as merely a successive number of independent, mechanical stages is akin to one's failure to see the panorama of the forest because of trees that block the view. Intellectually learning the steps of the revival process is helpful and necessary but only introductory in understanding true revival. Recall in the last chapter the description of what true revival was like in one of George Whitefield's revival meetings.

> Suddenly those present in the meeting become aware that someone has come amongst them, they are aware of a glory, they are aware of a presence. They can not define it, they can not describe it, they can not put it into words, they just know that they have never known anything like this before. Sometimes they describe it as 'days of heaven on earth.'[1]

This is the grand vista that is revealed when there is a special outpouring of the Holy Spirit. We encounter His divine presence and for a time see and experience a bit of heaven instead of just a burdensome form of godliness and religious activity. The special outpouring of the Holy Spirit in the church is a transforming experience that lasts far beyond the moment in both the individual and the church body.

In all the histories of revival you will not see any occasion where the church has suddenly passed from great sin and separation from God into great revival. In the larger sense revival is not instantaneous but follows a *course of events* that are very similar to that of the natural and divine processes that occur in the creation and development of the life of a child in a mother's womb and the baby's subsequent birth. Although there are very definite and identifiable stages in the creation, gestation, and birth of a baby, there is also a seamless quality as the baby transitions from the moment of conception to a fully-formed, independently-functioning human being. So too is there a seamless, unifying quality in the process of revival.

Once again think of the *stages of revival* discussed in the last chapter: recognition of the deplorable state of the evangelical church, the development of a hunger for more of God and a burden for the lost, prayer for revival, conviction of the sinner, repentance, confession of sin, forgiveness, individual and corporate spiritual revival, restoration of relationship, and blessing of God's people. This process occurs in varying degrees within the individual and in the church as a whole. When we couple these stages with the fact that there are special seasons of revival, we begin to understand that revival is not a single event that occurs because of the progression of a static set of sequential steps. Rather, revival is a dynamic, pulsating, and transforming series of events that can be thought of as multiple revivals occurring at the same time. In other words, one revival may in reality be a series of revivals at various stages but occurring simultaneously and which feed the next level of revival, whether occurring individually, at the local church level, or throughout the nation. For example, an individual may be experiencing a personal revival at an early stage while the local revival in which he participates is in the fully-matured later stages. Likewise, a mature revival in one local church may be carried to another church across the country and which begins to blossom into the early stages of a new revival. Hopefully, this description gives a better understanding of the vitality or dynamism of the outworking of true revival.

What general course of events should the church anticipate when seeking revival?

Every revival or awakening that ever happened was preceded by two occurrences. First there must be a growing consciousness in the heart and mind of one or more individuals of the pervasiveness of sin in the church and departure of the presence of God. This consciousness grows in the hearts of a few in the church to the point that they are greatly burdened by the sin and desperate condition of the church. The burden leads to intercessory prayer and petition to God to rid the church of sin and restore His presence. This is preparation for revival, but it is not revival. In the next chapter we shall examine what intercessors for revival should be seeking in their prayers. But this chapter will be confined to a discussion of the general course of events that take place during revival. These events to a significant degree parallel the events that took place in the book of the Acts of the Apostles in the first century.

As the general course of events in revival are described in this chapter, it must be remembered that in all revivals the individuals participating in or who come under the influence of revival do not start at the same point or necessarily rise to the same level of personal spirituality during revival.

To distill the essence of this course of events is to understand that revival "is nothing but God hearing the people and answering them by giving the manifestation of his glory and his strength and his power."[2] But again, we must add flesh to the bones of this plain description of revival. The following is the general course of events during a season of revival which begins with a special outpouring of the Holy Spirit.

- Stirrings of revival

When God has been stirred by the persistent and plaintive cries of the intercessor, there arises a faint, tentative quickening in the pulse of the church. The worship and preaching may have a new robustness. People are strangely roused and hopeful, and there is a growing sense of unity among the believers. There is also an increasing restlessness and anxiety among backslidden Christians and the spiritually lost because of an awakened conscience and conviction about their sinful condition. Once again the Holy Spirit has quietly, almost unobtrusively returned to the midst of God's people. All of these things happen when preparations for revival have been made.

- The Church becomes conscious of a presence and a power in her midst

There may be moments in the midst of worship, a preaching service, or a prayer meeting in which a holy hush settles over those gathered. Every heart, saint or sinner, becomes suddenly aware that a holy presence has come into their midst. This is as it was on the day of Pentecost.

> And when the day of Pentecost was fully come, they were all with one accord in one place. And suddenly there came a sound from heaven as of a rushing mighty wind, and it filled all the house where they were sitting.

> And there appeared unto them cloven tongues like as of
> fire, and it sat upon each of them. And they were all
> filled with the Holy Ghost, and began to speak with
> other tongues, as the Spirit gave them utterance. [Acts
> 2:1-4. KJV]

Even if there is anticipation that revival is at the door, it will still surprise as it comes suddenly when a special outpouring of the Holy Spirit descends upon His people. The people have recognized their great need and have sought God for renewal and restoration. This has brought people together in one accord regarding their situation, that is, they were of one mind or one impulse. It is this essential posture of humility and brokenness that opens the door to revival. Christ does not revive unrepentant people or churches that continue in the grip of pride and disunity.

The second thing we see is that revival is accompanied by a demonstration of His power and authority. Various phenomena may occur. These may be "cloven tongues like as of fire" or "speaking in tongues" similar to that which occurred in the upper room, or there may be various other manifestations of His presence. The power and glory of His presence may be so intense and overwhelming that many may faint and fall prostrate because it is too much for their physical bodies.[3]

Book II is an overview of the history of the great revivals and awakenings that have occurred in the evangelical church since the early 1700s. One notices in these accounts of the overpowering of the consciousness of many who come into His glorious presence during revival. This seems to be an exceptionally common if not an almost universal occurrence. A more in-depth discussion of the physical manifestations accompanying revival will follow in later chapters.

We close this description of the second event in the course of revival by saying that almost all who have experienced seasons of revival as has been described above no longer have just an intellectual or reasoned belief in God. Rather, God has become an indisputable reality because He came down into their midst. This writer experienced many revivals of yesteryear, both as a child and as a young man, and can attest to revival's transformative power that leads one from mere head knowledge of belief in God to a heart knowledge of the reality of God.

- The church is given a great assurance concerning the truth

The special outpouring of the Holy Spirit that leads to revival not only sweeps away doubts about the reality of God but also gives assurance concerning the truth. Here we look to the disciples as our example. Following Christ's crucifixion and burial, the disciples were in a terrible state of fear and disbelief even though Christ had taught and warned them of the things that were to come. Although Christ's resurrection restored a measure of their trust and fidelity to Him, they were still shaken and uncertain. But then the day of Pentecost came and with it came an unshakable assurance in God, Jesus Christ, and the spiritual realm.[4] No longer would their faith in Him waver. This is what revival does for the believer. Minds are illuminated. Hearts are strengthened. Faith increases. The narrow path becomes firm under foot as those born in revival strap on the full armor of God.

- The church is filled with a great sense of joy and praise

When revival comes there is such great joy and happiness that the people of God cannot contain their praise and thanksgiving. This occurred within the newly born church after being filled with the Holy Spirit on the day of Pentecost.

> And they continued stedfastly in the apostles' doctrine and fellowship, and in breaking of bread, and in prayers. And fear came upon every soul: and many wonders and signs were done by the apostles. And all that believed were together, and had all things common;
> And sold their possessions and goods, and parted them to all men, as every man had need. And they, continuing daily with one accord in the temple, and breaking bread from house to house, did eat their meat with gladness and singleness of heart, Praising God, and having favour with all the people. And the Lord added to the church daily such as should be saved. [Acts 2:42-47. KJV]

There are several things to be gleaned from these verses. First, there was a great sense of unity and singleness of purpose. They were unwavering in their faithful commitment to the house of the Lord, teaching of the apostles, fellowship, and prayer. They praised God in all their activities. They had favor with all people and as a result the Lord added to the church daily such as should be saved. What a wonderful picture of a Christ-centered people in the church, in their homes, and in the community at large. All of this occurred for one reason—they were all filled with the Holy Spirit.

This brings us to a comparison of what happened at the birth of the church on the day of Pentecost and what has happened in all revivals since that day. The writer of Acts 2:4 is very plainspoken and unequivocal. "And they were *all* filled with the Holy Ghost, and began to speak with other tongues, as the Spirit gave them utterance." [emphasis added] *All* in attendance were believers and faithful followers of Jesus Christ. Many if not most of the one hundred and twenty gathered in the upper room very likely had witnessed the ministry of Christ; were present or in close proximity on the days of His crucifixion, burial, and resurrection; and had been among the five hundred or so people who saw Christ during the forty-day period before His ascension.

The faithful one hundred and twenty had gathered in the upper room specifically at Christ's instruction. They were expectant and hopeful for the gift of the baptism in the Holy Spirit as promised by Christ in Acts 1:4-5. What occurred to them on the day of Pentecost was not a revival in which death is made life again but a birthing of the church and a new life in the Spirit. The gathering was not an evangelical service but a commissioning and empowerment service. And here we see the difference between what happened at the day of Pentecost when *all* were filled with the Holy Spirit and what happens in revival when *some* are filled with the Holy Spirit.

This is not a condemnation of the church for failing to live up to the standard which was established on the day of Pentecost. When the newly born church left the upper room, they stepped onto their mission field, and mission fields are always hostile environments. The church exists in a hostile environment and therefore must have seasons of revival so that Christians can be continually energized and prepared for spiritual warfare and to be salt and light unto the world. However, the local church rarely finds all of its members fully revived as did those emerging from the upper room on the day of Pentecost. Since the day of Pentecost individual members of the body of Christ (the Church) and local congregations find themselves at various stages in their spiritual lives. Also, when a revival occurs it must be remembered that not all Christians may be revived to the same extent. Some may be refreshed and continue with the abiding presence of the Holy Spirit within. Others may be baptized in the Holy Spirit. Certainly the local church is far stronger and better prepared to accomplish His purposes in the world when the great majority of its congregants have been baptized in the Holy Spirit.

When the local church experiences revival, it must be remembered that it may also have unrepentant sinners in their midst who receive salvation and the abiding presence of the Holy Spirit at the moment of their spiritual birth. Some of the repentant sinners may also experience the separate and distinct work of the Spirit when they are "clothed with power" by being baptized in the Holy Spirit (see: Luke 24:49). Yet, others will resist the wooing of the Holy Spirit and the conviction of sin and thus remain unrepentant.

From this discussion one can see and understand the critical importance of the baptism in the Holy Spirit for *all* disciples of Christ. Three things happened in Acts 2:1-4. They were in unity, they experienced a manifestation of the presence and power of the Holy Spirit, and they were all filled with the spirit. The primary purpose of the believer's baptism in the Holy Spirit is to prepare and enable Christians to accomplish His purposes on earth. The baptism in the Holy Spirit infuses a holy boldness and the power of God's Spirit into a Christian's life so they can be more effective in spreading the gospel throughout the world.

- Worship and thanksgiving with gladness and singleness of heart

This is the fifth element which occurs in the general course of revival. As revival unfolds and intensifies, worship and thanksgiving are transformed from Christian obligation to a passionate desire to meet together with other believers to worship and praise God. Worship and thanksgiving in revival mirror the church in its early days following the day of Pentecost. As they had gathered in "one accord" on the day of Pentecost, they continued daily "with one accord." It was an inward urge of a people to come together to share in fellowship, worship, prayer, and thanksgiving. This is what happens in every season of true revival and re-awakening. But a church's fellowship, worship, prayer, and thanksgiving do not end when the season of revival has run its course.

Regrettably, these seasons of revival have become a thing of the past in many churches over the past three or more decades. Having not had true revival for so many years, some churches resort to "doubtful, worldly methods, to try to gather crowds and to bring people together." These methods are nothing more than a religious pacifier for those congregations when there is no real hunger or desire for revival among the leadership or the people.[5]

- Revival of power and boldness in the proclamation of the truth

39

As has been previously noted, all revivals are a sovereign move of God. Man cannot create revival. Thus, we may safely say that preaching does not cause revival. However, preaching has always been an integral part of every revival and awakening in history. The intercessors' prayers for revival are supported and encouraged by Holy Spirit anointed preaching of the Word of God. All who preach the Word ought to first ask for the anointing that can only come from the Holy Spirit. It is not the person preaching or the words spoken that makes the difference but the anointing of the Holy Spirit. Following his baptism in the Holy Spirit, the great evangelist D. L. Moody said, "I went on preaching the same old sermons as I had been preaching before. But, they were absolutely different." The sermons were the same but yielded different results because there was a demonstration of the Spirit and the power.[6] In times when revival is sought or when revival is occurring, the anointing of the Holy Spirit will empower, assist, and direct the minister, evangelist, or other persons to preach the essential Holy Spirit-directed message for that moment.

Spirit-powered preaching will invariably bring conviction and repentance as it did when Peter preached his Pentecost sermon. Soon after the outpouring of the Holy Spirit on the day of Pentecost, the once fretful Peter fearlessly preached with great power and authority to the people, their rulers, and governors.

> Therefore let all the house of Israel know assuredly, that God hath made the same Jesus, whom ye have crucified, both Lord and Christ. Now when they heard this, they were *pricked in their heart*, and said unto Peter and to the rest of the apostles, Men and brethren, what shall we do? Then Peter said unto them, Repent, and be baptized every one of you in the name of Jesus Christ for the remission of sins, and ye shall receive the gift of the Holy Ghost. [Acts 2:36-38. KJV] [emphasis added]

But as revival progresses, Holy Spirit anointed preaching will also bring wondrous joy and peace to the Christian, increase knowledge and understanding of the Word, and encourage and direct the faithful disciple of Christ in all matters of life.

However, as revivals in the evangelical church have largely disappeared over the last thirty years or more in most churches, the proclamation of the truth with power and boldness has been replaced by a timid church that is fearful of giving offense. Weak-willed ministers and churches dispense cheap grace, employ Philistine seeker-sensitive methods of evangelism, and seek to have "conversations" with the world in an effort to find common ground at the expense of preaching an unwavering allegiance to the inerrant Word of God. The timid church has become a powerless church because it has substituted surgery drinks and light snacks (health, prosperity, and happiness) for the bold and powerful proclamation of the milk and meat of the inerrant Word of God.

From his prison cell Dietrich Bonhoeffer, the soon to be martyred German theologian during World War II, wrote of the German church's failure to make a bold and powerful declaration of the truth and the terrible consequences that followed.

> We have been silent witness of evil deeds; we have been drenched by many storms; we have learnt the arts of equivocation and pretense; experience has made us suspicious of others and kept us from being truthful and open...Will our inward power of resistance be strong enough, and our honesty with ourselves remorseless enough, for us to find our way back to simplicity and straightforwardness?[7]

Two of those reasons God sends revival are based on fear. First, revival restores a healthy fear of God among His people. Second, God sends revival so that His people will no longer fear man and the power of organized sin in the world. When true revival occurs, it will produce power and boldness in the proclamation of the truth.

- The world outside the church is attracted by curiosity

To this point we have charted the general course of the events of revival occurring within the church. Once revival is in its full season, the church rightly becomes concerned about sharing the revival with the masses outside the church. But this is where many churches usually get it wrong. The first thing that occurs is that the church tends to forget who brought revival in the first place. So they begin by substituting man's ideas for the work of the Holy Spirit. They reason that if they are to attract the mayor, the banker, and the school superintendent, the church must subdue the manifestations of the Holy Spirit and curb any perceived excess exuberance of the people. They piously claim that these changes must be imposed to maintain "decency and order." In other words, revival must be organized, programmed, ritualized, and advertised. But man's methods and ideas cannot replace the life-giving power of the Holy Spirit. When the counterfeit is substituted for a move of the Holy Spirit, it always kills revival in the church. Thereafter, those in the church will never be successful in spreading life-altering revival to those outside the church.

If the church wants to fill the church with the lost found outside the church, the first thing to remember is that revival is not of men's making. The church must do what it did in the first place—pray for revival and leave the rest to the Holy Spirit. The curious will come— some to mock and some who will find Christ. On occasion there may be interest from the media, but they will generally be found seated among the skeptics and scoffers. Think of what was said about those who were filled with the baptism of the Holy Spirit on the day of Pentecost. "And they were all amazed, and were in doubt, saying one to another, What meaneth this? Others mocking said, These men are full of new wine."[8] [Acts 2:12-13. KJV] In spite of the detractors that may flock to revivals to see and report the spectacle to all, Dr. Lloyd-Jones wrote that those experiencing revival should take no heed for the conclusion of the story of every true revival has always been the same since the apostle Peter's day.

> There is always that kind of interruption, almost a disorder, what somebody called a divine disorder. And then, that in turn leads to repentance. "O," says Peter, "repent and be baptized every one of you in the name of Jesus Christ for the remission of sins." And they did. It is not a mere question of decision when you have revival, it is deep repentance, it is reformation. People receive a new life and they leave the old life. When revival comes the whole neighbourhood is changed and moral conditions are revolutionised.[9]

In this chapter we have identified and examined the general course of events found in all revivals. At every juncture in this course of events we see God's fingerprints which mark the presence of true revival—"the falling of the Holy Ghost upon the Church, the shedding forth of the Spirit of God again, and the Church being given a new baptism of power, and of authority, and ability to witness and to preach."[10]

42

Reasons revivals cease

There are dozens of reasons that revivals end, but Mathew Backholer believes that in one way or another all of those reasons fall into three main categories. However, only one of the three offers a satisfactory conclusion.

The first reason revivals end prematurely is because of sin among the members of the church but especially the leadership. As revival progresses, the church may do things it ought not or not do things it ought. These are sins of commission and omission.[11] Needless to say, sin in whatever form it takes is destructive and especially destructive during times of revival. Inattentive or complicit church leadership may let sin wheedle its way into the church in numerous ways which can damage or stop revival. To make a list of these would be useless if not impossible; however, there are certain general hindrances to both the occurrence and continuance of revival which the church should be especially wary. These will be discussed in a later chapter.

The second reason revivals end prematurely is due to the breaking of physical laws. Anyone who has ever participated in a revival of any length knows that it can be very exhausting, both emotionally and physically. Here we are speaking of irregular hours, lack of sleep, neglect of a balanced diet, and balancing faithful attendance and revival fervor with the demands of work, family, and other necessary activities of life.[12] It is during times of protracted revival that Satan will use human frailties to undermine and damage both the revival and the fruits thereof in the lives of men and women and their families in the church body.

The third reason revivals end is because they only last for a season, but their effects can last for years or decades. When the church is revived, the revival may gradually or suddenly come to an end.[13] This is because the church that was in spiritual decline, decay, or death but has been revived and brought back to life. In one sense revival has focused the church inwardly for a season of repentance, healing, and restoration. When revival ends it must become outwardly focused as it once again becomes salt and light to the world. This is the only worthy end of revival.

5

Vibrancy and Compelling Nature of Holy-Spirit Led Revival

In Chapter 3, the student of revival learned of the process or steps by which revival occurs. In Chapter 4, the general course of events that begin and progress throughout revival was examined. In this chapter it is hoped that the reader will receive a greater depth and clarity of understanding of revival as he or she examines the three phases of prayer that occur in preparation for and during the course of events that occur while in revival.

The spirit of the world has plagued mankind since Satan tempted Eve in the Garden and sin entered the world. The consequences of sin are felt by all mankind, but those who do not have a saving relationship with God generally fail to identify sin as the cause of mankind's pain, suffering, and death or know of sin's origin. When gross sin and failure becomes increasingly common in the heart of a Christian or becomes endemic within the church, the faithful, discerning Christian who knows the Word of God is troubled by the burden of sin that dwells in the lives of their fellow Christians and the church as a whole. This burden for the sins of others may grow to the extent that it includes the sins of an entire community or even the nation.

In all of church history the very first thing that happens and leads to revival is that a single Christian or a group of like-minded Christians begin to feel a growing burden because of sin oppressing the church. As the weight of the burden grows, they decide to do something about it. The burdened Christians *turn to prayer*, either individually or with a like-minded group of fellow Christians. It is our task in this chapter to reveal how the vibrancy and compelling nature of revival operates in the lives of individuals and the church *through prayer* at whatever stage in the revival process they may be found. Dr. Martyn Lloyd-Jones and other revival historians have identified three phases of intercessory prayer that occur before and during revival.[1]

Stage 1 -Drawing apart for prayer and intercession for revival

The first phase of prayer occurs when the burden bearers separate themselves and retreat to meet with God and intercede for revival. Throughout all of history, the common and inextricable thread running through all spiritual revivals and awakenings are Christians who bathed their petitions for revival with concerted, heart-felt intercessory prayer. We need only to look to the history of the great evangelical revivals and awakenings of the last three hundred years to find those giants of prayer and intercession for revival such as Jonathan Edwards, John Wesley, and George Whitefield of the First Great Awakening (1720-1783); Isaac Backus and Charles Finney of the Second Great Awakening (1794-1842); Jeremiah Lamphier of the Third Great Awakening (1857-1858); and Evan Roberts of the Welsh Revival (1905) that spread around the world. Frank Bartleman of the Azusa Street Revival (1906-1909) described this intense intercession for revival as "soul travail."[2]

Such drawing aside for intercessory prayer stands in contrast to man's efforts to create revival. Intercessory prayer for revival does not require committees to be organized, advertising campaigns to drum up support, a musical program, and preaching designed to tickle the ear. One of the reasons for the demise of revival beginning in the third decade of the twentieth century was the refusal by many evangelical churches to recognize the departure of the presence of God in their churches. Discernment in many modern-day evangelical churches has deteriorated to the point that it does not perceive anything is amiss or how far the church has departed from the pattern of New Testament Christianity. The departure of the Holy Spirit from many evangelical churches is masked by the numbing narcotic of incessant activity sustained by a plethora of programs, endeavors, entertainment, community projects, attracting seekers and making converts rather than disciples, preaching a therapeutic gospel to improve people rather than saving the soul, and pursuing a social gospel bent on building an earthly kingdom for Christ but which is devoid of eternal significance.

Here we must not confuse the busyness and activities of the modern church with the efforts of men such as Isaac Backus who in 1794, during his great distress at the immorality and irreligion abounding in the new American nation, sent letters to all of the pastors in the various states calling for concerted intercessory prayer for revival. In one sense, that was a national drawing aside for intercession, and this concerted effort eventually brought about the Second Great Awakening in America. Those who carry the burden of sin for those within and without the church must seek out other like-minded Christians to join in concerted prayer for true revival.

But it must be reiterated that no revival has ever been an official movement of the church. Both before and after the Reformation, much of the official church was opposed to revival. But there were men who saw the great sin within the official church and by necessity had to draw aside to intercede with God for the church's deliverance. These were men such as Wycliffe, Luther, the Puritan Fathers, the Wesleys, and Whitefield. In their drawing apart for prayer and intercession, it was not their intent or purpose to establish a new church nor is it the purpose of those seeking true revival. As Lloyd-Jones wrote, "...when God is preparing the way for revival, this is how he always seems to do it. He puts this burden upon certain people, who are called apart, as it were, and they meet together quietly, unknown, and unobtrusively, because they are conscious of this burden."[3]

This drawing apart for intense intercessory prayer produces something even more important than an understanding of the dismal state of the church. It is the desire for greater consecration and holiness that is necessary so that one may come into His presence and know His glory. This invariably leads to separation, and Lloyd-Jones explains why this is important.[4]

> Now there are two things that always happen in this early stage of revival. The people who are concerned about revival in the true sense, are not just out for a little bit of excitement, or interest, or some happiness, or phenomena, or coming with an attitude of 'something marvelous is going to happen and we are going to have a great good time.' That is not how to think about it at all.

> The first indication of a true and genuine concern is that we are aware of our unworthiness and uncleanness. We have got to separate ourselves.[5]

While the small group has separated themselves, the remainder of the people who have not dedicated themselves to prayer for revival and consecration begin to look on with wistful interest and have a vague awareness that something is happening but do not know what it is. Nor do they understand the urgency within this small group of intercessors who resolutely believe that nothing less than the divine intervention of God will change the Laodicean spirit within the church. God takes notice of the intercessors' actions and is pleased. He begins to offer encouragement through manifestations of His presence which is the first

47

indication of a coming revival. "There seems to be a new quickening. The worship of the church becomes warmer, something comes back which had gone, a warmth and a tenderness. There is a growing sense of encouragement. There is a new wistfulness, a new sense of expectation, a new freedom given in the prayer of the people."[6]

For intercessors in all revivals there is a period of agony as they pray, plead, and petition God for revival and deliverance from the burden of sin which they carry. But a point eventually arrives when God gives the assurance that they have been heard. The situation will change, something is going to happen. Although it may take a long time, the entire church begins to be affected. This is the first stage of prayer which is built on intercession and holiness in the presence of God on behalf of the remainder of the church and the lost souls beyond.

Stage 2 – True revival is seeking something extra and not business as usual

Many in the church, having never known or been taught about true revival, will assume that all there is to revival is being conscious of God's presence among them, doing the regular work of ministry that leads to conversion of the lost, and generally being blessed. However, this is only the beginning of revival. There is something more, something extra, something unusual. Revival is never a restoration of the ordinary but something amazing and exceptional. Although intercessors are encouraged by the return of the presence of God and general direction of the church, revival has not arrived. They want something more.[7] For the intercessors, this is the second phase of prayer in their quest for revival.

But what is this "something more"? In other words, what are those things for which those concerned about revival should ask? Dr. Lloyd-Jones has identified three things.

- Personal assurance – Seeking a special *manifestation* of God's presence.

The first thing that happens to men and women upon whom God has laid a burden for revival and intercessory prayer is that they "…feel a desire for a deeper knowledge of God…a hunger and thirst for something bigger and something deeper…" They find no satisfaction with the routine, the mundane, and business-as-usual in the spiritual life of the church. It is not sufficient to simply know that the presence of the Holy Spirit resides in the church. Those that long for the blessing of God in

48

revival desire "a very living and real consciousness of the presence of the Holy Spirit in the Church." God's incomparable love must be demonstrated and manifested in a way that leaves no doubt or hesitation. We must have certainty which only comes through a clear, unusual, and additional manifestation of His love. Without such assurance there can be no revival.[8]

John the apostle wrote of the importance of the knowledge of God. "Now this is eternal life: that they may know you, the only true God, and Jesus Christ, whom you have sent." [John 17:3. NIV] The Holy Spirit communicates a knowledge of God in several ways. One of those ways occurs during a season of a special outpouring of the Holy Spirit that revives the church and brings the submissive Christian into a deeper knowledge of God, not just knowing about God but truly knowing God. As he basks in the nearness of His manifest presence, the Christian cannot help but know God in a deeper, more intimate way. How does this occur? For the Christian, there is a renewal or restoration of intimacy in relationship with the Father which may lead to levels of love and knowledge not previously known and which may lead to the baptism of the Holy Spirit for those not previously filled. For the sinner present during those times of special manifestation of His presence, it will bring conviction that may lead to repentance, forgiveness, and fear of the Lord which is the beginning of wisdom and knowledge (see: Proverbs 9:10).

- Prayer for power

One of the signs of the beginning of revival is that the church realizes that it can do nothing without a manifestation of God's power. The prayer for power is not a matter of pride which is the root of most sin in the world since Satan's deception of Eve in the Garden. In all of the history of the church prior to revival, be it for Old Testament Israel or in the New Testament, there was always a prayer for power. This need is clearly evident to intercessors. Recall that in the first stage of prayer for revival, intercessors recognized the great magnitude of decline of the church and its power, the strength of Satan and his minions, and escalating incursion of worldly systems into all areas of the culture including the church. Yet, the church remains oblivious to its inward decay and nearness of destruction. Without a manifestation of God's power, the church can do nothing.[9] The apostle Paul wrote to the Corinthians of their situation and remains a pattern for the church today.

And I was with you in weakness, and in fear, and in much trembling. And my speech and my preaching was not with enticing words of man's wisdom, but in *demonstration* of the Spirit and of power. That your faith should not stand in the wisdom of men, but in the power of God. [1 Corinthians 2:3-5. KJV] [emphasis added]

Paul used the word "demonstration" but that is a synonym for "manifestation." The power of the church was once sustained by faithful preaching of the milk and meat of God's Word. But the worldly churches' wisdom and enticing words are not substitutes for the Word of God. Worldly wisdom and enticing words cannot build faith, spiritual muscle, and strength to not only withstand Satan and his followers but to carry the battle into the enemy's strongholds. This is why intercessors for revival must seek a mighty manifestation of the power of God.

- Special authentication of the church and her mission

When seeking revival, the third occurrence for which intercessors must pray is the special authentication of the church and her mission. As Dr. Lloyd-Jones explained, the church is meant to be separate, unique, and set apart. If it is not, how is the rest of the world to know that Christians are really God's people? The weakened church has become a matter of derision and mockery in most of the world and especially in the West. The world's perception of the church of Jesus Christ will not change until there is a mighty manifestation of His power which cannot be explained in human terms, something that will captivate the whole world; something so overwhelming, divine, and unusual that the church will be seen as the exclusive and separate people of God.[10]

The results of a spectacular outworking of revival is found in every great revival and awakening as documented in the history of evangelical revivals found in Book II. In each of these revivals the exaltation and authority of His church and her mission was marvelously displayed before a sinful and mocking world and changed the course of history.

Look at the modern evangelical church. It seems that its primary concern is bridging the gap between the church, the world, and other religions. Efforts at fellowship, blending in, and seeking common ground with the people and things of the world in the name of ecumenicalism and unity are an abomination in the sight of God. The uniqueness of the church has disappeared in modern times, but this is not the path upon which revival will be found.

> Do not be yoked together with unbelievers. For what do righteousness and wickedness have in common? Or what fellowship can light have with darkness? [2 Corinthians 6:14. NIV]

However, as the book of Matthew tells us, such separateness must never be confused with abandonment of the world.

> You are the salt of the earth. But if the salt loses its saltiness, how can it be made salty again? It is no longer good for anything, except to be thrown out and trampled underfoot. "You are the light of the world. A town built on a hill cannot be hidden. Neither do people light a lamp and put it under a bowl. Instead they put it on its stand, and it gives light to everyone in the house. In the same way, let your light shine before others, that they may see your good deeds and glorify your Father in heaven. [Matthew 5:13-16. NIV]

The manifestations emitting from just one revival has the candlepower to illuminate the entire world with the power and majesty of Jesus Christ and the unique and special character of His separated people and their mission.

These manifestations are something the world cannot do. To repeat what was written in the second chapter, all authentic revivals and awakenings have a common theme or pattern which "is always the repetition of the phenomena of the Acts of the Apostles..." What are the manifestations found there?

After Jesus' ascension His followers returned to upper room in Jerusalem and for nine days continued in one accord in prayer and supplication. On the day of Pentecost, Christ's promised gift of the baptism of the Holy Spirit suddenly came with manifestations: the sound of the rushing mighty wind, the appearance of cloven tongues like as of fire, and the infilling of the Holy Spirit and speaking with other tongues as the spirit directed (see: Acts 2:1-4).

In Acts 4 we see a repetition of Pentecost. Near the beginning of Chapter 4, we learn that about five thousand men had heard the word and believed. The Jewish religious leaders were highly upset and forbad

Peter and John from preaching and threatened them with prison. Peter and John returned to their fellow believers and reported all that had occurred. When they had heard all, the group raised their voices in prayer.

> And when they had prayed, the place was shaken where they were assembled together; and they were all filled with the Holy Ghost, and they spake the word of God with boldness. And the multitude of them that believed were of one heart and of one soul: neither said any of them that ought of the things which he possessed was his own; but they had all things common. And with great power gave the apostles witness of the resurrection of the Lord Jesus: and great grace was upon them all. [Acts 4:31-33. KJV]

These are only two examples of the New Testament manifestations of the power and working of the Holy Spirit. The sound of the rushing mighty wind, the tongues of cloven fire, and the shaking of buildings are only a few of the manifestations of revival recorded in the New Testament. It is important that intercessors for revival understand that these manifestations did not diminish or stop after the passing of the first century church. The signs and wonders, miracles, and the operation of the gifts of the Holy Spirit are just as important today for they continue to be an attestation of the uniqueness and power of His separated people and their mission to a lost and hell-bound world.

Stage 3 – The glory of God revealed

The first stage of prayer for revival is focused on the return of the abiding presence of the Holy Spirit to the church. As God begins to respond to those prayers, the spiritual life of the church begins stirring, but this is not revival. In the second stage of prayer we saw that those interceding for revival wanted something more than just a return to normalcy between God and the church. They wanted an assurance of their position in Christ, a special outpouring of the Holy Spirit in which His power and presence would be supernaturally demonstrated. They desired a deeper knowledge of God that would lead to a greater closeness, affection, and tender relationship with their loving Father. This is revival.

And yet even in the midst of revival, even though God mercifully allows His children to see His manifest presence, His power, and to dwell in the sweet knowledge of His the loving nearness, there is still a greater level of the knowledge of God that some intercessors seek. And that is to know the *fullness* of His glory. Donald Stamps in his commentary on the glory of God describes it this way. "The glory of God reveals to us the *fullness* of his uniqueness and holiness (i.e., purity, perfection, completeness and separation from evil) and his transcendence (i.e., the fact that he is different from, independent of, and in every way greater than anything he has created)."[11] [emphasis added] Put another way, it is a revelation of God's nature and attributes. That is what Moses asked of God.

> And he said, I beseech thee, shew me thy glory. And he said, I will make all my goodness pass before thee, and I will proclaim the name of the LORD before thee; and will be gracious to whom I will be gracious, and will shew mercy on whom I will shew mercy. And he said, Thou canst not see my face: for there shall no man see me, and live. And the LORD said, Behold, there is a place by me, and thou shalt stand upon a rock: And it shall come to pass, while my glory passeth by, that I will put thee in a clift of the rock, and will cover thee with my hand while I pass by: And I will take away mine hand, and thou shalt see my back parts: but my face shall not be seen. [Exodus 33:18-23. KJV]

Now Moses had witnessed God's mighty power demonstrated again and again in the Israelite's deliverance and flight from Egypt. He saw God's great mercies and loving kindness to the Israelites during their sojourn in the wilderness and communed with God many times while in His presence. But Moses was not satisfied. He wanted to know more about God. He knew that God was the Great I AM, but he wanted to see the fullness of the glory of God. Yet, Moses did not understand the magnitude of what he was asking because no man is capable of seeing God's highest glory and live. However, it pleased God to give Moses a partial glimpse of the fullness of His glory. God's purpose in allowing Moses to have a partial glimpse of the fullness of His glory was to radically change Moses by that revelation.

David Wilkerson has given insight as to what the glory of God should mean to Christians and how it should affect their lives.

Today, Jesus Christ is the express image of who God is. When our Lord became flesh, it was as a full revelation of the heavenly father's mercy, grace, goodness, and readiness to forgive. God wrapped up everything of his nature and character in Jesus. And any revelation of his glory to us now is meant to change us into an expression of Christ![12]

This is the final stage in praying for revival—that we should be like Jesus.

———

In succeeding chapters we shall examine the various characteristics of revival, the physical manifestations, the distinction between revival and evangelism and mass evangelism in particular, the hindrances to revival, and the intensifying drought of revival in the evangelical church since the 1960s and especially in the last thirty years. Finally, we shall examine in some depth the elements necessary for revival as given in the second book of Chronicles. "If my people, who are called by my name, will humble themselves and pray and seek my face and turn from their wicked ways, then I will hear from heaven, and I will forgive their sin and will heal their land." [2 Chronicles 7:14. NIV]

6

Characteristics of Revivals and Awakenings

Some characteristics of revival have consistently occurred in all evangelical revivals since the early 1700s. Other characteristics may vary from revival to revival. In this chapter both types will be examined. The various characteristics are not listed in any particular order of importance nor are they meant to be all inclusive.

Revival is sent by God to all of mankind

Revival is meant to be experienced by all of mankind. When God created the human race through Adam and Eve, mankind was specially set apart, gifted, and distinct from all other forms of life on the planet. He implanted within Adam and Eve an astonishingly complex biological mechanism that eventually produced the human race with an immense degree of differences and characteristics: gender, height, weight, intellect, personality, temperament, and coloration of the skin, hair and eyes to name just a few. Each of these differences contain vast numbers of variations and sub-variations such that no single human being among the nearly eight billion on the planet are totally like any other human.

To complicate matters even further, we must add environmental and cultural influences such as geography, climate, diet, education, family and social practices, life experiences, and a host of other variations that cause each human to be a unique individual in all of human history. Yet, the writer of Psalms assures us that God intimately knows each of His creations even before he or she was formed in their mother's womb.

> My frame was not hidden from you when I was made in the secret place, when I was woven together in the depths of the earth. Your eyes saw my unformed body; all the days ordained for me were written in your book before one of them came to be. [Psalm 139:15-16. NIV]

God does not bring us into life without a purpose. God intends for us to accept Jesus Christ as our Savior and to fulfill His plans and purposes through obedient and faithful service. That is why revival is meant for all mankind in spite of the uncountable differences between each and every human being that ever lived. What evidence do we have to support such a conclusion? Even a cursory examination of recent history reveals that the mechanism of revival has led to the rapid and remarkable spread of the Christian faith throughout the world during the last two hundred and fifty years to all races and classes of people regardless of their economic status, age, temperament, and a host of other factors by which people are different.

True revival brings blessing and judgment

True revival produces either a blessing or judgment depending on the true state of peoples' hearts that have come into the presence of God during revival and either repent or continue in disobedience.

> For it is time for judgment to begin with the family of God; and if it begins with us, what will the outcome be for those who do not obey the gospel of God? [1 Peter 4:17. NIV]

Revival is first for the body of Christ, and during times of revival there must be a deep penetrating self-examination, humility, repentance, and a turning from sin. These actions are necessary before any measure of spiritual revival can take place within the church and a subsequent unleashing of the power of Christian influence in the larger community. Nominal Christians and unbelievers who are not part of the body of Christ may find themselves in His presence during a special outpouring of the Holy Spirit. They will react in one of two ways. Some will feel the weight of conviction, acknowledge their sin, and repent. Those that remain unrepentant and willfully continue in habitual sin will attempt to escape from the presence of God. But God's judgment will overtake them. Unfortunately, many nominal Christians and unbelievers may languish in the pews of spiritually barren churches for years because the Holy Spirit and His convicting power are nowhere to be found. It is too generous to call these nominal churches and nominal Christians "seekers" because they do not seek the presence of God which invariably brings exposure of their spiritual condition and the painful "cleansing and purging" of sin.

Revival is controversial

Revival always brings a degree of controversy. For the majority of modern-day evangelicals, true Holy Spirit-inspired revivals do not often conform to their flawed theological understanding of revival or to their neat, stereotypical ideas of what decency and order should look like during revival. Opposition to revival and all of its messy details come from both inside the church and from the enemies of Christ outside the church. Satan and his minions will always attempt to infiltrate revivals and hinder the moving of the Holy Spirit, usually in one of two opposite ways: by instilling in certain individuals a spirit of criticism of the physical phenomena or by causing a display of excess exuberance beyond the leading of the Holy Spirit.

Physical phenomena inevitably occur during revivals and are the most controversial aspects of revival. These phenomena occur to varying degrees during revival when the Holy Spirit touches people with His convicting power or they experience some other supernatural manifestation of the power of God. However, opportunists and exhibitionists (some may be foolish Christians) will be used by Satan in an attempt to imitate the genuine through excesses and deceptions that bring unbelief or reproach to the work of the Holy Spirit. This occurs in all revivals, but the Christian hungering for an outpouring of the Holy Spirit must focus on the glory of God and not the counterfeit excesses and unbiblical practices.[1] These will be discussed more fully in the chapters on hindrances to revival and physical manifestations in revival.

Revival lasts for a season

As discussed previously, it must again be emphasized that revival is an act of God to bring the church into a state of spiritual restoration and recovery from a state of spiritual decline. Revivals may come gradually or suddenly and end the same way. However, a church's joy, peace, fellowship, worship, prayer, and thanksgiving do not end when the season of true revival and reawakening has run its course. The church also continues to be blessed as well as concerned about sharing the gospel with the masses outside the church

Although men cannot do things to cause revival nor make revival continue, man can cause revival to cease. As noted in Chapter 4, revivals may end prematurely because of the continuation of sin or the occurrence of human frailties among many of the revival's participants.

By human frailties, it is meant a lack of wisdom in balancing "spiritual adrenaline" or "spiritual hyperactivity" occurring in revival and the physical and emotional stresses experienced outside of revival services. Because of this lack of balance, the participants may begin to suffer from lack of rest, sleep, proper diet, and exercise as well as efforts to meet the demands of one's family, job, and life in general.[2]

But again, it must be emphasized that both revival of the church and evangelical conversion of the lost is an act of God and *not* merely some psychological exercise in which a revival and evangelical conversions continue as long as the proper stimulus is applied to the "religious types" susceptible to emotionalism, spiritualism, or belief in the supernatural.[3]

The results of revival are long-lasting

True revival is not meant to be what we might term "a periodic religious fix" to return the Christian to the top of his or her spiritual roller coaster. True revival is meant to revive and empower each born-again Christian so that when the season of revival passes, he or she can experience and live a spiritually transformed and renewed life (i.e., a holy life) and do the works commanded by Christ here on earth.

During the Great Awakening, from about 1730 to 1745, historians have estimated that about fifty thousand people joined the evangelical churches. When the Revival of 1857-1858 occurred, about a half million people joined the Christian churches. What is meant when we say people "joined the churches" in those days is far different than what is meant when someone joins the church today. During the four major religious awakenings in American history, those that joined the church were generally not admitted immediately. They were examined, tested, observed, instructed, trained in the Word, and observed until they gave clear evidence of their conversion and regeneration at which time they were admitted into full membership and the life of the church.[4]

The results of this careful attention to discipleship following conversion are revealing. During the second half of the Second Great Awakening, a blue-ribbon committee was formed to study the life of those converted under the revival ministry of Charles Finney. Ten years after their conversion under Finney, it was found that eighty-five percent were still faithfully serving Christ.[5] How things have changed in the last half of the twentieth century to the present. The great emphasis is on making a decision for Christ. Of course this is the key turning point in any convert's life, but the church today has largely dispensed with the remainder which is discipling the new Christian. That is the reason for the abysmal statistics which show that only one-half of one percent of those who make decisions for Christ in modern evangelistic meetings will be living as Christians two years later.[6] In 1951, Billy Graham made the following statement.

> In the past evangelists have not always seemed willing to face the fact that the so-called "converts" passing through their enquiry rooms are not all converts...Furthermore, many evangelists, including myself, used to spend ninety-five percent of their efforts in persuading men to *decide* for Christ. Now I am convinced that it takes ninety-five percent of evangelistic effort [follow-up] to get men to *follow* Christ, as compared with five percent necessary for decision.[7] [emphasis in original]

How do we reconcile the one-half percent conversion rate with the growth in numbers sitting in the pews of many modern American churches? To paraphrase one of the leaders of the Church Growth movement, they have given the sinner some "slack" and allowed them to join in the life of the church in an effort to fill their pews with the hope that at some point in the future the sinner-seeker will "make a decision for Christ." But what is the end result of all of this? Udo Middelmann in his *The Market Driven Church* gives the answer.

> ...we simultaneously mimic the ways of the world in hopes of packaging our faith into "Christianity Lite"—a spiritual candy we can toss at nonbelievers rather than confronting the hostile reactions that can occur when we proclaim the real gospel of Jesus Christ. Pandering to the culture with prepackaged truth nuggets hasn't made us *more* effective; it has made us *ineffective*.[8] [emphasis in original]

The only effective way to make a new convert a long-term Christian convert is discipleship, and the most effective way to achieve discipleship is through a genuine revival of the church. But even in times of revival, there will be the occasional counterfeit convert. Christ illustrated in the parable of the sower what may occur when various individuals hear the message about the kingdom. Some have no understanding of the message, and the evil one snatches away what was sown in the heart. Many receive the message with joy, but it does not take root. Thus, the message quickly withers away under persecution. Yet, others are drawn away from the message by the worries of this life and the deceitfulness of wealth.

It must be reiterated that the sinner must always be encouraged to attend church and be welcomed therein. That said, sinners must not be allowed to languish for months and even years without hearing a consistent and powerful presentation of the unadulterated Word of God. Such sinners coming under the presence of the convicting power of the Holy Spirit will either repent or flee.

God uses a variety of people to bring revival

God uses many different types of people to lead people into revival. Some have been great orators and great intellects while others are the humblest servants and shiest youth. Thomas Kidd in his book on *The Great Awakening* described Jonathan Edwards (1703-1758) as the most important preacher of that era and one of the most brilliant intellects in American history.[9] Edwards entered Yale at the age of thirteen, graduated at seventeen, spent two additional years studying divinity and getting his M.A. in 1723. He became a tutor at Yale (1723-1726), and at the age of twenty-six in 1728 he was an associate at his grandfather's Northampton, Massachusetts church. In 1729, upon the death of Edwards' grandfather, he became the senior pastor of the church.[10] Edwards began to challenge the theological liberalism that was invading the colonial churches. Edwards strongly opposed Enlightenment rationalism, and by 1733 Edwards was dealing with his church's youth which he believed had drifted from the tenets of the faith. By December 1734 there began to be an excitement that was stirred by a recent number of conversions among the youth, and thus began the awakening of 1734-1735, one of the pivotal events during the early years of the Great Awakening.[11]

Now we move to the other end of the social-academic-intellectual spectrum. Evan Roberts was born in Wales in 1878. After his father was injured in the mines, Evan began working in the coal mines before his twelfth birthday. He left the mines after twelve years and became a blacksmith for two years before entering Newcastle Emlyn Academy in September 1904 to prepare for the ministry. While at the Academy, he attended a revival meeting held by Seth Joshua and was profoundly moved by God and knew that an extraordinary work was about to take place in his life. He had a vision that Wales, known as the land of revival, was about to have its mightiest revival of all. He felt compelled to be a part of it and decided to leave school and go back to his home church to speak to the youth. On the evening of October 31, 1904, he conducted a meeting with seventeen youth that remained after the regular prayer meeting. This was followed by other meetings in area churches, and within a week crowds exceeded the capacity of the churches in which he spoke. By the end of the year Roberts was consistently drawing crowds of 2,500 to 3,000. Revival spread throughout Wales through the efforts of other ministers. Evan Roberts' vision that one hundred thousand would be won for Christ was fulfilled within a matter of months, but the Welsh revival of 1904-1905 also spread to the remainder of British Isles, North America, parts of Europe, Scandinavia, India, and the Orient.[12]

God also uses those not called to full-time ministry to spark revival. Flossie Evans was a timid young Welsh girl who attended a youth meeting in the late winter of 1904. In response to her pastor's request for testimonies from the young people about their various spiritual experiences, Flossie hesitantly rose to speak and said with a tremor in her voice said, "I love Jesus Christ, with all my heart." The assembled young people were very moved and blessed by her sincere declaration. The pureness of Flossie's words spoken from an obedient heart had released the Holy Spirit's power and blessings. News of the New Quay young people's prayer meeting soon spread throughout the area and opened the door for revival in Wales.[13] Six months later Evan Roberts would fan the flames of revival.

When, where, and how revivals begin

Just as there are many types of people God uses to preach and carry forth the message of revival, so too is there great variety as to when, how and where revivals occur.

Revival may be local or wide spread, come suddenly or gradually, and may depart the same way. Revival often breaks out in prayer meetings and spreads to the entire church. These meetings may begin with only a single intercessor fervently praying for revival, a handful of intercessors, or dozens gathered together and entreating God for an extraordinary outpouring of the Holy Spirit, revival of the church, and a general awakening of the moral and spiritual fiber of a nation. Revivals may also be birthed during a season of revival preaching as God's Word is powerfully presented which arrests the hearts of the rank sinner and backslidden Christian and makes way for the convicting power of the Holy Spirit. Revivals also may encourage and comfort the spirits of downtrodden or distraught Christians struggling with living life in a fallen world. Finally, revival may occur in large evangelical gatherings such as those that occurred under the ministries of George Whitefield, John Wesley, and others who preached revival to thousands of people at one time. Revival may occur in large cities such as the one which began at the Union Prayer Meeting held in lower Manhattan that led to the Revival of 1857-1858. Revival may begin in the smallest hamlets such as the tiny villages of Wales under the preaching of Evan Roberts. These small revivals quickly coalesced into the great Welsh Revival of 1905 that spread around the world within a year.

There is no limit to the times when revivals emerge, the length of the season of their blessing, or time of their departure (the when); the places God sends revival (the where); and the variety of conditions and circumstances that God uses to bring about revival among His people (the how).[14]

Regardless of the when, where, and how revivals occur, it must be remembered that an outpouring of the Holy Spirit is always preceded by those who carry the burden of sin found in the church. The burden leads them to intercede with "soul travailing" prayers for repentance, revival, and restoration of the Glory of God among His people. These burden bearers are born of the cross of Christ and have been found to be tried and true. They have humbled themselves, prayed, sought the face of God, and have shunned sin. They are heart-broken over the dismal state of the church and the rampant sin and lawlessness in their communities and nation. They are greatly burdened by the sin abounding in every sphere of life which mocks God and His holiness. A righteous anger swells in their chests as they survey the destruction and death caused by Satan and his minions in the lives of their families, friends, co-workers, and the nameless masses of downtrodden, sin-bound humanity. As these burden bearers fall to their knees with distraught, desperate hearts in an agony of prayer for God's intervention, they become those that stand in the gap, the watchmen on the wall. Their prayers ascending to the Father become the heavenly prelude to revival.

True revival favorably impacts society outside of the church

When it is said that revival favorably impacts society outside of the church, it must be emphasized that this means true revival. In the opposite way, counterfeit revival (and the actions of a few during true revival) bring reproach to the church and the things of God. The greater the revival of the church, the greater the impact there will be on society. There are many remarkable stories of how cities, regions, and nations have experienced dramatic spiritual and moral uplift during and following times of widespread revival in the church. A more in-depth examination of this impact is given in the history of revivals and awakenings found in Book II. One example mentioned here is a description given by a Christian editor who wrote of the social impact of the Awakening of 1905 across America.

> We find evidence of a revival of righteousness in the popular and pulpit protest against the "sharp practice" and "double-dealing" of insurance managers, the indignation against rate swindling, oppressive corporations, dishonest officials of banks and trust companies; the public wrath against political scoundrels and the successful overthrow of many such; and the elevation of power of fearless, honest, competent men in many states and cities.[15]

Just one instance of this revitalization of the spiritual and moral health of the nation is found in a newspaper story written by a secular New York City journalist. He wrote that the 1905 Awakening had brought to the City of Schenectady, New York, "stronger and better citizens, brighter and happier homes, a cleaner city life, and the strengthening of all the churches and other agencies for good."[16] When transformations such as this one are repeated hundreds and perhaps thousands of times across a nation, whole societies are awakened to Christ as sinners are redeemed and Christian men and women are revived and return to their homes, jobs, and communities carrying the good news of Jesus Christ with them. Even when the season of revival passes, the revived church will carry on Christ's work for which they have been invigorated and empowered.

Other characteristics of revival

What follows is a brief and incomplete listing of other characteristics which flow from revival and its aftermath. No single book on revival can be written that includes every characteristic of every revival that has ever occurred. Each outpouring of the Holy Spirit during revival is a unique expression of God's love and mercy specially crafted for each of His special creations.

- Increased zeal for God

The revived body of Christ and new converts crowd into the church, and when the work of the kingdom is laid before them, there are many willing hands ready to take up the tasks. For most, these are not reactions to fleeting emotions of the moment but deep and lasting commitments in service to God. Such are the depths of commitment that there is a large increase in numbers called to full-time ministry.[17]

- Increased concern for personal holiness

In seasons of revival and the return to the life of the church following revival, those who have experienced a special outpouring of the Holy Spirit in the body of Christ (the Church) will have a new aversion to sin and things of the world which is brought about by a sharper conscience that leads to quick conviction over even minor offenses. Many will regularly search their hearts and confess their sins to God and sometimes publicly to their brothers and sisters in Christ. There will be a renewed desire to read the Bible, pray, and attend the house of God with regularity. Even interest in innocent, non-sinful secular activities and hobbies diminish in importance as the things of God take precedence. The general attitude of Christians shifts from seeing how close a Christian may get to the world without crossing the line. Their focus is now on the holy life that will bring them ever closer to Christ.[18]

- Greater expressions of the Christian character in family and public life

During and after revival, the general level of crime will drop as Christians demonstrate the holy life and hold accountable those who stand opposed to God and His kingdom. Honest dealings and restoration where necessary will be the standard for Christians and not the exception. There will be a greater freedom to be identified as a Christian and to share Christian testimonies and other expressions of devotion to God in the public square. Christians will be eager to hear the Word preached with renewed forthrightness and to advance from the milk to the meat of the Word. Society will be greatly benefited by the increased participation of Christians in ministries, organizations, and societies whose missions uplift the culture by meeting the material, emotional, and physical needs of the less fortunate members of society.[19]

- Evidence of the supernatural permeates every facet of revival

Revival is a move of the Spirit of God, a special outpouring of the Holy Spirit which is independent of the efforts of men. Although God is attentive to the pleading prayers and petitions of his people for revival, the bringing and blessings of revival are in every aspect dependent on the actions of the supernatural God. Thus everything to do with true revival must be supernatural. During seasons of revival God may cause some to have dreams and visions, some to prophecy especially regarding turning from sin and the nearness of the Second Coming. Others may experience immediate healings, deliverance from demonic powers, angelic singing, heavenly music, and supernatural light. The supernatural presence of God may cause some to be in such agony by the conviction of sin that they fall to the ground unconscious and unable to move for hours. For varying periods, some sinners may lose their ability to speak, walk, or see. Christians may be so overwhelmed by the supernatural presence of God that they are unable to walk and must be helped or carried from the meeting (sometimes called being "drunk in the Spirit").[20]

———

Revival may always be seen as the front lines in the war between the kingdoms of light and darkness, and throughout the history of revival, physical manifestations occurring in revival are always the most controversial and counterfeited aspect. As we saw in the last section, the presence of the supernatural invariably lead to physical manifestations among many who are present at revival meetings, and these manifestations may be different for Christians and sinners. The subject of physical manifestations is so large and its correct understanding is so important that it will be dealt extensively in the next two chapters. The pervasive presence of physical phenomena during revival and the controversies that surround them are easily recognized as one reads the history of revivals in Book II.

7

Physical Phenomena that Accompany Revival

Before we begin an examination of this extremely complex and difficult but most important subject, it is necessary to reiterate what was written in Chapter 2. In its most elemental form, an evangelical revival or awakening is an outpouring of the Holy Spirit in the body of Christ (the Church) which brings about a *revival of New Testament Christianity*. All authentic revivals and awakenings are "…always the repetition of the phenomena of the Acts of the Apostles…" The wondrous New Testament narrative of the establishment of the church, the periodic revival of believers within the church, and the conversion of sinners may be said to be the pristine pattern for all who follow the way of the Cross.[1] It is within this framework of understanding that we must approach the subject of physical phenomena accompanying revival.

This is not to say the phenomena occurring in the New Testament are complete to the last detail and exclude all others. For example, the New Testament authors described a number of miraculous healings. However, that does not mean that all healings thereafter are limited to those specific ailments, injuries, or conditions mentioned in the New Testament. Rather, those healings serve as a *pattern* for the church in seeking healing for all manner of illness—mental, emotional, and physical diseases and injury. In a similar manner, the New Testament authors describe numerous phenomena surrounding the establishment of the church, revival of believers, and conversion of sinners which also serve as a pattern for other phenomena that may occur as a result of an outpouring of the Holy Spirit. However, the kinds or types of phenomena that do occur as a result of a special outpouring of the Holy Spirit are not limitless. Second, the phenomena that occur have boundaries and limitations set by the Holy Spirit, and these may vary from place to place and from time to time as guided by the Holy Spirit. Violation of these boundaries and limitations bring distortion, confusion, and damage to the work of revival and dishonor to God's holiness. In times of true revival Satan always attempts to inject the revival-killing poisons of self, fleshly excess, counterfeit phenomena, and demonic influence.

In every great revival, physical phenomena have been present to varying degrees, but they have been especially prominent in revivals since the birth of evangelicalism. The emergence of the widespread physical manifestations during revival in the early 1700s brought about the evangelical church, but the evangelical church also saw the continuing need of periodic revivals of believers within the church. The Northampton revival of 1734-1735 at Jonathan Edwards' church saw numerous miraculous and ecstatic manifestations of the Holy Spirit, signs and wonders, visions, healings, and other phenomena. These phenomena were also present during virtually all of the major revivals that occurred during the eighteenth century. Edwards strongly affirmed these manifestations but attempted to address those whose emotional expressions led to excess "enthusiasm." Edwards defended those who had visions which he called "impressions." He stated that they had not seen these visions "with their bodily eyes" but were dramatic pictures in their minds. Even though Edwards was at a loss to explain the visions, he did not dismiss them because the visions were accompanied by "a great sense of the spiritual excellency of divine things." Yet, Edwards repeatedly cautioned visionaries to distinguish between the "vain and imaginary for the truly spiritual."[2]

The great question of the genuineness of ecstatic expressions of worship is found in the *motives* of worshipper. This was Edwards' test: did the ecstatic expressions lead the worshipper to a greater appreciation of God's glory or did such expressions descend into mere self-glorification? Those expressions which led to a greater comprehension of God and His glory were incidental to the operation of the Holy Spirit in persons susceptible to them because of their particular mental and emotional makeup.[3] Put another way, Edwards is saying that we may conclude that those ecstatic expressions of worship may vary from one individual to the next depending on their respective emotional and mental makeup. But whether emotionally volatile or reserved, those expressions that lead to self-glorification must be judged as being driven by emotionalism gone to excess.

Here we must be careful to distinguish between (1) the mental and emotional makeup of individual and (2) an individual's sensitivity to the leading and operation of the Holy Spirit. The two are not necessarily the same. In other words, we must not automatically conclude that a person with a higher level of emotional and mental effusiveness is therefore more sensitive to the moving and operation of the Holy Spirit or conversely that a typically reserved person is less sensitive. Said another way, we must not confine sensitivity to the leading and operation of the Holy Spirit during times of revival only to those who are more emotionally and physically excitable. Those who are constitutionally reserved in their emotional and physical demeanor may be just as sensitive to the leading and operation of the Holy Spirit whether in times of revival or otherwise.

True revival will bring physical manifestations born of deep sorrow and conviction of sin

The process of conviction, confession, and repentance in revival is painful, the universality of which is demonstrated by a brief look at the history of revivals. During the long history of revivals and awakenings, conviction, confession, repentance, and forgiveness, physical (bodily) manifestations are invariably present. Mathew Backholer wrote of many physical manifestations that had been present in all revivals. Many of these manifestations occurred as a result of deep conviction of sin during revivals held by some of the most famous preachers of the First Great Awakening during the middle third of 1700s. Backholer gives a brief account of some of the manifestations that occurred during the preaching of John Wesley and George Whitefield.

> Some of these manifestations were of the flesh (which John Wesley rebuked), the majority was of God, when those under deep conviction of sin cried out, in screams and deep anguish of soul, some slumped to the ground, while others convulsed, shook, or trembled. Some of the manifestations were clearly demonic and the people concerned were delivered from the oppression of the devil when they cried out to God.

> John Wesley on the 7 July 1739 had to talk to George Whitefield "of those outward signs which had so often accompanied the inward work of God." Wesley continued in his *Journal*, "I found his objections were chiefly grounded on gross misrepresentations of matter of fact. But the next day he had opportunity of informing himself better: for no sooner had he (Whitefield) begun (in the application of his sermon) to invite all sinners to believe in Christ, than four persons sunk down close to him, almost in the same time. One of them lay without sense or motion. A second trembled exceedingly. The third had strong convulsions all over his body, but made no noise, unless by groans. The fourth equally convulsed, called upon God, with strong cries and tears.

From this time on I (Wesley) trust, we shall all suffer God to Carry on His work in the way that pleaseth Him."[4]

Less than a year later, George Whitefield's objections would be completely overcome concerning the continued occurrence of the perplexing physical manifestations occurring during his revivals. Whitefield's biographer, John Pollock, reported of the occurrences at Whitefield's Philadelphia meeting on May 10, 1740, and at Nottingham, Delaware, four days later which assured Whitefield of the divine cause of the physical manifestations.

He (Whitefield) began a brief prayer before addressing the assembly but to his own astonishment could not stop. Petitions, praises, raptures poured from his lips: "A wonderful power was in that room." Soon the girls were sobbing and confessing and weeping for sins…When he ceased to pray no one noticed [as] every girl in the room was totally absorbed in prayer and confession, an amazing medley of sound…"They continued in prayer for above an hour, confessing their most secret faults; and at length the agonies of some were so strong that five of them seemed affected as those who were in fits." George crept away. He wondered how much was the devil trying to disrupt the gospel, how much the genuine, unfathomable power of God.

…when Whitefield preached on 14 May to twelve thousand people who had gathered in a clearing near Nottingham, Delaware, "thousands cried out, so that they almost drowned my voice." George did not doubt this time that the Spirit of God was present in fire and love and force. Men and women dropped as dead, then revived, then fainted again, as George preached on, swept up into contemplation of Christ's "all constraining, free and everlasting love" until, as he reached a last appeal to come to the Cross and receive the grace of God, George himself fell in a swoon.[5]

These manifestations occurred as a result of deep conviction and repentance and were present and characteristic of all great awakenings and revivals from the birth of evangelicalism. Charles Finney, the great revivalists of the Second Great Awakening in America wrote of manifestations that occurred in one revival in a particularly ungodly place.

> I had not spoken to them in this train of direct application more than a quarter of an hour when all at once an awful solemnity seemed to settle down upon them. The congregation began to fall from their seats in every direction and cry for mercy. If I had had a sword in each hand I could not have cut them off their seats as fast as they fell.[6]

During the Welsh Revival of 1858-1859, the manifestations described in the following accounts occurred as a result of deep conviction of sin and were typical of those found in many revival prayer meetings.

> It was in its terrors that the eternal became a reality to them first. They seemed plunged into depths of godly sorrow...For some weeks it was the voice of weeping and the sound of mourning that was heard in the meetings. The house was often so full of the divine presence that ungodly men trembled terror-stricken; and at the close, sometimes they fled as from some impending peril...[7]

During the Welsh Revival of 1904, it was not his eloquence but the tears of Evan Roberts that affected his audience.

> He would break down, crying bitterly for God to bend them, in an agony of prayer, the tears coursing down his cheeks, with his whole frame writhing. Strong men would break down and cry like children...a sound of weeping and wailing would fill the air.[8]

Revival is a form of re-birth or being born again whether one is a life-long sinner, a backslidden Christian, or an individual Christian or a body of believers who have lost their first love. Given the often painful elements of revival (burden bearing, soul travail through intercessory prayer, conviction of sin, confession, repentance, and salvation), the process of revival as well as being spiritually born again may be compared to the painful process of natural childbirth. The actions, sounds, agonies, and subsequent joys originating from both are often indistinguishable.

The purpose of physical phenomena during revival

Those who seek revival of the church in a sanitized, orderly, refined manner without the discomfiture of physical phenomena are seeking in vain. Revival, like the birthing process, is a messy and painful affair. Revival comes only through the divine outpouring of the Holy Spirit, and He will dictate its terms and conditions, messy or otherwise.

In these so-called enlightened times there are legions of religious leaders mainly found in the apostate seminaries and liberal churches but increasingly in evangelical churches as well who deny the need for revival and especially the physical phenomena accompanying revival meetings. Many of these same people have attempted to explain away or openly deny much of the New Testament and have entirely dismissed the Old Testament as too harsh and primitive to be relevant to modern times.

Those that dismiss the necessity of physical phenomena during revival often begin by questioning the *purpose* of these phenomena. But in the same context one must then question the purpose of love in a marriage relationship. Love for one's spouse is not only a feeling but may also be an outwardly observable physical expression of the marital relationship. The obvious physical aspects of love in a marriage relationship are not hidden away but visible testimony to the world through the tender expressions of that love memorialized in a couple's vow that they will "from this day forward, for better, for worse, for richer, for poorer, in sickness and in health, to love and to cherish, till death do us part." As these vows are lived out in a marriage relationship, their love becomes a visible reality which cannot be hidden away or discarded. Love plainly exists apart from any definable non-physical purpose that may be present.

Similarly, expressions of physical phenomena during a revival are the result of an individual's encounter with the manifest presence of the Holy Spirit during a special outpouring. Such an encounter has the potential to become an eternal relationship with God. Thus, we may say that these physical phenomena are a reaction to an encounter with God. Like visible manifestations of love, physical phenomena in revival are an outward testimony to a supernatural encounter with the Holy Spirit.

However, we must not say that God does not have purposes for physical phenomena that occur during revival. To illustrate one of those purposes, we must return to our example of love. Not only is love an expression of the marital relationship, these expressions have a purpose apart from the man and woman bound by their marital vows. The love that is shared and demonstrated by a couple through many years of a beautiful marriage serves as a model for children, family, friends, and others.

In the same manner, physical phenomena that occur during a revival are not only an expression of an encounter with God, they speak to the onlookers, both in the church and in the world. Here we return to the day of Pentecost when a violent wind filled the whole house where the disciples and others had gathered. Tongues of fire rested on each of them and all were filled with the Holy Spirit and began to speak in other tongues as the Spirit enabled them. These phenomena were observed by certain God-fearing Jews from all over the world that had gathered in Jerusalem at that time.

> Now there were staying in Jerusalem God-fearing Jews from every nation under heaven. When they heard this sound, a crowd came together in bewilderment, because each one heard their own language being spoken. Utterly amazed, they asked: "Aren't all these who are speaking Galileans? Then how is it that each of us hears them in our native language? ... Amazed and perplexed, they asked one another, "What does this mean?" Some, however, made fun of them and said, "They have had too much wine." Then Peter stood up with the Eleven, raised his voice and addressed the crowd: "Fellow Jews and all of you who live in Jerusalem, let me explain this to you; listen carefully to what I say. These people are not drunk, as you suppose. It's only nine in the morning! No, this is what was spoken by the prophet Joel... [Acts 2:5-8, 12-16. NIV]

Then Peter continued preaching to the multitude and explained the meaning of the physical phenomena in light Joel's Old Testament prophesy. Human nature has not changed, and just as in Peter's time when the Holy Spirit was poured out as on the day of Pentecost, the curiosity of men and women will be attracted by the unusual or extraordinary. Many will deny the truth and reject what they see. Others will jeer and mock. Yet, some will have their hearts pricked by what they see, repent, and seek forgiveness.

Not only are the physical phenomena of a bodily nature during revival, sometimes the Holy Spirit supernaturally intervenes in nature to demonstrate his power and presence. On the day of Pentecost alone, God used a mighty wind, tongues of fire, and men and women speaking in unknown languages to the amazement of the gathered crowds. Paul and Silas found themselves in prison for preaching the gospel. At midnight they were praying and singing hymns as the other prisoners listened. "Suddenly there was such a violent earthquake that the foundations of the prison were shaken. At once all the prison doors flew open, and everyone's chains came loose." [Acts 16:26. NIV] Because of that mini-revival and the supernatural occurrences that accompanied, their suicidal jailer believed in the Lord Jesus and was saved, both spiritually and physically.

Revival in an age of mass communication

Modern technology and means of communication are both a blessing and a curse as they relate to revival. Prior to the twentieth century, news of revival spread by the re-telling of eye-witness accounts, written correspondence, newsletters, newspapers, and pamphlets and books. This all changed in the age of electronic broadcast media when time-delayed reports of revival were replaced by broadcast reports, either through live coverage or through recorded and edited reports. As a consequence, it is often the dramatic physical manifestations that receive most attention in audio and visual media. As various media compete for large audiences, it is the human tendency to focus on the unusual, dramatic, or bazaar.[9]

Unfortunately, evangelists, pastors, and other church leaders recognize this tendency and have embraced certain methods and practices during revival that pander to the desires and emotions of the audience. This includes the encouragement of or participation in certain spectacular physical phenomena during revival that are not from God. The inner working of the Holy Spirit in saving souls and changing the lives of individuals are often not immediately visible and therefore less spectacular. So it is a human tendency to link the revival with the manifestations and not the inner work occurring within the heart and soul. Thus, the measure of spirituality and "success" of a revival is too often linked with physical manifestations which are assumed to be evidence of God's blessing on certain ministries. Other less discerning men and women of God begin copying these tactics. But it must always be remembered that physical phenomena that are experienced by people during revival are a direct response to the power, presence, and operation of the Holy Spirit and not man's imitation or manipulation.

Revival and mass evangelism

It is important to distinguish true revival from the modern depersonalized efforts of mass evangelism. This distinction was unnecessary for revivals prior to the age of mass electronic communication that began with radio and television in the third decade of the twentieth century.

True revivals are always evangelistic but mass evangelism generally has not led to revival of the church or general awakening of the community. True revival revitalizes the body of Christ, i.e., the church. An awakening occurs when the revival of the church spills into the larger community and beyond which stirs an interest in the Christian faith among nominal Christians and unbelievers. The term "modern revivalism" is often used interchangeably with "professional mass evangelism," but the two are not the same in methodology or results.[10]

Perhaps the defining moment of modern mass evangelism occurred in 1949 as a result of an eight-week Los Angeles crusade held by a thirty-one year old Southern Baptist preacher by the name of Billy Graham. Graham's larger and commendable goal was to "revive revivalism." According to historian Paul Johnson, Graham's "stress was not on sinfulness so much as opportunity, renewal, and peace of mind, epitomized in his *Peace with God* (1953)."[11] The Los Angeles crusade set the pattern for other massive crusades held by Graham and other well-known evangelists over the next several decades.

However, in the quest to revive revivalism, something unforeseen happened. These massive crusades soon became marvels of planning, organization, and staffing reminiscent of complex military battle campaigns. In 1957, Graham had been the most celebrated evangelist for almost a decade when he and his organization conducted the famous 1957 Manhattan crusade which featured a 4000 member choir, 3000 ushers, and thousands of counselors for those who had made a decision for Christ. For sixteen weeks Graham preached to 20,000 per night at Madison Square Garden. On one mid-summer day the crusade was taken to Yankee Stadium and broke all attendance records when 100,000 attended. The crusade ended on Labor Day weekend with an open-air meeting surrounded by skyscrapers at 42nd and Broadway's Times Square which attracted a crowd comparable in size to the one at Yankee Stadium.[12]

The growth of high-profile mass evangelism paralleled growth in church affiliation by Americans between 1940 and 1960. In the two decades between 1910 and 1930, forty-three percent of Americans identified themselves with particular churches. Beginning in the 1930s the percentage of Americans affiliated with particular churches had grown to 49 percent in 1940, 55 percent in 1950, and 69 percent in 1960 but declined to 62.4 percent in 1970 following the turbulent decade of the 1960s.[13] It can be reasonably assumed that mass evangelism supported growth of the church in the 1940s and 1950s, but other evidence does not support a contention that mass evangelism was the primary cause of growth in church affiliation.

The difference between revival and mass evangelism

The fundamental difference between revival and mass evangelism is their respective sources from which they spring. Evangelistic crusades of whatever magnitude arise from great human effort and activity: organization, publicity, great choirs, well-known evangelists, and a host of other details that come together at an evangelistic meeting. But revivals are exactly the opposite in that the activity is generated by the revival under the impetus and direction of the Holy Spirit in response to the prayers of burdened believers who have besieged heaven with their prayers.

The spontaneous spiritual movements throughout the history of revivals bear little to no resemblance to the highly orchestrated professional mass evangelism campaigns of the modern era. Although evangelistic crusades are needed and have their rightful place in accomplishing God's mission for the church, they must never be considered a substitute for true revival. Both revival and evangelistic campaigns are of great benefit to a healthy and thriving church, but the languishing church that has lost its first love must have revival.

Revival historian Dr. J. Edwin Orr has said that there can be no justification for treating modern mass evangelism as being synonymous with revival.

> Christians, individually or collectively, may engage in evangelism or social action, the former the presentation of the Good News of Jesus Christ with the object of bringing men to vital faith in God, which is their great commission, and the latter application of Christian truth to human situations, whether individual or social. Thus

> evangelism and social action *may* issue from a revival or
> awakening, or they *may not*, if hindered by
> circumstances.[14] [emphasis added]

In other words, revivals may or may not produce evangelism and social
action. But can evangelism produce revival? To answer this question, a
second question must be asked. In what type of meetings do revivals
originate? An examination of the history of revivals and awakenings will
show that revival may arise from a single individual praying alone.
Jeremiah Lamphier prayed alone for some time in New York City before
being joined by others. From one individual committed to prayer for
revival was birthed the great Revival of 1857-1858. Sometimes revival
comes through the prayers of two or three who have gathered together to
bombard heaven for a heaven-sent revival. Sometimes revival may arise
from a single preaching service. And sometimes a series of meetings
built around a planned campaign of evangelism may be seized by the
Holy Spirit, becomes a revival, and take a new direction entirely.[15] But
modern history records few if any significant, lasting revivals that have
arisen from modern professional mass evangelism campaigns.

Other than peripheral support for the church, it appears that
professional mass evangelism has done little since the end of the 1950s
to build the church of Jesus Christ through discipleship and retention of
confessed converts harvested in mass campaigns. The truth of this
statement is confirmed by an examination of the retention rates of those
"committing to Christ" during these crusades. It has been reported that
ninety 98.5 percent of those who made commitments to Christ in modern
evangelistic meetings of today will *not* be living as Christians within two
years. In other words, the retention rate of those committing to Christ is
only 1.5 percent. In contrast to this dismal statistic, a blue-ribbon
committee studied those who made professions of faith in the revival
meetings of Charles Finney in the first half of the nineteenth century
found that 85 percent were faithfully serving the Lord after a decade![16]

Evangelistic campaigns focus on winning the lost. The focus of
revival is to revive the church. Only when there has been a mighty move
of God in reviving the church can a community, district, or nation
receive a great and lasting moral uplift. As we have said, the ultimate
purpose of revival is for the glory of God, and the more God is glorified
in the church, the more He will be glorified through a general moral
uplift of the general culture. This has been proven in every great revival
or awakening in the history of evangelicalism.

8

Manifestations – The Distinguishing Marks of a Work of the Spirit of God

As noted in the previous chapter, the manifestations and phenomena occurring in the New Testament are not meant to be complete to the last detail and exclude all others. Rather, the New Testament manifestations and phenomena serve as a pattern throughout church history for other manifestations and phenomena that may occur as a result of an outpouring of the Holy Spirit. However, as previously noted, the kinds of manifestations and phenomena that do occur as a result of a special outpouring of the Holy Spirit are not limitless. There are boundaries and limitations set by the Holy Spirit, and these may vary from place to place and from time to time as guided by the Holy Spirit. The letter and Spirit of the Word are always sovereign but may not give a complete picture of the Christian's experience as he or she responds to a special outpouring of the Holy Spirit. Therefore, it is right and proper that Christians "test the spirits" with regard to these manifestations as John the apostle cautioned. "Dear friends, do not believe every spirit, but test the spirits to see whether they are from God, because many false prophets have gone out into the world." [1 John 4:1. NIV]

To that end this chapter will rely heavily on a small book published by Jonathan Edwards in 1741. Edwards is considered by many as one of the greatest minds of the eighteen century and a pillar of The First Great Awakening. He was pastor of the church at Northampton, Massachusetts, during the famous Northampton revival of 1734-1735. Based on a sermon he preached in Boston, Edwards wrote *The Distinguishing Marks of a Work of the Spirit of God* which is perhaps the most brilliant, discerning, articulate, and possibly unsurpassed discussion of manifestations that occur during spiritual revivals of New Testament churches. In the introduction, Edwards wrote:

> In the apostolic age, there was the greatest outpouring of the Spirit of God that ever was; both as to his extraordinary influences and gifts, and his ordinary operations, in convincing, converting, enlightening, and sanctifying the souls of men. But as the influences of the true Spirit abounded, so counterfeits did also abound: *the*

*devil was abundant in mimicking, both the ordinary and
extraordinary influences of the Spirit of God,* as is
manifest by innumerable passages of the apostles'
writings. This made it very necessary that the church of
Christ should be furnished with some certain rules,
distinguishing and clear marks, by which she might
proceed safely in judging of the true from the false
without danger of being imposed upon.[1] [emphasis
added]

Both Edwards and the apostle John's first letter make it plain
that Christians should be concerned with all manifestations that occur
during revival in order to distinguish the true Spirit from the false.
Discernment in these matters is important not only in matters of
prophesy, miracles, and other manifestations of the Spirit during revival
but also in the ordinary day-to-day influences of those manifestations on
the minds of the people.[2]

Edwards described the distinguishing scriptural evidences or
marks of a true work of the Spirit of God, i.e., true revival. These are
positive characteristics found throughout the Bible which point to a
Christ-like nature abounding of a work in both the lives of individual
participants and the overall demeanor of the work as it progresses.
Edwards identifies five marks of a true move of God: the exaltation of
Jesus Christ, the overcoming of Satan's kingdom, a love of the
Scriptures, people are convinced of the truth of the gospel, and an
expressed and evident love of God and man. When the term "true work
of the Spirit of God" is used in this book, it should not be thought to
imply that the Holy Spirit also does works that are not a true work.

*The distinguishing evidences from Scripture which confirm that a work is
of the Spirit of god*

1. A sure sign that the work is from the Spirit of God is plainly
   evident when the operation of the work is such as to heighten the
   participant's esteem of Jesus "…who was born of the Virgin, and
   was a crucified without the gates of Jerusalem; and seems more
   to confirm and establish their minds in the truth of what the
   gospel declares to us of his being the Son of God, and the
   Saviour of men…"[3]

Edwards is saying that a true revival will contain a number of people who have been genuinely drawn to or "esteem" Jesus Christ. However, among those are people who may not have accepted Christ as their Lord and Savior. This is not evidence that a revival is not a true work of the Holy Spirit.[4] In previous chapters we have given accounts of many who came under the convicting power of the Holy Spirit or had shown particular affection for Christ during revival but who did not ultimately accept Christ as savior and make Him the Lord of their lives. It must always be remembered that Satan is the great enemy of God and man. The devil and his followers may entice men who were once drawn to Jesus and lead them away to another christ or some mystical christ such as a light within.

2. A sure sign that the work is from the Spirit of God and not a false spirit is obvious when "…the work operates against the interests of Satan's kingdom, which lies in encouraging and establishing sin, and cherishing men's worldly lusts…"[5]

Edwards' teaching is clear that Satan is the god of the world and that his kingdom is the world, but Christ said, "My kingdom is not of this world." Therefore, the Holy Spirit operates to lead men away from the things of the world, but Satan does just the opposite.

> Do not love the world or anything in the world. If anyone loves the world, love for the Father is not in them. For everything in the world—the lust of the flesh, the lust of the eyes, and the pride of life—comes not from the Father but from the world. [1 John 1:15-16. NIV]

Thus, the direction taken by the work of a spirit is ample evidence to determine whether it is a true or false spirit. If the spirit at work among the people leads them away from the pleasures, cares, and concerns of the world; heightens their focus and concern for things eternal; and causes a realization of the awfulness of sin and its works of misery, guilt, and destruction; then it may be deemed to be a true work of the Holy Spirit. To every degree that a work of the Holy Spirit is invaded and diminished by the things of the world, this can be attributed to Satan and his effort to sow tares into a true work of the Spirit of God.

3. A sure sign that the work is from the Spirit of God is clear when the spirit operates to place in the hearts of men a greater regard for the Holy Scriptures and its truth and divine origin.[6]

One of Satan's most devastating tactics in his war to corrupt the souls of men is to diminish or destroy their belief in and reliance upon the Word of God. As men ignore, limit, challenge, marginalize, or pervert the Bible and its direction for their lives, they open themselves to a spirit of delusion which leads away from light to Satan's kingdom of darkness.[7]

Love and respect for the inerrant Word of God during times of revival is vitally important for it is during these times when people see or experience manifestations as a consequence of the special outpouring of the Holy Spirit. The Word of God is the foundation of the church, and without a love of God's truth, men's hearts are inclined toward delusion.[8] New Christians, those with limited knowledge of the Scriptures, those lacking a measure of discernment, and those who are especially caught up in their enthusiasm for manifestations experienced during revival have a greater tendency to diminish or ignore the supreme importance of the written Word of God and replace it with deviant rules and theologies or some other light from within. Revival is diminished or terminated when regard for the truth of the Holy Scriptures becomes significantly marginalized or made subordinate to manifestations during times of a special outpouring of the Holy Spirit.

4. A sure sign that the work is from the Spirit of God is apparent when the spirit operates in a spirit of truth as opposed to a spirit of error.

When a work of a spirit is observed, it can be determined whether it is the spirit of truth or the spirit of error that counterfeits the operation of the Holy Spirit. A spirit of truth leads people to light and convinces them of things that are true, but Satan is the father of lies and leads people into deception and darkness. Paul says, "But everything exposed by the light becomes visible—and everything that is illuminated becomes a light." [Ephesians 5:13. NIV] As light prevails over darkness the Christian finds liberation from the power and control of Satan. "For he has rescued us from the dominion of darkness and brought us into the kingdom of the Son he loves." [Colossians 1:13. NIV] Thus, we can say that when a spirit brings light and exposes error, it is the true Spirit of God.[9]

5. A sure sign that a work is from the Spirit of God is obvious when
    that "work among a people operates as a spirit of love to God
    and man."[10]

The importance that God places on love is found in the book of
Matthew when Jesus responded to a Pharisee's question as to the greatest
commandment in the Law.

> Jesus replied: 'Love the Lord your God with all your
> heart and with all your soul and with all your mind.' This
> is the first and greatest commandment. And the second is
> like it: 'Love your neighbor as yourself.' All the Law
> and the Prophets hang on these two commandments.
> [Matthew 22:37-40. NIV]

Perhaps more than any other, the spirit of a work of revival is determined
by its adherence to these two commandments.

A true work of the spirit is one that leads toward the type of love
spoken of by Christ in His response to the Pharisee. When the true work
of the Spirit of God is working among the people, they begin to realize
and have an appreciation for the incomprehensible love of God about
which the apostle John wrote. "This is how God showed his love among
us: He sent his one and only Son into the world that we might live
through him. This is love: not that we loved God, but that he loved us
and sent his Son as an atoning sacrifice for our sins." [1 John 4:9-10.
NIV] When the work of the spirit drives people toward a realization of
God's incomprehensible love for man and the price He paid to make
possible the redemption of his special creation, it must unquestionably be
"evidence of the work and influence of a true and divine spirit."[11]

But Satan is a master craftsman at counterfeiting a work of the
true Spirit. Edwards speaks of a counterfeit love that leads people into a
spirit of delusion.

> There is commonly in the wildest enthusiasts, a kind of
> union and affection, arising from self-love, occasioned
> by their agreeing in those things wherein they greatly
> differ from all others, and from which they are objects of
> the ridicule of all the rest of mankind. This naturally will
> cause them so much the more to prize those peculiarities
> that make them the objects of others' contempt...it is

only the working of a natural self-love, and not true
benevolence, any more than the union and friendship
which may be among a company of pirates, that are at
war with all the rest of the world.[12]

Here Edwards is alluding to an elitism or a "holier than thou"
attitude that arises among those who cherish their pretentious
peculiarities as a result of self-love and not a love for God or other men.

Standing in contrast to this self-love is the divine supernatural
love of God expressed through the Christian virtue of humility which
"renounces, abases, and annihilates the Adamic nature of self-love." A
Christ-like love and humility that flows through the people during a true
work of the Spirit stands in stark contrast to the malice and pride that is
inherent in self-love and the mark of a false spirit at work among
people.[13]

Signs that are wrongly used to discredit a true work of the Spirit of God

Edwards described nine revival characteristics which some have
used to discredit true revivals. Edwards calls these "negative signs" by
which he meant signs that *cannot* be used to judge a work of God and
specifically what signs are *not* evidence that a work is *not from the Spirit
of God*. Since manifestations associated with revival are Satan's most
effective means to undermine and destroy true revival, he injects false,
self-centered, or excessive manifestations which are presented as
evidence that a revival is not a true work of the Spirit of God.

1. A true work of the Spirit of God *cannot* be discredited because
    the manner in which the work is carried out is unusual and
    extraordinary.

Such an unusual and extraordinary work must pass the test of the
Scriptures. However, those judging a work tend to substitute experience
for the Word of God. In other words they are saying, "We haven't
experienced that before, so it can't be a work of the true Spirit." As
Edwards succinctly explained, "The Holy Spirit is sovereign in his
operation; and we know that he uses a great variety; and we cannot tell
how great a variety he may use, within the compass of the rules he
himself has fixed. We ought not to limit God where he has not limited
himself."[14]

Edwards makes several arguments in defense of the unusual and extraordinary occurrences in a true work of the Spirit of God. These arise from a variety of circumstances: the swiftness of the change in atmosphere as the Holy Spirit makes his presence known; an overwhelming conviction because of one's sinful nature; the overwhelming magnitude of the glories of God glimpsed during a special outpouring of the Holy Spirit; and the expression during revival of a variety of human emotions such as fear, sorrow, desire, and love. Each human being is a unique creation of God and will react differently as they come into God's presence.[15]

Edwards points out that, "It may be reasonably expected that the extraordinary manner of the work then, will bear some proportion to the very extraordinary events, and that glorious change in the state of the world, which God will bring to pass by it." Therefore, the extraordinary power and degree of influence of a work of the Spirit during a revival is not an argument against but rather in favor of a true work of the Holy Spirit, as long as the occurrences and manifestations are in conformity with the "rules and marks of Scripture."[16]

As the boundaries of Scripture are approached during revival by certain manifestations of a lesser degree, it may not be easily distinguished whether the nature of the minor occurrence falls within or without those boundaries.[17] In such cases godly leaders and wise counselors should approach these matters with restraint, caution, and discernment. If it is an issue of suspected tares among the wheat, it may be well to ignore them for a season rather than cause greater damage by uprooting the offending tares.

2. "A work is *not* to be judge by any effects on the bodies of men; such as tears, trembling, groans, loud outcries, agonies of body, or the failing of bodily strength."

    "The influence persons are under, is *not* to be judged of one way or other, by such effects on the body; and the reason is, because the Scripture nowhere gives us any such rule."[18]

Some contend that a work of the spirit is not from God because it contains bodily manifestations not recorded in the New Testament but which arise from an individual's being overwrought or excessively emotional. But Edwards stated that there is no rule of Scripture by which men are to judge a work by outward effects upon the body. Edwards argues that the extraordinary manifestations described above may be considered a normal human reaction (1) for the child of Christ as he comes into proximity to the wondrous glories of God's presence and (2) for the sinner or backslidden Christian as the Holy Spirit exposes and convicts the destitute souls of lost men and women. Given the nature of mankind, it would be unusual or even remarkable if individuals under a divine outpouring of the Holy Spirit did *not* have various extraordinary reactions. Depending on their spiritual state, these bodily reactions may include loss of bodily strength, the body being seized and thrown into great agonies or rapture, and loud outcries of despair or jubilation.[19]

Edwards had no objections to these manifestations. He argued that neither man's reason nor the New Testament excludes such things given (1) the nature of man, (2) what the Scriptures informs us in general concerning the nature of eternal things, and (3) the nature of the convictions of God's Spirit. Thus, there is "no need that any thing should be said in particular concerning these external, circumstantial effects."[20]

However, a note of clarification must be added to Edwards' statement. As previously noted, revivals all through the history of the evangelical church have had elements that were not a true work of the Holy Spirit. But beginning in the twentieth century, there have arisen a significant increase in false revivals led by false prophets and teachers who perform great signs and wonders. These revivals have been accompanied by many wild and outlandish manifestations that are recognized as having a false and anti-biblical nature. Because of a departure from sound doctrine and lack of spiritual discernment, many Christians and their leadership have been and will continue to be deceived. These works of these false teachers will be discussed in later chapters.

> For false messiahs and false prophets will appear and perform great signs and wonders to deceive, if possible, even the elect. See, I have told you ahead of time. [Matthew 24:24-25. NIV]

3. A true work of the Spirit of God *cannot* be discredited because "it occasions a great deal of noise about religion."[21]

Some people wrongly believe that a true work of the Spirit of God cannot be vigorously passionate and expressive. But where vigor and emotion are suppressed, the work of the Spirit will subside as the church quickly slides into a sedate, ritualistic work centered on forms of godliness and self-importance. Similar to his arguments in the last section, Edwards states that it is not possible for a people to be caught up in a revival led by the Holy Spirit without causing a "notable, visible, and open commotion and alteration amongst that people." A true work of the Spirit of God will cause people to be affected with much "noise and stir" such as when the apostles "turned the world upside down" (see: Acts 17:6. KJV).[22]

4.   A true work of the Spirit of God *cannot* be denied by claiming people's minds have been overcome by their own thoughts and imaginations.

Some people deny that a work is a true work of the Spirit because of the presence of prophetical visions, divine revelations, and signs from heaven of what shall come to pass. These people claim that such manifestations are nothing more than overwrought imaginations of many in a time of revival and a basis for discrediting a true work of the Holy Spirit. To the contrary, Edwards argued that a true work of the Holy Spirit causes people to use their God-given faculty of imagination (inspiration, vision, creativity) without which man would not be able to comprehend the things invisible or eternal. Yet, when properly controlled, imagination is subservient and helpful to other faculties of the mind. Even when not well controlled during times of revival, especially among the more ignorant or new to the Scriptures and things spiritual, God makes use of imagination in their circumstances by dealing with them as babes. In such cases God may use their confusion, impropriety, misunderstanding, or error to bring loving correction, instruction, and spiritual growth.[23] Such is the care and nurture of a loving heavenly Father.

5.   A true work of the Spirit of God *cannot* be denied by claiming that manifestations are not from God but merely a human means of producing revival.

Edwards is not saying that all manifestations are a true work of the Spirit of God. Again, the spirit that produced the manifestation must be tested. However, some claim that those experiencing manifestations are merely copying the example set by others. Therefore, manifestations become self-perpetuating in times of revival and not from the Spirit of God. In other words, man, not God, is the source of manifestations and an example for others to copy. But this is false reasoning for God uses many means of carrying out his work on the earth. Edwards wrote,

87

"There never yet was a time of remarkable pouring out of the Spirit, and great revival of religion, but that example had a main hand."[24]

A second argument used by some is that the Word of God is the principal means of propagation of the work of God and that men should be influenced by reason rather than example during revival. However, even though the Word of God and preaching are the principal means for spreading the faith, it is also the foundation for other means to operate and be made effective.[25] Words convey ideas to others, but actions including manifestations during revival may do it more fully and effectively. For confirmation of the importance of actions in addition to words, we point to Christ's command to follow His examples concerning Holy Communion and water baptism. Nevertheless, it must be remembered that, apart from the Word of God, many things visible to the eye remain unintelligible and that includes manifestations during revival that fall outside the boundaries set by the Holy Spirit and Scripture.

6. A true work of the Spirit of God *cannot* be denied because of the great imprudences and irregularities in the conduct of those associated with the revival.

Edwards speaks of imprudence which is more broadly defined as profligacy (carelessness, indiscretion, foolishness) and gullibility (credulity, innocence, naïveté). When speaking of irregularities he meant indiscretions, wrongdoings, or misdeeds. The end purpose of revival is to make men and women holy. Yet, some attempt to discredit a revival as not being true work of the Spirit of God because many of those participating in and under the influence of revival have sin in their lives. This is obviously a flawed argument. To the contrary, Edwards wrote that revival contains "…a mixed multitude of all sorts—wise and unwise, young and old, of weak and strong natural abilities, under strong impressions of mind—there are many who behave themselves imprudently." The first century churches of the New Testament demonstrated many of these imprudences and irregularities.[26]

Even great individuals including the apostle Peter who were used by God to carry on the work were guilty of imprudences and irregularities. Such failures do not prove that a revival is not a work of God. If such great men were guilty of these failings, is it not surprising that those with lesser abilities and lacking the special guidance of the Holy Spirit should be guilty of the same imprudences and irregularities?[27]

Although Edwards describes zeal as an excellent grace, he cautions that zeal is one that must be closely watched and guarded against corruption, pride, and human passion which are easily and subtly mixed with this virtue. In times of great revival, zeal may carry its participants to extremes of censuring others that differ from them in some points regarding the Scriptures.[28] The extremes of zealousness were evident in the first century church, in the fourth century church during the reign of Constantine when Christianity became the official religion of the Roman Empire, during the Reformation in the 1500s and1600s, and during all Protestant revivals and awakenings since the beginning of the evangelical church in the early 1700s. During these times of over-zealousness, many in the church were often guilty of exercising improper and severe discipline to the point of persecution of all who failed to measure up to the contemporary standards of the times.

7. A true work of the Spirit of God *cannot* be denied because there may be many errors in judgment and some delusions of Satan intermixed with a true work of the Holy Spirit.

Some argue that because many errors in judgement and satanic delusions are intermixed with a revival that it cannot be a true work of the Spirit of God. However, godly men and women are still earthly vessels subject to human frailties while living in a fallen world. Perfection will not be totally achieved until Christians reside with Him for eternity after their time on earth is completed. Thus, Christians are still subject to the wiles of the devil and may stumble into errors of judgment and delusions of Satan. Edwards succinctly sums up the fallacious argument that errors in judgment and satanic delusions void the authenticity of a work of the Spirit of God.[29]

> Many godly persons have undoubtedly in this and other ages, exposed themselves to woeful delusions, by an aptness to lay too much weight on impulses and impressions (manifestations), as if they were immediate revelations from God, to signify something future, or to direct them where to go, and what to do.[30]

8. A true work of the Spirit of God *cannot* be denied because there are persons under the influence of a work of the Spirit of God who fall into gross error or scandalous practices. "That there are

some counterfeits, is no argument that nothing is true: such things are always expected in a time of reformation."[31]

In all of church history there is no instance of any great revival of the church that does not contain many counterfeits. During the time of the apostles and thereafter there have been many great men who seemed to be (and may have been) subjects of a great work of the Spirit but fell away into gross heresies and abhorrent practices. Some of these may have been great officers, teachers, and eminent members of the church. Just because the devil leads some into gross error or scandalous practices during revival is not evidence that the work is not a true work of the Spirit being gloriously poured out upon the people during revival. Even Christ had Judas in His inner circle.[32]

9. A true work of the Spirit of God *cannot* be denied because the work is promoted by ministers who forcefully convey with much pathos and earnestness the terrors awaiting the unrepentant sinner.

Those who oppose a forceful presentation of the gospel generally do not have a strong sense of the dreadful and never-ending torments of hell and the great number who are in immediate danger of spending eternity there. To preach of hell and eternal separation from God to lost sinners with a casual, mañana attitude and manner of speaking is to contradict the very message they are attempting to convey. According to Edwards, "This is not the way of mankind in temporal affairs of great moment, that require earnest heed and great haste, and about which they are greatly concerned."[33]

In these modern times, many preachers who reject such forceful presentations of the gospel often do so because they wish to downplay the law in favor of an inoffensive, seeker-sensitive message. This was an issue in Edwards' time. But Edwards also warned that those who forcefully preach the terrors of the law but forget Christ fail to preach the gospel. Both the gospel and the law should be preached for "Christ is the end of the law for righteousness." Edwards succinctly summarized the connection between preaching the law and the gospel, "The gospel is to be preached as well as the law, and the law is to be preached only to make way for the gospel, and in order that it may be preached more effectually."[34]

As previously stated, revivals are controversial, and no aspect of revival is more contentious than that of physical manifestations. We close this chapter with two admonitions. The first is to repeat John's instruction, quoted at the beginning of this chapter, which is to test the spirits to determine whether they are from God. Although this testing may bring contention and disagreement, it is a necessary requirement during times of revival.

> Dear friends, do not believe every spirit, but test the spirits to see whether they are from God, because many false prophets have gone out into the world. This is how you can recognize the Spirit of God: Every spirit that acknowledges that Jesus Christ has come in the flesh is from God, but every spirit that does not acknowledge Jesus is not from God. This is the spirit of the antichrist, which you have heard is coming and even now is already in the world. [1 John 4:1-3. NIV]

The second admonition is from Jonathan Edwards writing near the conclusion of his work, *The Distinguishing Marks of a Work of the Spirit of God.* Here he instructs Christians to avoid being over-zealous in dealing with people opposing a true work of the Spirit of God.

> And another thing that I would entreat the zealous friends of this glorious work of God to avoid, is managing the controversy with opposers with too much heat, and appearance of angry zeal; and particularly insisting very much in public prayer and preaching, on the persecution of opposers.[35]

9

Hindrances to True Revival

A sick man needs a medical doctor who will accurately diagnose his illness or infirmity, prescribe a remedy, and make application thereof. So too must the ailing church seek the divine physician who has already diagnosed the spiritual malady affecting His bride. The church may find a description of its afflictions and the prescription for its spiritual malaise in the Bible. The remedy for the spiritual ailments of the church is that which we have called "revival."

The path to spiritual health for the body of Christ is not an easy one for it is fraught with various hindrances as it struggles along the road to recovery. In this chapter we shall look at hindrances to true revival from two perspectives: hindrances that prevent or hamper the *coming* of revival and hindrances that cause a revival that is a work *in progress* to be hampered and eventually cease.

Conditions that hinder the coming of true revival

The leadership and congregants of many churches may recognize their spiritual disquiet but are oblivious to the reasons or obstacles which block the coming of true revival. Even those who are prayerfully interceding for a special outpouring of the Holy Spirit may be unaware of the depth of the church's decline and the reasons for its worldliness, shallowness, spiritual poverty, and powerlessness. The following list is not meant to be an exhaustive report of the hindrances to revival, but they appear to have been significant roadblocks to revival of the modern church over the last half century. A number of these afflictions of the modern evangelical church have been discussed in *Evangelical Winter – Restoring New Testament Christianity*.[1]

- The lukewarmness of the modern church is a hindrance to the coming of revival

In the first verse of the first chapter of the Revelation of Jesus Christ, we find John in the Spirit on the Lord's day. Christ sent an angel to John and instructed him to record the Word of God and the testimony of Jesus Christ. Christ's revelation was of the condition of the seven churches in Asia and insights into future events concerning the end-time tribulation and judgments. One by one, John revealed each of their works (good and bad) and the essence of their hearts. Put another way, God looked into the deepest recesses of the hearts of the Asian churches and diagnosed their spiritual condition. The issues addressed in each of the churches were common to all churches of that day and continue to be down to the present time.[2]

Laodicea was the worst of all of the seven Asian churches, and Christ found nothing to commend it. Its great sin was that it was lukewarm—neither hot nor cold. Its indifference arose from self-conceitedness and self-delusion. It believed itself rich and in need of nothing but in reality was wretched, pitiable, poor, blind, and naked. Christ reminded them of where true riches may be found, without which severe punishment would follow.[3]

The condition of the Laodicean church is an accurate and revealing picture of the modern American church and sadly includes many evangelical churches. They are rich, prideful, apathetic, and deluded as to their spiritual condition. In one sense their pride, prayerlessness, contentment with the world, and lukewarmness stand as polar opposites of the principles necessary for revival as laid down by God in 2 Chronicles 7:14: humility, prayer, seeking the face of God, and turning from man's wicked ways. Those conditions necessary for true revival will be more fully examined in the Chapter 14.

Thus, one of the great hindrances blocking a special outpouring of the Holy Spirit is the church's lukewarmness and its accompanying elements of pride, spiritual indifference, apathy toward God, and comfortableness in their sinful state.

- The coming of revival is hindered when the church ignores the presence and work of the Holy Spirit

As a consequence of the pursuit and application of man's wisdom in building the church, many modern churches have dismissed the irreplaceable power and presence of the Holy Spirit which accounts for their powerlessness, spiritual poverty, and shallowness. Christ instructed His disciples to first "tarry" and then after they had been endued with power from the Holy Spirit (that occurred on the day of Pentecost) they would be ready to do the work of the church. However, many in the body of Christ and its leaders are more interested in doing church than being the church. Put another way, they focus on man's knowledge and methods to build the church and fail to wait upon the Holy Spirit and His enduement of power. Revival will always be hindered when the Holy Spirit is not sought after, welcomed, relied upon, and made the center of church life.[4]

- The coming of revival is hindered when the modern Church Growth movement's principles and methods are substituted for the power of the Holy Spirit in building the church

In their quest to fill the pews and coffers of the local church, pastors, preachers, teachers, and other church leaders rush to various meetings and conferences that glowingly advertise speakers, books, and courses promoting the benefits of new techniques and methods of attracting crowds to the local church. To that end the gospel is bent, trimmed, and modified to meet the desires of the consumers of religion that have been conditioned to treat the church as a shopping mall at which its various tenants constantly tout their array of wares and benefits of attendance and membership. Building the Universal church has been replaced by pursuit of numerical and financial growth through scientific marketing techniques designed to assemble the right team, build the right facilities, develop the right programs, craft an appealing message, and choose the right media. But growth of church attendance and membership must never be confused with true kingdom growth.

This modern consumer-oriented mindset has greatly hindered the pursuit of true revival in the church. Beginning in the last half of the twentieth century, many preachers, evangelists, pastors, and others in church leadership began applying man-conceived church growth techniques. These are merely background noise to distract the church from the spiritually barren desert which many churches inhabit.

- The coming of revival is hindered when the gospel is cheapened

The heart of a cheap gospel is found in the preaching of the world's definition of nonjudgmental love which produces a counterfeit or cheap grace. Erwin Lutzer in his book *When a Nation Forgets God* reveals the cost of a cheap gospel.

> Cheap grace is the deadly enemy of our Church...In such a Church the world finds a cheap covering for its sins; no contrition is required, still less any real desire to be delivered from sin...Cheap grace means the justification of sin without the justification of the sinner...Cheap grace is grace without discipleship, grace

95

without the cross, grace without Jesus Christ, living and incarnate.[5]

Recall from an earlier chapter that one of the prime conditions necessary for revival of the church is that the church must critically examine itself, both individually and corporately. When this examination reveals its miserable condition and separation from God, the prayer and burden for revival will grow and lead to conviction of sin in the hearts of men. Thus, conviction is an indispensable element necessary for revival of the church. And conviction is the product of intense, sustained intercession coupled with the influence of pungent preaching that opens the door to the presence and convicting power of the Holy Spirit. However, when the Bible is no longer the central source for preaching and teaching that leads to conviction of sin, the coming of true revival will never occur because the gospel is cheapened by preaching and teaching the world's definition of nonjudgmental love.

- The coming of revival is hindered when weak or misleading preaching leads to a painless cross which is an oxymoron

For many modern Christians the message of the cross of Calvary is too confrontational and must be muted if not altogether silenced to minimize its offensiveness. The message of the old cross has been rewritten to smooth its abrasiveness and soften its demands. The message of the new cross is a thing of comfort and beauty instead of an instrument of death to self. The old message, having been modernized and adapted, seamlessly blends with the church's fascination with the world's humanistic concepts of self-esteem instead of the reality of the fallen nature of man.

But the message of the cross found in Matthew's gospel still means today what it meant two thousand years ago. "If any man will come after me, let him deny himself, and take up his cross, and follow me." [Matthew 16:24. KJV] At its core the new cross rests on ego and selfishness and is the great enemy of the old cross of Christ. But ego, selfishness, and the message of a new cross will never lead to conviction, repentance, forgiveness, and true revival of the body of Christ.

- The coming of revival is hindered when false teachers and false doctrines are not confronted but allowed to remain in the church

Paul warned of a time when many in the church would not endure sound doctrine but seek teachers of fables instead of truth.

> For the time will come when people will not put up with sound doctrine. Instead, to suit their own desires, they will gather around them a great number of teachers to say what their itching ears want to hear. They will turn their ears away from the truth and turn aside to myths. [2 Timothy 4:3-4. NIV].

In his letter to the Romans, Paul commands the faithful to be aware of those who depart from sound doctrine and act accordingly.

> I urge you, brothers and sisters, to watch out for those who cause divisions and put obstacles in your way that are contrary to the teaching you have learned. Keep away from them. For such people are not serving our Lord Christ, but their own appetites. By smooth talk and flattery they deceive the minds of naive people. [Romans 16:17-18. NIV]

False teachers and doctrinal heresy flourish in the church when the truth of the Bible and its meaning are diminished or abandoned. There has never been a time in church history since the beginning of the Reformation that the church has been so immersed in a tidal wave of false teachers and false doctrines and which are now surging into the evangelical church. Truly, the church is near the end of the last days.

Evidence of this tsunami of false teachers and preachers can be seen in the vast numbers that populate the media and evangelical pulpits of America. Like their liberal forerunners, large numbers in the evangelical church during the latter half of the twentieth century and to the present day have replaced many of its doctrines with another gospel or have abandoned New Testament Christianity altogether. These false teachers forfeit the unambiguous truth of God's Word in the name of cultural relevance through an accommodation of the spirit of the world within the church. But as Os Guinness states in his book *Prophetic Untimeliness-A Challenge to the Idol of Relevance*, such accommodation leads to a Christian faith that dispenses "...a license to entitlement, a prescription for an easy-going spirituality, or a how-to manual for self-improvement."[6] It is a false religion, a weak and unrecognizable shell without the sustaining truth and power of New Testament Christianity.

Unless the church and its leaders return to and preach the inerrant and unadulterated Word of God and stand against those false teachers who do not, true revival will never come to that people.

- The coming of revival is hindered when "foolish preaching" is substituted for the "foolishness of preaching"

Paul described his calling as an apostle of Jesus Christ. "For Christ sent me not to baptize, but to preach the gospel: not with wisdom of words, lest the cross of Christ should be made of none effect." [1 Corinthians 1:17. KJV] In the next verse Paul explained that the impact preaching had on its hearers depended upon whether they were lost or saved. "For the preaching of the cross is to them that perish foolishness; but unto us which are saved it is the power of God." [1 Corinthians 1:18. KJV]

Paul's belief as to the purpose of preaching is far different than that of many evangelical pastors and evangelists of today. Paul believed that preaching anything other than the cross is a contradictory message and may be called *silly or foolish preaching* and not the *foolishness of preaching* to which he adhered.

Writer Peter F. Jensen stated, "It is the chief function of the sermon to unleash the word of the Lord in the midst of *his* people. It is the chief means by which the Lord directs, rebukes, sustains, and invigorates *his* people."[7] [emphasis added] And the chief method of unleashing the Word is expository preaching which according to the great E. M. Bounds "...was true preaching—preaching of a sort which is sorely needed, today, in order that God's word may have due effect on the hearts of the people..." He wrote these words over one hundred years ago but lamented at the lack of expository preaching in his day.[8] What would he think about the far greater decline of expository preaching in today's churches?

The abandonment of expository preaching for other types, particularly topical preaching, is perhaps the major reason for the dramatic decline in biblical literacy among evangelicals in America which appears to be at its lowest point since the beginning of evangelicalism in the early 1700s. Certainly, this decline has been exacerbated by declines in the number of preaching services and Sunday school classes offered as well as a decline in attendance at both.

Yet, the majority of Christians desire the strong meat of the Word found in biblically-sound expository preaching. A survey of 1,103 congregations and their pastors was conducted over a period of twelve plus years on the topic of why churches fail. The pastors and congregations were asked forty-four questions whose answers indicated either the health or dysfunction of the churches surveyed. The results indicated a significant disconnection between what the congregations felt important and what they actually received from their leadership. The survey revealed that 78% of the congregation felt the ability to teach the Bible effectively was important (ranked first in importance of the top twelve listed). Only 26% of the pastors felt the ability to teach the Bible effectively was important (ranked tenth in importance of the top ten listed). The overall results of the survey generally pointed in the direction of dysfunction and breakdown among those churches surveyed.[9]

Without unleashing the Word through the foolishness of preaching, the coming of revival will be hindered. Over the last thirty to forty years in evangelical churches in America, there has been a considerable amount of foolish preaching. As the survey has shown, the fault lies with the pastors, preachers, and teachers and not with their congregations who deem solid, effective biblical teaching as the most important thing they want from the leadership of their churches. Recall Peter Jensen's words, "It is the chief function of the sermon to unleash the word of the Lord in the midst of *his* people." [emphasis added]

- The coming of revival is hindered by fear

In Chapter 1 it was noted that revivals that by their very nature are controversial, and this controversy arises on three levels. First, people fear revival because it is fundamentally a supernatural event brought by the Holy Spirit, and people fear the unknown. Many people are uncomfortable with a religion that goes beyond the familiar forms of godliness practiced in many churches. Second, some fear revival because it is viewed as being "of the devil" and a form of mass hysteria. Third, some church leaders fear true revival because it means surrendering control to the Holy Spirit, the status quo is shaken up, and the light of God's Word is allowed to shine into the dark corners of the church where the spirit of the world often resides.

- The coming of revival is hindered when churches have mixed the light with the dark through misguided efforts to promote ecumenicalism to the detriment of truth

Paul warned the Ephesian church that Christians cannot be silent or neutral in the presence of evil and must expose evil behavior. "Have

99

nothing to do with the fruitless deeds of darkness, but rather expose them." [Ephesians 5:11. NIV]

One of the great hindrances to the coming of revival is the quest for unity among various factions that claim to be part of the Universal church. The principle or aim of promoting unity among the world's Christian Churches is called ecumenicalism which is highly prized and sought after. It has become accepted theology that the great problem with the church is that it is "the divided Church."[10] However, the Bible and church history shows that God sends revival even when the church is divided. Revival brings people together in great spiritual unity but also invariably creates new and fresh divisions with those who dislike, criticize, and condemn revival. Those that promote ecumenicalism beyond those churches adhering to the Bible attempt to beat down or remove doctrinal obstacles in order to establish a "big-tent" view of what the church should be.

Those who promote ecumenicalism in which the tenets of the Christian faith must be subordinate to the greater goal of unity with denominations and religions in opposition to the tenets of the Christian faith are joined in a false unity. The outworking of Satan's Trojan horse of ecumenicalism requires that the church recognize the priority of unity *without limit*. Acceptance of this false unity within the church has become the norm rather than the exception, and this limitless ecumenicalism is promoted at the highest levels of leadership in both evangelical and non-evangelical churches.

Following the 1950s and 1960s, the ecumenical movement was effectively advanced by incorporation into the church's message certain themes of the humanistic spirit of the world: relativism, tolerance, and inclusion. This compromise and accommodation leads to ignoring, changing, abandoning, or adding doctrines, beliefs, and activities in ways that conflict with two hundred and fifty years of evangelical thought, belief, and practice that mirrored first-century New Testament Christianity.

Paul cautions that Christians should not be mismatched with unbelievers. "Do not be yoked together with unbelievers. For what do righteousness and wickedness have in common? Or what fellowship can light have with darkness?" [2 Corinthians 6:14. NIV] In his commentary, Matthew Henry expounds on Paul's admonition.

> It is wrong for good people to join in affinity [kinship or relationship] with the wicked and profane...We should not yoke ourselves in friendship with wicked men and

unbelievers...Much less should we join in religious
communion with them. It is a very great absurdity.
Believers are made light in the Lord, but unbelievers are
in darkness; and what comfortable communion can these
have together?[11]

Martyn Lloyd-Jones has said that "...no revival has ever been
known in the history of churches which deny or ignore certain spiritual
truth."[12] Revival will never come to those churches that persist in
denying spiritual truth by mixing the light with the dark.

Conditions that hinder a true revival in progress

When Satan fails to block the coming of revival, he always
continues his mischief and interference during revival. Again, the
following is not an exhaustive list of hindrances found during seasons of
revival, but they appear to be commonly found in many revivals.

- Revivals are hindered when the Spirit is quenched

During revival there is an unavoidable tension present among
Christians caused by the Bible's instruction to test the spirits but at the
same time not quench the Spirit. Paul presents this challenge in his letter
to the Thessalonians. "Do not quench the Spirit. Do not treat prophecies
with contempt but test them all; hold on to what is good, reject every
kind of evil. [1 Thessalonians 5:19-22. NIV]
The Holy Spirit must be allowed to anoint and move as he
wishes but at the same time Christians must judge and discern the spirits.
Obeying these twin commands requires a delicate balance especially
when dealing with sincere believers that occasionally and unknowingly
have crossed the line into excess. To rescue these erring believers, they
must be teachable and receive correction.[13]
For those who have tested the spirits and found something from
the flesh or Satan, discernment may lead those testing the spirits to err on
the side of patience and gentleness so as not to quench the Spirit if the
excesses are relatively minor, unobtrusive, and play out at the edges of
revival. It must be remembered that if a particular expression or
manifestation is of God, then man should not and cannot stop it. If the
relatively innocuous expression or manifestation arises from man, it will
fail in time. Wisdom dictates that premature removal of these tares may
be avoided along with the potential damage to the precious wheat during

revival. However, if the questionable manifestations are grievous and have become widespread, disruptive, and divisive, solid spiritual leaders draped with the mantle of God's authority must boldly bring open correction.[14]

- Revival is hindered when there is an improper use or overemphasis on identifying, bestowing, or imparting spiritual gifts by the laying on of hands and naming, supposedly by prophecy, specific gifts

Although not confined to revival, the improper use of the laying on of hands to identify, bestow, or impart special gifts by misguided individuals or false teachers is often found in revival. However, it must not be forgotten that it is the Holy Spirit that empowers the gift He bestows, and no individual should assume the Holy Spirit's role. Paul talks about gifts bestowed by the laying on of hands (see: 1 Timothy 4:14, 2 Timothy 1:6), but the biblical record does not record the name of a specific gift received by Timothy nor does it imply that Paul or the other elders imparted the gift. The Holy Spirit identifies and bestows the gift, not the individual laying on hands and praying for the empowerment.[15] Those that attempt to usurp prerogatives of the Holy Spirit invariably hinder a revival.

- Revivals are hindered when there is an abuse of impartations or impositions of personal leadings by means of gifts of utterance

There are very rare instances of Spirit-prompted personal advice which may be contrary to common sense but are unquestionably of divine origin. This practice is subject to misuse at any time, but it is especially susceptible to abuse during times of revival by zealous but untrained or spiritually immature individuals. If from God, the reality of the prophesied words will be confirmed by the Holy Spirit in the heart of the one set apart for the Spirit's work.[16]

- Revivals are hindered when there is an excessive fixation on Satan and demonic spirits

This fixation is of special concern during the excitement of spiritual warfare during times of revival. Most of the problems arise from a misunderstanding of the spiritual position of a child of God. Satan can attack, oppose, and oppress believers, but he cannot take possession of a born again Christian. In other words, believers cannot be possessed by demons and therefore in need of having them cast out. However, there may be one or more individuals present during a revival and other times that are demon possessed. This condition may be made known to a Spirit-filled believer by the Holy Spirit. Also, the Holy Spirit may give discernment to a Spirit-filled believer as to the presence and source of demonic activity during revival.[17] Although believers are engaged in periods of spiritual warfare of various intensities, the vast majority of spiritual issues and concerns of life faced by people, both in and out of revival, are not caused by demonic possession but are the result of man's sinful nature and living in a fallen world.

- Revival is hindered when false teachers and false doctrines become a significant presence during seasons of revival

Not only may false teachers and false doctrines hinder the coming of revival, such teachers and doctrines can also invade revival causing confusion, doubt, and division among its leaders and the laity which if left unchecked, will bring damage to the revival and reproach upon the church. Several examples are examined in the next chapter.

John Wesley, one of the great pillars of the First Great Awakening in both America and England, declared, "At the first, revival is true and pure, but after a few weeks watch for counterfeits." God often does many unexpected things in revival, and the devil soon attempts to interject the counterfeit to create a "cloud of confusion, rumors, and false manifestations." Soon even "pro-revival" ministries may be tempted to add to what the Holy Spirit is doing and thereby discredit the entire move of God. These additions quickly descend into all manner of soulish, shallow, and showy activities often designed to wrap people "in a warm, positive, 'feel-good' cocoon – all of this God hates."[18] Yet, most Christians are unable to distinguish this type of false teacher or false doctrine from the genuine.

- Revivals are hindered when the church has no knowledge or understanding of past revivals and history of the church

Dr. Martyn Lloyd-Jones, the great English minister of the gospel during the mid-twentieth century, wrote of the importance of reading church history and studying the past so that one may learn of its message. That is why the last half of this book is devoted to the history of revivals and awakenings since the late 1600s and early 1700s. Dr. Lloyd-Jones believed that modern Christians mistakenly assume that the problems faced today are new and unique to the present generations and which the world and the church have never before encountered. Thus, the history of the church including past revivals is ignored or discarded because it is thought that they have little if anything to teach us.[19]

Christians and the church in general who subscribed to this mindset mimic the humanist worldview in which history is considered excess baggage that must be tossed out to make way for new, bold, and progressive ideas. This is called the Whig theory of history which states that the most advanced point in time is the point of its highest development. This fits nicely with humanists' progressivism whose foundation is the Enlightenment belief of the perfectibility of man, a "...belief that critical and autonomous human reason held the power to discover the truth about life and the world, and to progressively liberate humanity from the ignorance and injustices of the past."[20]

However, Lloyd-Jones reminds us that God never changes— "God is from everlasting to everlasting." And this is true for man for his Adamic nature has never changed. If we look at the Old Testament we find God's chosen people in a seemingly perpetual cycle of victory and defeat, holiness and sin, degeneration, and revival. Christianity and the church throughout history have followed the same cycles. Before the apostles had died, the churches they founded began to follow the same cycles as their Old Testament predecessors.[21] The reason that Christians and the church as a whole should pay attention to the past and the history of the church is that when the church is in the valley of rebellion, despair, and defeat, it should not seek new solutions but look to those never-failing biblical prescriptions and lessons of history that brought revival to the church.

10

Test the Spirits in Revivals and Manifestations

Distinguishing between true and false revivals and manifestations

- Test the spirits

1. Make sure the spirit acknowledges that Jesus Christ has come in the flesh.

    Dear friends, do not believe every spirit, but test the spirits to see whether they are from God, because many false prophets have gone out into the world. This is how you can recognize the Spirit of God: Every spirit that acknowledges that Jesus Christ has come in the flesh is from God, but every spirit that does not acknowledge Jesus is not from God. This is the spirit of the antichrist, which you have heard is coming and even now is already in the world. [1 John 4:1-3. NIV]

2. Recognize the spirit by the fruit it produces

    By their fruit you will recognize them. Do people pick grapes from thorn bushes, or figs from thistles? Likewise every good tree bears good fruit, but a bad tree bears bad fruit. A good tree cannot bear bad fruit, and a bad tree cannot bear good fruit. Every tree that does not bear good fruit is cut down and thrown into the fire. Thus, by their fruit you will recognize them. [Matthew 7:16-20. NIV]

3. Does the spirit speak in accordance to God's Word, the Bible? Does the spirit acknowledge the Bible's authority? Does the spirit put anything above the Bible or degrade the Bible?

    But there will also be false prophets among the people, just as there will be false teachers among you. They will secretly introduce destructive heresies, even denying the sovereign Lord who bought them-bringing swift destruction on themselves. [2 Peter 2:1-2. NIV]

Now the Berean Jews were of more noble character than those in Thessalonica, for they received the message with great eagerness and examined the Scriptures every day to see if what Paul said was true. [Acts 17:22. NIV]

- Practice discernment

Andrew Strom lists five basic keys to discernment:

1. Know your Holy God intimately. When the Christian draws close to God they bask in His glory, His holiness, and His love. The luster of the counterfeit fades in comparison to the genuine.

2. Know your Bible. Knowing the Bible is important so that one may spot those things that are not supported by or are clearly opposed to the Scriptures. Knowledge of the Scripture enhances one's discernment.

3. Be a "lover of truth." Being a lover of truth means more than head and heart knowledge. The lover of truth must stand for truth, speak for truth, and take action for truth where necessary. Standing, speaking, and taking action gives legs to one's discernment.

4. Maintain a purity of heart and humility. An impure heart is often at the mercy of darkness and wrong motives. Such a heart becomes easy prey of the world as they are more susceptible to deception. Yielding to deception destroys discernment.

5. Listen to the "inner witness" of the Holy Spirit. This is the still, small voice that must never be over-ridden by the noise and lure of the world and its evil systems, peer pressure, or the reputations of "trusted" leaders or other individuals in the church (see: 1 Kings 19:11-13).[1] Above all, this inner witness of the Holy Spirit is the supreme source of discernment.

- True revival and legitimate manifestations lead the worshipper to a greater appreciation of God's glory.

When examining a revival and the manifestations therein, does the worshipper develop a greater appreciation for the glory and majesty of God or is there at some point a sense of shame and embarrassment for demeaning the character and nature of God and the body of Christ?

Recall Martyn Lloyd-Jones's description of what it was like for those captured by God's radiant presence when He came among His people during special outpourings of the Holy Spirit. It was described as "days of heaven on earth" in which time no longer had any meaning or any real existence as they were in a spiritual realm (Chapter 3). These people were raised to new heights of appreciation and thanksgiving for God's marvelous glory.

But what of the two woman in the so-called Toronto Laughing revival? One crawled around on all fours, snorting and pawing the ground like an angry ox or bull and the other supposedly stuck to the floor by "Holy Ghost glue" while wallowing around for hours against her will.[2] These women were obviously consumed by the carnal wildness of their experience and oblivious to any notions of God's glory.

- True revival and legitimate manifestations generally fall within the normative patterns of spiritual experience as revealed in the New Testament and history of the church during true revival

Strange manifestations may be evidence of exhibitionism, self-glorification, self-gratification, or demonic activity that fall outside the boundaries and patterns of normative spiritual experience found in the New Testament and history of the church during true revival. These extra-biblical manifestations and the revivals in which they are found should be viewed cautiously and examined closely.

- True revival and legitimate manifestations must focus on God and His plan and not man's programs, agendas, or manifestations

Beware of any revival that becomes popularly known for a predominant manifestation during a revival, e.g., "laughing" revivals and "healing" revivals. The occurrence of such manifestations (either real or false) is often the reason that many people visit such revivals. Certainly there are healings and other supernatural interventions of God in the personal lives of individuals that occur during revival, but the essential purpose of a revival is to glorify God and not to seek a particular manifestation. The same caution should be used when coming under the teaching or influence of any preacher, teacher, or revival leader that is predominantly associated with questionable revivals and manifestations or in close association with those known to be involved with such works.

- True revival and legitimate manifestations have an aura of God's holiness about them which rejects "soulishness," hype, and emotional manipulation

Revival ministries dependent on personality, cleverness, and showmanship appear to be the rule in much of American evangelicalism while those who preach with the truth and authority of the Word of God under the anointing and power of the Holy Spirit are in the minority.[3] Although popular and well-known ministers and ministries may be at the forefront of revival, the believer must always be mindful that the Holy Spirit is the only source of true revival and His plan must dominate every facet of revival.

Corrupting true revival

The church of Jesus Christ was born of the Spirit. On the day of Pentecost the church was created and commissioned as a supernatural organization by God's Spirit. It is the Universal church comprised of men and women who believe Jesus is the Son of God, follow His commands, and act in accordance with the leading and direction of His Spirit. Where God's people are gathered, the Spirit is present.

Thus, we see that the church is a supernatural entity not formed, operated, or defined by mere men or their mundane plans and programs. In every generation after its commissioning the church, the body of Christ, must continually seek renewal, better known as revival. That is the principal theme of this book. Because Satan is the great faker and counterfeiter, the church must also continually test the "spirits" to detect and be warned of false revival and ungodly manifestations.

Signs and wonders

The trademarks of the vast majority of Satan's attempts to corrupt true revivals and to produce false revivals are (1) subversion of the truth of God's Word as Satan did with Eve in the garden and (2) the infusion of both counterfeit and real physical manifestations that mimic the genuine during special outpourings of the Holy Spirit. This mimicry of true revival through lies and false manifestations is not a new wrinkle in the unfolding tableau of evangelical history but has been present since the first century and especially since the beginning of the evangelical church in the early 1700s.

Signs and wonders including various miracles and healings are wonderful to behold and experience when they are from God, but the problem with most Christians and non-Christians is determining whether a particular sign or wonder is from God or Satan. Signs and wonders are often present in true revival. But Satan also uses both counterfeit and real signs and wonders to bring turmoil and confusion during true revivals and to deceive and lead people astray during false revivals which bring reproach upon the church. Christians may distinguish between these opposing signs and wonders by looking at their source.

Generally, signs and wonders mentioned in the Old Testament refer to the deliverance of the Israelites from their enemies. In the New Testament, signs and wonders were used to confirm the preaching of the Gospel by the apostles. However, the terms "signs" and "wonders" were also used in the New Testament to warn the people of false teachers, leaders, and prophets.[4]

> For false messiahs and false prophets will appear and perform signs and wonders to deceive, if possible, even the elect. So be on your guard; I have told you everything ahead of time. [Mark 13:22-23. NIV]

> The Spirit clearly says that in later times some will abandon the faith and follow deceiving spirits and things taught by demons. [1 Timothy 4:1. NIV]

One of the great failings of Christians is the unquestioning acceptance of signs and wonders that actually happen. In other words, many Christians believe that a sign or wonder is from God if it is a genuine event or incident that has actually occurred and not accomplished by slight-of-hand or trickery. But the Christian must always test the sign or wonder as to whether it is counterfeit or real. Two of the principal tests included above ask two questions to determine if the sign or wonder is from God: (1) Is the sign or wonder supported and confirmed by the Bible or some other gospel, and (2) does it glorify God and promote the Gospel or publicize and elevate a particular person and/or his personal ministry/agenda?[5]

David Dombrowski gave an example of Satan's use of signs and wonders to deceive people.

Yet, for many people today (including many Christians), if a strange, paranormal manifestation occurs, that is evidence enough that it must be from God without any recognition or acknowledgment that dark supernatural forces can do these things. For example, the manifestations of holy laughter, "slaying in the Spirit," jerkings, convolutions, twisting, contortions, and animal-like behaviors have all been witnessed under the "ministering" of eastern gurus who draw on kundalini energy (serpent power) to do their work.[6]

There are a number of manifestations and occurrences that have been almost universal in every true revival since the beginning of the evangelical church. Many people would tremble and weep under the fear of God's manifest presence. People cried out in anguish when their hearts were convicted and fell to the ground as if under a great weight of sin. When people's hearts were flooded with joy upon receiving forgiveness, they would often shout, sing, or dance with unrestrained enthusiasm and thanksgiving. These manifestations are not different than what happened on the day of Pentecost when there were "tremendous cryings of distress over sin or 'trembling" under the fear of God, outbursts of joyous forgiveness, mass speaking in 'tongues", dreams, visions, dancing for joy, and similar actions."[7]

Manifestations in true revival are *not sought* but are the end product of conviction of sin, repentance, forgiveness, and an incomparable joyousness of heart. Manifestations and experiences that *are sought* carry their own distinguishing marks: an air of unrestrained emotionalism (carried beyond normal human emotion to the point of exhibitionism, a casting off of restraint, or a kind of wildness); convulsive laughing fits which last until it has run its course, sometimes to the point of exhaustion; strange and involuntary contortions, twitching, jerkings, or dancing; barking like a dog or imitation of other animal noises and actions; those who seek blessings, touches, or experiences rather than seeking God (the emphasis is on self and not God); and other bizarre or aberrant phenomena.

With regard to physical phenomena that may be observed in true revival, what was said in an earlier chapter bears repeating. The New Testament authors describe numerous phenomena surrounding the establishment of the church, conversion of sinners, and the revival of believers which also serve as a *pattern* for other phenomena that may occur as a result of an outpouring of the Holy Spirit. This pattern was not meant to be complete to the last detail and thereby exclude all other phenomena. However, there are boundaries and limitations set by the Holy Spirit which must not be breached when following the scriptural pattern. These boundaries and limitations may vary from place to place and from time to time as guided by the Holy Spirit. Violation of these boundaries and limitations bring distortion, confusion, and damage to the work of revival and dishonor to God's holiness.

We began this chapter by discussing the tools that are used to distinguish between true and false revival and their manifestations. In the remainder of this chapter three occasions will be examined as to how *true revivals* have, in a manner of speaking, nearly gone off the rails or have been prematurely ended through the rise of elements of heretical preaching, false manifestations, and deception. Examples of *false revivals and manifestations* will be examined in the next chapter.

- The Great Awakening – Radical evangelicals 1841-1844

One of the greatest damages to the First Great Awakening happened because of abuses by sincere, pro-revival preachers who became known as radical itinerants. Their extreme preaching and behavior brought great controversy and bitter disputes to the revival movement in the early 1740s.[8] By 1741, there was a growing division between the moderate revivalists and their more radical counterparts. These disputes between radical itinerants and all of the established powers of Connecticut and Massachusetts including Jonathan Edwards became a serious split in 1742. James Davenport was one of the most virulent of the radical itinerants. The moderate revivalists labeled Davenport's "wild enthusiasm" as being "beyond legitimate evangelical limits." As these excesses and extremes played out, a point was reached in March 1743 when even Davenport's most devoted supporters began to question his tactics and extreme actions. As a result Davenport fell into a "repentant despondency." However, historian Thomas Kidd wrote that "Davenport's ministry was not over, but his days as a radical were."[9] In 1744, the chastened Davenport made a public apology for his excesses.[10]

In 1742, Jonathan Dickinson wrote *A Display of God's Special Grace* to address the problem of revival excesses. He believed the excesses were not necessary for revival to occur but neither were the excesses cause to condemn revivals. He defended the "preaching of terror and the ecstatic joys of converts as potentially authentic parts of the conversion process" although he admitted that some during revival had suffered "from animal Impressions, or from diabolical Delusions." Additionally, he believed that there were occasions to doubt another person's salvation but objected to those that condemned serious Christians, be they established ministers or laity.[11]

As the radical evangelists reined in their excesses and extremes, they went through a period of maturation but did not abandon the key tenets of their belief which were freedom of private judgement and power to establish independent churches free from the dictates of competing ecclesiastical and legislative authorities. By the 1760s, the chastened and less-radical evangelicals had become the most vigorous and productive arm of revivalism.[12]

- The Second Great Awakening – Excesses and Extremes in Kentucky 1800-1801

In the early days of the Second Great Awakening, there were similar examples of excesses and extremes. By 1800, revival had reached the western extremities of civilization in Logan County in southern Kentucky, an area known for its wild and irreligious people including escaped murderers, counterfeiters, highwaymen, and horse thieves. Through the efforts of Presbyterian minister James McCready and others, revival broke out in the summer of 1800.[13] The revival brought forth a great wave of conviction and repentance which continued throughout the period of revival. Great cries of anguish pierced the air as sinners came under conviction. This was often followed by great cries of joy as they experienced God's forgiveness of their sins.[14]

Next came the Cane Ridge revival in August 1801 located a few miles northeast of Lexington, Kentucky. The Cane Ridge revival was different in that people came from great distances and included rich, poor, black, and white who joined in prayer together. It was reported that ten thousand people had gathered and were ministered to by over twenty Presbyterian, Methodist, and Baptist preachers. The scene was often chaotic and unwieldy as several ministers preached at one time from various locations among the crowd.[15] Andrew Strom wrote that it was the Cane Ridge revival that brought about the "beginning of excesses that had been generally condemned…ever since the wild antics and frenzies of James Davenport and others…"[16]

Strom quoted T. W. Caskey, an eyewitness, who described the earlier manifestations at the Cane Ridge revival.

The whole congregation by some inexplicable nervous action would sometimes be thrown into side-splitting convulsions of laughter and when it started, no power could check or control it until it ran its course. At other times the nervous excitement set the muscles to twitching and jerking at a fearful rate and finally settled down to regular, straight-forward dancing. Like the 'Holy Laugh" it was simply ungovernable until it ran its course. When a man started laughing, dancing, shouting or jerking, it was impossible for him to stop until exhausted nature broke down in a death-like swoon…"[17]

Caskey reported that a number of the revival's participants began to question whether the manifestations were truly a work of the Holy Spirit. As a result they began to search the Scriptures and 'test the spirits,' it was only then that the more bizarre and extreme manifestations began to vanish and allowed the revival to continue for another six years.[18]

- The Welsh Revival 1904-1905 – The loss of leadership and the anointing

Many revival historians believe the revival in Wales during a brief period in 1904-1905 was one of the most powerful revivals of all time. In September 1904, Evan Roberts had just entered a Bible school for training to become a minister. That same month Roberts, just twenty six at the time, attended a local revival meeting and had a life-altering encounter with God. He left school and began preaching.[19] Within eight months revival had spread throughout Wales, and an estimated one hundred and fifty thousand people had applied for church membership. Dr. Edwin Orr estimated that during the brief span of the revival in Wales, a quarter of a million people may have been converted. The Welsh revival caused many others to pray and seek revival around the globe. Within one to two years the Christian church was experiencing great revivals in at least twenty countries.[20]

Roberts had been an intensely devout young man and became even more so following his life-altering encounter with God in September 1904. Although God's anointing was on Roberts, the responsibilities associated with leading such a great and rapidly expanding work of God was a great strain for the relatively untrained and inexperienced young man. He suffered greatly because of the strain.

During this period when he was the acknowledged leader of the great revival in Wales, he began to think that his fame and position were "stealing glory from God." As a result of his mistaken perception, he abruptly retired from public preaching and appearances and devoted himself to prayer and seclusion. The revival was only about a year old, and there was no one with the leadership or anointing to carry on the work and keep the counterfeits out. Soon the revival was filled with many deceptions and false manifestations. Andrew Strom said that the Welsh revival "probably had the 'messiest' ending in history." And for the small country of Wales once known as the land of revivals, there has not been another widespread revival to the present day.[21]

————

   In the last part of this chapter an examination was made of corrupting influences found in true revivals of the past. In the next chapter an examination will be made of false revivals that originated from corrupt leaders and never by a special outpouring of the Holy Spirit.

11

False Prophets, False Revivals, and False Manifestations

False revivals arise from false teachers and preachers

Jesus told His disciples that one of the signs of the end of the age was that "... many false prophets will appear and deceive many people." [Matthew 24:11. NIV] Donald Stamps commentary on this verse gives great insight as to the manner in which these false prophets and their deception will beguile their way into the church at the end of the last days.

> As the last days draw to a close, false teachers and preachers will be very common. They will gain influence in the church by claiming to have "new" revelations and solutions to serious problems. Yet they will deny proven teachings of God's written Word as the answer to these issues. Much of Christianity will be in a spiritually rebellious and unfaithful condition. Those who are totally committed to living by the truth and standards of God's Word will be in the minority.
>
> Many who claim to be loyal Christians will accept "new revelation" even though it conflicts with God's Word as revealed in the Bible...
>
> Throughout the world, millions will be involved in the occult, astrology, witchcraft, Spiritism, and Satanism. Through these activities, the influence of demons and evil spirits will multiply greatly.[1]

The following are accounts of false revivals devised by false teachers and preachers which brought and continue to bring great harm to the true church of Jesus Christ, especially as the church's attention is drawn away from understanding and seeking true revival. Generally, these false revivals have been birthed and promoted by a mixture of false teaching and aberrant and ungodly manifestations.

- Millerism 1831-1844

Toward the end of its second phase, a heretical movement arose in the church that effectively ended the Second Great Awakening. Here the enemy of revival was not aberrant manifestations but the spread of false doctrine that brought great reproach upon the church and a decline in the religious life of America between 1842 and 1857. In 1831, William Miller, a farmer and sincere well-meaning Baptist, began preaching a message that the Coming of the Lord would occur on March 21, 1843. Over the next twelve years before the predicted date of Christ's return, Miller had gathered a following variously estimated to be between one hundred thousand and one million. As the date approached, many of the Millerites, as they were known, sold their possessions, camped out in fields, or waited in white garments on nearby hilltops for Christ's return. As the day came and went, along with two subsequent dates marked for Christ's return in 1844, the Protestant church as a whole was considerably diminished and frequently ridiculed. As a result, faith in religion seriously declined and the church experienced sizable losses during the period 1845-1855.[2]

- Latter Rain 1948-1949

Part II of this book contains a discussion of the Welsh Revival of 1904-1905 and one of its greatest derivatives, the beginning of modern Pentecostalism in 1906. The great Pentecostal upsurge of vitality and enthusiasm for God spread around the world and prepared the church for the challenges it would face in the modern world of the twentieth century and beyond.

Every great move of God is met by Satan's counterattack in which he often attempts to penetrate and corrupt the very heart of the movement blessed by God. Satan uses people's desire to see and experience demonstrations of God's power to deceive them, but in their enthusiasm for signs and wonders they fail to consult God's Word and to test the spirits to determine the source of the manifestations.

Over time every Christian movement has allowed deception to enter and pervert the Word and will of God. Many Reformed, orthodox, and liberal churches veered into the "social gospel" that abandoned many if not most of the truths of the Bible and embraced a form of godliness but denied the power thereof. Many in fundamentalist churches sank into harsh legalism not intended by God or supported by the Scriptures. Many

Pentecostals also have been deceived by extreme emotionalism, have failed to test the spirits, and have placed experiences above the authority of the Bible.

Satan's attack on Pentecostalism came in the form of the aberrant teachings of Kingdom theology which had its beginnings in the Latter Rain movement during the late 1940s. The following is an overview of the basic tenets of Kingdom theology found in the Latter Rain movement and its various iterations that continue under several names down to the present day.

> The basic premise of Kingdom Theology is that man lost dominion over the earth when Adam and Eve succumbed to Satan's temptation in the Garden of Eden. God "lost control" of the earth to Satan at that time, and has since been looking for a "covenant people" who will be His "extension," or "expression," in the earth and take dominion back from Satan. This is to be accomplished through certain "overcomers" who, by yielding themselves to the authority of God's apostles and prophets for the Kingdom Age, will take control of the kingdoms of the world. These Kingdoms are defined as all social institutions, such as the "kingdom" of education, the "kingdom" of science, the "kingdom" of the arts, and so on...

> Necessary to the Kingdom Age is "the Restoration of the Tabernacle of David," defined as the completion of perfection of the Bride of Christ - a church without spot or wrinkle...Critical to hard-core Kingdom Theology is the denial of "the Rapture" – the teaching that the Church will one day be caught up to meet the Lord in the air so that we will be with Him in Heaven when God's wrath is poured out upon the earth.[3]

At this point it is important to make an important distinction between the tenets of Kingdom Theology and the great necessity for the body of Christ and the organized church to speak truth and life into the various spheres of culture. One of the greatest sins of the evangelical church during the last sixty years is its failure to actively engage all facets of society including the government, business and economics, human and physical sciences, arts, entertainment, various media,

117

education, and popular culture. For decades the American evangelical church has been largely silent in the public square about *societal, moral, and political issues.* When pastors and other church leaders are silent, they erroneously separate the gospel and the kingdom from the culture outside the walls of the church, whether intentional or not, and have left the nation's culture to be framed without the influence of a biblical pattern. But it must be remembered that whatever area the church does not influence will soon try to destroy the church itself.

It is proper and right for Christians to strive to return the nation back to its godly heritage; however, it is important for the church and state to follow the biblical model as to their proper roles in society. The nation was founded on a biblical worldview, and we get a picture of this worldview in operation from the observations of Alexis de Tocqueville in his *Democracy in America* written in 1831, one of the most influential political texts ever written about America. "Americans so completely identify the spirit of Christianity with freedom in their minds that it is almost impossible to get them to conceive the one without the other..." Tocqueville went on to say that the peaceful influence exercised by religion over the nation was due to separation of church and state.[4] But unlike the modernists' definition of the separation of church and state, Tocqueville's separation was a separation of the spheres of power and not a separation of government from ethics and moral guidance supplied by the moral suasion of Christianity. Christian ethics and moral guidance increase throughout society when godly Christian men and women attain positions of authority in government and become salt and light to those around them. Too often this distinction is lost or blurred when some Christians develop a mindset that ruling the kingdom here on earth will be a monolithic or top-down affair. However, the biblical rule of the kingdom described by Tocqueville is not immediate, direct, or monolithic but must always be accordance with the biblical roles of the church and state in society.

As the Pentecostal movement coalesced around various denominational organizations, there was a growing resistance among some Pentecostals that became known as the "New Order of the Latter Rain." Like Millerism of the 1830s, the Latter Rain movement started out as a true revival that began at the Sharon Schools and Orphanage in North Battleford, Saskatchewan, Canada, in February 1948. Several Pentecostal leaders claimed that a new outpouring of the Holy Spirit had begun. They denigrated other Pentecostals denominations as apostate, sought restoration of the offices of apostle and prophet, and promoted an extreme form of congregationalism which in practice resulted in a lack of accountability. This lack of accountability eventually brought disrepute to the movement as several self-proclaimed apostles and prophets exhibited poor morals and promoted questionable doctrines. The Assemblies of God played a major role in confronting the extremes of the Latter Rain. As a consequence of the opposition by the Assemblies of God and other denominations, many who embraced the Latter Rain movement left those denominations. However, the Latter Rain movement soon lost momentum, became marginalized, but continued to exist among various small independent churches and ministries. Years later these churches embraced the more radical elements within the charismatic, Word of Faith, and Apostolic-Prophetic movements.[5]

The Latter Rain teachers blended Pentecostal fervor with false teaching and ungodly supernatural manifestations that were heavily influenced by occult activity. Many who were touched by these ungodly manifestations were ignorant of the similarities with various occult manifestations.[6]

Variations of the teachings of the Latter Rain movement continue to exist down to the present day under various names (including Manifest Sons of God, Shepherding/Discipleship, Positive Confession, and Dominion theology). The effect of the Latter Rain movement upon the major Pentecostal denominations was minimal after the mid-1950s. However, pastors and the laity must be made aware that the successors of the Latter Rain movement who continue to preach its false teachings are growing in influence once again among Pentecostal as well as traditional non-Pentecostal denominations.[7]

Within Pentecostalism and other evangelical denominations of today we continue to see true revival with both manifestations from God and occult manifestations from Satan. What makes it extremely difficult for the average layman sitting in the pew is that godly but deceived leaders of many evangelical churches have tended to mingle and share pulpits with, fellowship with, and follow the teachings of an intertwined, highly influential, and well-known group of leaders who are false teachers and preachers, lead false revivals, and preach another gospel. More importantly, there are many seemingly clueless godly evangelical church leaders who give homage to these false teachers and preachers and fail to publicly challenge their false doctrines, heresies, and teachings. In other words, these highly regarded false teachers are lying to the people, and the people's own pastors are not warning them or exposing their lies.

- Latter-day false prophets claiming apostolic and prophetic authority

A major source of false revivals over the last thirty-five years has resulted from what Mary Danielsen in her small booklet calls *The Perfect Storm of Apostasy*. Danielsen's booklet focuses on the Kansas City prophetic movement which had its roots at the Kansas City Fellowship during the mid-1980s. By the early 1990s the movement began to coalesce around several key leaders known as the Kansas City prophets: Mike Bickle, Bob Jones, John Paul Jackson, Rick Joyner, and Paul Cain. Draped with a self-proclaimed covering as a great move of God, these and other false prophets and teachers are "prophesying and prognosticating the path or direction of people's lives and the church as a whole." Danielsen believes the Kansas City prophetic movement and its various offshoots appear to be a perfect storm of apostasy because it continues to embrace and teach many of the tenets of dominion theology (e.g., Latter Rain, Manifest Sons of God, Joel's Army, Kingdom Now, elements of the prosperity gospel, and heretical interpretation of the five-fold ministry). These elements have been woven together such that the teachings of the personalities claiming special apostolic/prophetic authority are often viewed as superseding the authority of the Bible.[8]

The founder of the Kansas City prophets was Mike Bickle. While in Egypt in 1982, Bickle claims to have received a prophecy directly from the Lord in which He audibly spoke to Bickle these words, "I will change the understanding and expression of Christianity in one generation." Thereafter, Bickle moved to Kansas City and began Kansas City Fellowship.[9] Under Bickle, the Kansas City prophets became a worldwide movement that Bickle believed was meant to bring about a new order. Together, the Kansas City movement and Vineyard churches would become a training center for end-time prophets and apostles. Bickle also believed that God would raise up three hundred thousand leaders in the last days to become "Joel's Army" to oversee the end-time church and supervise all end-time prophecies, signs, and wonders.[10]

The other members of the Kansas City prophets had equally strange and heretical beliefs and teachings. Bob Jones claims to have had a vision when he was nine years old. In this vision, the angel Gabriel supposedly came to Jones and presented him with a bull skin mantle to represent his future role as a "seer." His ministry included many visions and interpretations of strange spiritual experiences. Paul Cain believed that he was visited by Jesus at age eight and again at eighteen and was called to a healing ministry. According to a 2005 *Chrisma* article, Cain admitted to involvement in long-term homosexual activity while Jones was exposed in 1991 as having been involved in sexual misconduct. Cain and Jones' ministries were closely linked with Bickle.[11]

Rick Joyner played a significant role in the Kansas City prophetic circle. He was a Supreme Council member of The Knights of Malta, an ecumenical order which included Orthodox, Evangelical, Catholic and Protestant members. This order was sanctioned and blessed by the Vatican. The knights are required to vow that they will be guided by the Sovereign Order of St. John of Jerusalem which began in 1090 and was the predecessor of the Knights of Malta.[12]

John Wimber went to Fuller Theological Seminary in Pasadena, California during the 1970s to study church growth. At Fuller, Wimber soon sought to incorporate signs and wonders as a means to achieve church growth, believing that the Gospel is largely ineffective without them. While at Fuller, Wimber met C. Peter Wagner, one of the founders of church-growth methodology along with Norman Vincent Peale and his disciple Robert Schuller and Schuller's disciples Bill Hybels (Willow Creek) and Rick Warren (The Purpose Driven Church). Wagner was greatly influenced by Wimber and also came to believe that the only means by which churches grow and produce revival is by the accompaniment of signs and wonders. Wagner is the father of what is now called the New Apostolic Reformation (NAR) which birthed the "territorial spiritual warfare" model which teaches that "every generation must 'take cities for God' and rid the planet of demons so Jesus can return."[13] Here again we see the heart of false teachings of dominion theology that permeates these ministries. The NAR teaches that there are modern day apostles and prophets that are equal or greater than those who wrote the Bible. For the church to come into the fullness of Christ, it must submit to the modern prophets and embrace their teachings.[14]

After resigning from Fuller in 1977, Wimber began to pastor a church he founded. Initially, Wimber sought a spiritual covering for his churches under Calvary Chapel, a group of fast-growing evangelical churches under the leadership of the late Chuck Smith. But soon Wimber sought spiritual power through a mixture of signs and wonders, psychology, and occult practices such as visualization and Eastern mysticism. Vineyard churches began to incorporate a variety of highly experiential practices that challenged the truth and authority of the Bible in many areas. Calvary Chapel's Smith challenged Wimber and others with regard to their bizarre practices, denigration of the Scriptures, and hyper-charismaticism. Smith effectively told Wimber and others that they had a choice of staying under the Calvary banner by systematically teaching the Scripture or to follow the pursuit of signs and wonders and the encouragement and endorsement of subjective truth as opposed to the objective truth of God's Word. Wimber chose the path of heresy and went on to found a group of Vineyard churches.[15]

- Toronto Blessing - 1994

One example of false revival and manifestations that came out of the Vineyard churches was the Toronto Blessing whose beginning is considered to be January 10, 1994, at the Vineyard Fellowship near Pearson International Airport, Toronto, Canada. Randy Clark from St. Louis, Missouri, was preaching a revival message that evening when it was claimed that the Holy Spirit was poured out on the congregation resulting in long periods of spontaneous, uncontrollable laughter among many in the congregation. Soon thousands of visitors from across the globe flocked to the church in hopes of receiving a similar experience and transporting the laughing revival back to their home churches. Within four years there were multiple thousands of churches around the world that were experiencing the so-called "Holy Laughter Revivals."

Clark was a disciple of Rodney Howard-Browne, a South African minister who is the reputed "Father" of Holy laughter. Howard-Browne claims to have had his first experience with the phenomenon of Holy Laughter in 1979. In 1989 while preaching in New York State, the congregation began to experience the same manifestation. This occurred again while he was preaching at a Lakeland, Florida, church. But it was the Toronto church that ignited the Holy Laughter Revival that spread rapidly around the world.[16]

Sustained, uncontrollable laughter was not the only unbiblical manifestation to be experienced during the Toronto revival. Howard-Browne gave an account of one woman who got "stuck" in the spirit by "Holy Ghost Glue" while she lay on the carpet. Although the woman tried to get up from the floor over a period of six hours, she kept saying, "I can't get up. I'm stuck to the floor." Other manifestations were even more bizarre. One woman claimed that Jesus took her through the events of her childhood as they relived them together. Another petite woman was "on all fours, snorting and pawing the ground like an angry ox or bull." Howard-Browne claimed that many had received gold fillings in their teeth at the Toronto congregation and at a South African church.[17]

Warren B. Smith made a detailed search of what the Bible says about laughter and found thirty-four references in the Old Testament and six in the New Testament. None of the references were even close to being a biblical precedent for "Holy Laughter" as a result of a special outpouring of the Holy Spirit.[18] But laughter is a normal expression of human emotion, and as one experiences great joy during such an outpouring there may be a moment's laughter as a result of that joy welling up within one's being. However, such occasions will not be marked by raucous and irreverent peals of continuous and uncontrollable laughter by large numbers of people. That is a manifestation of a spirit that is not from God.

The Holy Laughter phenomenon is just one of many similar false revivals and counterfeit manifestations that have deceived even the very elect in many churches that failed to test the spirits. Given the magnitude of the bizarre excesses, unscriptural nature of these revivals and manifestations, and their departure from the biblical patterns and boundaries provided by Scripture, it appears almost inconceivable that these deviant doctrines and abuses have spread so widely and burrowed so deeply into evangelical mentality in America. Yet, Paul warned of this deception in his first letter to Timothy.

> The Spirit clearly says that in later times some will abandon the faith and follow deceiving spirits and things taught by demons. Such teachings come through hypocritical liars, whose consciences have been seared as with a hot iron... If you point these things out to the brothers and sisters, you will be a good minister of Christ Jesus, nourished on the truths of the faith and of the good teaching that you have followed. [1 Timothy 4:1-2, 6-7. NIV]

- Todd Bentley and Healing Revivals

In April 2008, the Florida Healing revival began as a series of meetings held by Todd Bentley at Ignite Church pastored by Stephen Strader in Lakeland, Florida. As healings began to occur, the meetings were continued. Eventually the meetings were televised and news of the revival spread. People travelled from all over the world to attend, and Bentley specifically targeted the leaders in attendance so that he could give an "impartation of his anointing" which was to be taken back to their home churches. Because of the large crowds, the meetings were transferred to an eight thousand seat stadium.[19]

Andrew Strom has personally observed Bentley's ministry from its beginnings in the 1990s and its association with the prophetic movement. Strom states that Bentley was always on the forefront, the cutting-edge of the most extreme manifestations of the prophetic movement—"promotion of female angels, wealth-getting angels and every kind of dubious experience or 'anointing' you can imagine. And there was real 'power' behind it. That is what alarmed me. It wasn't just hype. People were having real 'power encounters' with this stuff."[20]

Bentley frequently talks of his experiences with an angel named Emma. Bob Jones, another Kansas City prophet, told Bentley that Emma was the angel that helped start the Kansas City prophetic movement in the 1980s. He described Emma as being a beautiful young woman about 22 years old but at the same time old in wisdom. Subsequently, Bentley was in a meeting in Beulah, North Dakota, when Emma supposedly came into the service. Bentley said that Emma floated a couple of inches off the floor and glided across the room carrying bags of gold. According to Bentley, Emma opened the bags and began sprinkling gold dust on people as she went up and down the aisles. Bentley also claims to have made several "Third Heaven" trips, and on one of these trips he visited the apostle Paul who lives in a small cabin.[21]

If one doubts that Bentley's extreme departures from the nature of true revival could actually still be a true revival, one need only to go to the Internet. Strom describes the course of events in two such videos of Bentley revival meetings.

> Todd speaks of the angel that is going to "visit the children" and then he begins to jerk and laugh uncontrollably more and more. He prays that a "drunken glory" will move across the whole place – and you can see it happen in the audience. In another video he has German preacher Stefan Driess on stage with him and they both weave drunkenly as Stefan describes the angel encounter that he just had. Todd then imparts his 'anointing' to Stefan by kneeing him in the stomach and Stefan falls to the ground, jerking uncontrollably. These bizarre manifestations and the 'angels' that accompany them seem to be all through the Florida revival. In fact angels are being given credit for many of the healings there. (Please watch the change in Todd's EYES during a lot of these manifestations also. Frightening!) One eyewitness describe the "impartation" lines in Florida

this way: "As far (and I mean as far) as I could see masses of people on the floor shaking, shivering, dazed looking, completely out or unconscious looking.[22]

Even though there are claims that some of the healings may possibly be genuine healings from God, how can they distinguish between which healings are from God and which are not when both apparently come from the same source? Would a child of God want to risk receiving their healing from a source that can't be trusted?

- Bill Johnson, Bethel Church and Bethel School of Supernatural Ministry, Redding, California

Bethel Church of Redding is one of the largest evangelical churches in North America and attracts many visitors from around the world who come to attend Bethel School of Supernatural Ministry whose purpose is to have a "global impact as a revival resource and equipping center." The Bethel Church juggernaut is a highly influential purveyor of New Age and quantum spirituality practices to evangelical churches throughout America.[23] Writer John Lanagan quotes Johnson's views on his association with the New Age from Johnson's 2006 book *Dreaming with God.*

> Many prominent pastors and conference speakers add fuel to the fire of fear by assuming that because the New Age promotes it, its origins must be from the devil. I find that form of reasoning weak at best. If we follow that line of thought we will continue to give the devil *the tools that God has given us for success in life and ministry.*[24] [emphasis added]

Effectively, Johnson has taken New Age theology, science, and worldview and attempted to recreate God as the universe and not a heavenly being. But labeling his extra-biblical New Age beliefs and practices as being stolen from God doesn't mean they are from God, the Father of Jesus Christ.

The Physics of Heaven is a book co-authored by Bill Johnson's administrative assistant Judy Franklin. Bill Johnson wrote two of the chapters, Johnson's wife Beni wrote another chapter, and Kris Vallotton, one of the Bethel pastors, wrote the Forward. The book as described on *Amazon.com* promises many things.

Some of the most influential and prophetic voices of the Spirit-empowered movement have joined together to help you start hearing the sounds of heaven and discover how natural elements—sound, light, energy, vibration and even quantum physics—are supernaturally bringing Heaven to Earth... *The Physics of Heaven* features revelatory segments such as: *Recovering Spiritual Inheritance, Sound of Heaven, Angelic Encounters, Quantum Mysticism, Authentic versus Counterfeit.* Unlock Heaven's healing energy, tap into the frequency of God's Kingdom, and access a new realm of divine encounters today![25] [emphasis in original]

Andrew Strom warns of other New Age practices covered in the book: "Vibrating in Harmony with God," "Good Vibrations," "The God Vibration," "Dolphins and Healing Energy," "The Power of Color," and "Human Body Frequencies."[26]

At the heart of this attempt to blend New Age theology and influence with Christianity is a rejection of the rapture. As Johnson's assistant wrote in *The Physics of Heaven*, "The greatest error we could ever commit is to think that the world is going to get so bad that He will snatch us out quickly before we all die...This is not...showing the world how powerful we are because *God has given us His power.*"[27] [emphasis added]

Those that adhere to dominion theology are viewed as power-oriented religions that have a perverted understanding of the Fall and redemption. For power religions the Fall is as much "about the loss of power and authority as it was about sin and alienation from God. Therefore, salvation is about restoration of power and authority, as well as forgiveness of sins." As a result, dominionists believe that when Adam fell he handed his God-given dominion over to Satan who became God of this world. God was not going to come in and take back the dominion He had given to Adam; Adam had to take it back.[28] How do dominionists such as Johnson suppose that Christians will take back dominion lost by Adam? John Lanagan quotes Dr. Orrel Steinkamp.

This dominion mentality is conceived as a gigantic *end-time revival* that will sweep the whole earth in its wake....An elite company of overcomers from out of the larger church will subdue all things and will be so

126

endued with *supernatural power* that the first church apostles will be envious of the latter day apostles.[29] [emphasis added]

Apparently this gigantic end-time revival will be the work of a select company of overcomers endued with super-supernatural power which is different from the power of the Holy Spirit bestowed on the church on the day of Pentecost.

The marks of the dominionists' gigantic end-time revival are defined by mystical experiences, unbiblical and extra-biblical practices, and the denigration of sound biblical doctrine. Those attending Bethel have been exposed to a number of these practices including visualization, contemplative prayer, meditation rituals, chanting, spiritual drunkenness, and grave soaking.[30] This last practice is sometimes called mantle grabbing and occurs when a person lies across the physical grave of a deceased preacher or evangelist (e.g., John Calvin, George Whitefield, and Charles Finney). Supposedly, the power of the Holy Spirit has been "trapped" within the body upon that person's death, and by lying on that person's grave the recipient person can "soak up," that is, to reclaim the coveted anointing (such as healing and prophesy) that has been trapped inside the deceased person and therefore unused and wasted.[31]

———

In this chapter the reader has been given merely a sampling of a much larger wave of apostasy, heresy, cultism, and worldliness that has inundated the church beginning in the twentieth century. In the next chapter an examination of how Satan invaded the evangelical church and substantially replaced true revival based on conviction, repentance, forgiveness, and sanctification with new false definitions of renewal and reformation based on mystical experiences and the philosophies and practices of the New Age and Eastern religions.

12

New Age Spirituality and Man's Fascination With the Mystical

In the last chapter an examination was made of several notable examples of false revivals, one in the nineteenth century and the remainder occurring after World War II. When the history of these revivals is measured against the standards discussed in Chapter 10 (Test the Spirit in revivals and manifestations) they are found to be false revivals and not from God. At their core these false revivals stand in fundamental opposition to the biblical character and essence of true revivals from the first century through the worldwide awakening during the first decade of the twentieth century.

The greatest facilitator of false revival and hindrance of true revival over the last seventy-five years is New Age Spirituality. In this chapter an examination will be made of its worldview, beliefs, practices, and how to recognize when New Age Spirituality comes into the local church. In the next chapter the reader will learn how that after World War II New Age Spirituality invaded the evangelical church, the last bastion of New Testament Christianity.

False teachers and perilous times at the end of the last days

The increase in the number of false revivals beginning in the last half of the twentieth century is a direct result of two significant events. First, there has been a substantial increase in the number of false teachers and prophets as the world enters the end of the last days. Second, there has been an alarming decline among Christians in the areas of biblical knowledge, sound teaching, and discernment. As a result of ignorance of the Bible and loss of discernment, many Christians have been deceived and are unwittingly embracing false revivals to fill the vacuum left by the departure of true revival from the American evangelical landscape. In his second letter to Timothy, Paul speaks of the proliferation of evil among men during the last days that will make this deception possible.

> This know also, that in the last days perilous times shall come. For men shall be lovers of their own selves, covetous, boasters, proud, blasphemers, disobedient to

parents, unthankful, unholy, without natural affection, trucebreakers, false accusers, incontinent, fierce, despisers of those that are good, traitors, heady, high minded, lovers of pleasures more than lovers of God; Having a form of godliness, but denying the power thereof: from such turn away. [2 Timothy 3:1-5. KJV]

The last days about which Paul spoke include the entire Christian era that began with the establishment of the church on the day of Pentecost following Christ's crucifixion and resurrection. However, at the end of the those last days (the church age) conditions will become ever-increasingly worse in the world including a rapid disintegration of moral standards and a great increase in false believers and false churches within God's kingdom.[1] As one observes the current magnitude and world-wide spread of the perilous times spoken of by Paul, it is virtually undeniable that the church is very near the end of the last days.

Recall that the Loadicean church was the last of the seven Asian churches that John wrote about in Revelation 3:14-21. This church is considered to be the church of the end times and has fostered unprecedented levels of apostasy, cultism, heresy, and worldliness.[2]

At the end of the last days great numbers of churches that claim to follow Jesus Christ as Lord and Savior will depart from biblical truth in both word and deed. This departure is called the Great Apostasy and means to "fall away" or abandonment and rebellion. Within the church, the apostasy will take two forms. The first is *theological* apostasy in which false leaders will depart from and reject part or all of the New Testament teachings of Christ and the apostles and replace them with various heretical teachings and doctrines. False leaders and teachers will promote a false salvation and cheap grace to replace salvation through Christ's atoning sacrifice at Calvary, repentance, turning from sin, and adherence to God's holy standards of living. False leaders and teachers will offer a gospel centered on the self and its needs and desires. The second type is *moral* apostasy in which wicked men sever their relationship with Christ and fully embrace sin and immorality. Although proclaiming right doctrine and adherence to biblical teachings, they will abandon the moral standards as taught by the New Testament in exchange for money, success, honor, and a large following.[3]

Paul also warned the Corinthian church against false teachers and preachers that would come among them and preach a different Jesus, a different spirit, or a different Gospel than the one they accepted.

> But I am afraid that just as Eve was deceived by the
> serpent's cunning, your minds may somehow be led
> astray from your sincere and pure devotion to Christ. For
> if someone comes to you and preaches a Jesus other than
> the Jesus we preached, or if you receive a different spirit
> from the Spirit you received, or a different gospel from
> the one you accepted, you put up with it easily enough.
> [2 Corinthians 11:3-4. NIV]

Donald Stamps' commentary about this verse explains how error enters
the church through Satan's false teachers.

> False teachers may admit that what is in the Bible is true,
> but they also claim to have additional revelations or
> knowledge equal in authority to Scripture. Such false
> teaching usually blends the Christian faith with other
> religious ideas or philosophies. This results in the
> following errors: (1) People put the supposed new
> revelation on the same level of authority as the original
> message of Christ as revealed in the Bible. (2) God's
> Word becomes less important, and Christ takes second
> place to human leaders or founders of a movement or
> church. (3) The false teachers claim to have deeper
> understanding of so-called "hidden revelations" in
> Scripture. They teach or reveal things that supposedly
> have been missed or overlooked by countless godly
> people and preachers throughout history.[4]

*New Age Spirituality –The heart of rebellion in the modern evangelical
church*

Over the course of human history Satan has predominantly
peddled his lies and deceptions to mankind in two forms: *spiritual*
humanism (you are God because God is in all things) and *secular*
humanism (man is his own god). Both promote an exaltation of self. For
the last three hundred years in Western civilization beginning with the
era of Enlightenment, the humanistic spirit of the world has shown its
secular face through appeals to science and reason. Men attempt to
exclude the supernatural as he tries to create the ideal society based on
the supposed never-ending progress of man's unfallen and fundamentally
good nature. But the folly and falseness of secular humanism's promises

died in the ashes of two world wars and the Great Depression during the first half of the twentieth century.

Although man's faith in progress and reason still dominates the leadership and institutions of Western civilization, in the 1960s there developed a growing alienation, restlessness, and disillusionment with the spiritually barren secular humanism, especially among the young who sought elsewhere for answers to the basic questions of life. For those disheartened by the barrenness of religion-free secular humanism, Satan resurrected spiritual humanism, painted a modern face on this ages-old spirit of the world, and dressed it in new clothes to fit the spirit of the age. Out of spiritual humanism was born the New Age movement whose spiritual ancestors are witchcraft, occult, and mystical Eastern religions.[5]

The decline of the power and cultural influence of the evangelical church beginning in the last half of the twentieth century indisputably corresponds with the simultaneous rise of *New Age Spirituality*. New Age Spirituality is the central force or tool used by Satan to empower his other assault weapons (*apostasy, heresy, and worldliness*) against the evangelical church during the end of the last days. The rise of New Age Spirituality also marked the beginning of the decline of those periodic seasons of revival of the church.

Recognizing New Age Spirituality in the evangelical church

New Age Spirituality may be said to fall under the broader definition of *cultism* – a spurious religion of encompassing numerous and generally pagan belief systems and practices. Billions around the world have become deeply involved in false religions, the occult, astrology, witchcraft, Spiritism, and Satanism. Through these activities the influence of demons and evil spirits has multiplied enormously. Many elements of cultism have surged into numerous areas of evangelical church life and practices through New Age Spirituality. Before an examination is made of how this happened, we begin with the words of Paul in his first letter to Timothy.

> The Spirit clearly says that *in later times* some will abandon the faith and *follow deceiving spirits and things taught by demons*. Such teachings come through hypocritical liars, whose consciences have been seared as with a hot iron. [1 Timothy 4:1-2. NIV] [emphasis added]

The deceiving spirits and things taught by demons are in essence New Age Spirituality which has invaded many parts of the evangelical church. Kevin Reeves defines the New Age as follows:

> New Age – In a religious context, an all-encompassing spirituality, sourced in ancient pagan practices that defies specific "doctrinal" definitions. It is geared toward New Age religion, which can incorporate teachings and practices from virtually any other religion or non-religion such as Buddhism, Taoism, Wicca, astrology, alchemy, veganism, homeopathic medicine, tarot cards, crystal gazing, etc.[6]

Many Christians will vehemently deny that they, their leaders, and their fellow congregants are involved in the practices of New Age religions. Yet, they are unaware that many of the seemingly innocuous beliefs and practices infiltrating the church are directly linked with New Age Spirituality. As a result, there are a number of New Age Spirituality's beliefs and practices once thought hostile to Christianity that have been repackaged and are now comfortably entrenched in many evangelical churches, e.g., contemplative prayer, visualization and yoga.

It is extremely important for those seeking true revival of the body of Christ in these dark days to understand the source of this darkness. Christians must not only know the tenets and beliefs of their faith, they must know the tactics and deceptions of the enemy in order to defend the faith and the faithful. In this chapter New Age Spirituality has been identified as Satan's driving force in attacking the church in modern times. To understand New Age Spirituality the Christian must know its language and definitions. What follows in the remainder of this chapter is an examination of the major themes of New Age Spirituality which will also serve as a brief but incomplete checklist for Christians wishing to determine the extent to which New Age Spirituality may have invaded their churches. [7]

Spiritual formation and spiritual disciplines

Spiritual formation is a process by which Christians supposedly can become more Christ-like which occurs when one is more fully adapted to and united with Christ. The process of becoming more Christ-like begins with the practice of certain spiritual disciplines. Some of these practices do not conflict with biblical instructions such as fasting, good works, and prayer, but those practices act as a cover or smokescreen for those that do. In addition to biblically sound practices, spiritual disciplines must always include *contemplative spirituality* which is the heart of Spiritual formation and the doorway for New Age Spirituality to enter the hearts of individual Christians and the life of the church. Some Christian leaders who endorse and practice spiritual formation recognize that the spiritual disciplines can be practiced by anyone—Christians, Buddhists, Hindus, and even atheists. Therefore, non-Christians can also become more Christ-like.[8] But disciplines, practices, and other works do not make one a Christian. Both the individual Christian and the church need not seek for better, newer ways of drawing close to Christ. There are no formulas, processes, series of steps, or mystical experiences necessary because a person becomes a new creation in Christ when they accept Him as his or her Lord and Savior. Those "good" spiritual practices found in the Bible do not need to be re-formed, re-packaged, and presented as something new and special to enhance one's access or nearness to Christ.

The degree to which spiritual formation (and practice of the associated spiritual disciplines) has invaded the vast majority of America's seminaries and Bible colleges is astonishing. There are about three hundred fifty Bible colleges and seminaries accredited by either the Association of Theological Schools or the Association for Biblical Higher Education. In *every case* these accrediting organizations require institutions seeking accreditation to incorporate spiritual formation into their infrastructures and the lives of their students. These accredited institutions in the United States and Canada are found in virtually every Protestant denomination including the Assemblies of God and various other Pentecostal churches, Nazarene, Baptist, Methodist, Wesleyan, and Reformed churches to mention only a few.[9]

Bible colleges and seminaries are readily embracing and teaching spiritual reformation because many administrators and faculty members believe it is the best way to train spiritual leaders.[10] One of the themes bandied about in Christian churches, colleges, and seminaries is that of being a *Servant Leader* or practicing *Servant Leadership*. To get people to embrace spiritual formation as a normal Christian practice, they are told that to become a good leader, they must practice Servant Leadership. These servant-leaders-in-training are taught to be good servant-leaders (i.e., followers) by not challenging their teachers with regard to the various New Age practices brought into the church through spiritual formation. Effectively, the aspiring servant leader is subtly pressured toward a suspension of discernment.[11]

Contemplative spirituality (Meditation and Contemplative prayer)

Contemplative spirituality is the heart-beat of the spiritual formation movement. It uses ancient mystical practices to induce altered states of consciousness. In Christian circles these various practices fall under the general heading of contemplative prayer. Because contemplative spirituality is such a broad subject and involves a wide range of mystical practices, it is best to begin with a few definitions.

- Meditation (New Age Spirituality)

New Age meditation is not continuous thinking about something but just the opposite. It involves ridding oneself of all thoughts in order to still the mind, essentially a state of mental drifting or non-thought. This condition is not to be confused with daydreaming where the mind dwells on a particular subject. New Age meditation leads the practitioner down a path to the point where the mind becomes thoughtless, empty, and silent. *Christ-Consciousness* occurs when a "state of awareness is reached in meditation in which one realizes one's own divinity and oneness with God, thereby becoming a "christ" or enlightened being."[12]

- Meditation and Contemplation (Biblical)

Meditation by most Christians involves a deep, continuous thinking about something or a normal thinking "process of reflection on the things of God and biblical precepts."[13]

- Creative Visualization

A practice in which a person can supposedly create one's own reality, especially during times of meditation. An image is created in the mind of a desired object or occurrence which supposedly will result in its physical fulfillment. In the Christian version, faith proclamations are joined with visualization techniques.[14]

- Altered State of Consciousness

"A meditative or drug-induced non-ordinary state of mind." By repeating a word or phrase (*mantra*) or concentration on one's breath or an object, the mind goes into an altered state of consciousness and all thought becomes absent. This absence of normal thought is called *the Silence*. In a religious context, this is a state where the seeker is drawn out of his normal thinking processes into *self-realization*. When one achieves self-realization, he or she has come into contact with the *higher self* and becomes aware of his divinity or connection with the divine or divine wisdom. However, rather than finding one's higher self during an altered state of consciousness, the person has opened himself up to (*channeling*) the inhabitation of supernatural entities or *spirit guides* (the Bible calls these demons or familiar spirits).[15]

- Contemplative Prayer

Contemplative prayer uses repeated words or phrases (mantra) and begins with *centering or centering prayer* with the purpose of taking the person deep within their center. Centering encourages a clearing of the mind of conscious thought in order to create a spiritual receptivity to God or the divine. Likewise, *breath prayer* is the practice of picking a single word or short phrase and repeating it in conjunction with the breath. Rick Warren encouraged the use of breath prayers in his multi-million best-selling book *The Purpose Driven Life*.[16]

One of the reasons for the ease with which contemplative prayer has invaded both evangelical and non-evangelical churches is that people are truly hungry for a genuine presence and touch of God. This hunger has occurred because many of them have not been taught with power and passion the life-sustaining truths of God's Word. A second reason is that true revival has been virtually non-existent in most evangelical churches for almost a half century. Many Christians are spiritually half-starved because they have not received the meat of the Word from the pulpit and have not experienced the periodic refreshing brought by a special outpouring of the Holy Spirit due to the absence of revival. As a result, many are turning to meditative/contemplative prayer practices of Eastern religions and the occult to find the God within. However, Christians must not succumb to the deceptions of Satan but take heed of Paul's words to the Colossians.

> See to it that no one takes you captive through hollow and deceptive philosophy, which depends on human tradition and the elemental spiritual forces of this world

rather than on Christ. For in Christ all the fullness of the Deity lives in bodily form, and in Christ you have been brought to fullness. He is the head over every power and authority. [Colossians 2:8-10. NIV]

New Age Spirituality – Beliefs and worldview

- Pantheism and panentheism

The belief system from which all New Age Spirituality flows is *pantheism* and *panentheism* which are endemic in both Eastern religions and the occult. Pantheism teaches that God *is* all things. The universe and all life are connected in a sum which is the total reality of God. All physical matter is seen as equal and includes man, animals, plants, other life forms, and all non-living physical matter. Distinctions or hierarchy do not exist at any level. Therefore, if "all is one," then all must be deity. Panentheism carries this one step farther. It teaches that God is *in* all things. God is both personal and is also universal, that is, in all of creation. In this universal view, panenthiests believe that God is in all people and when all people become one with him, all of God's creation will be saved. Being both personal and universal, there is a physical dimension but also a non-physical true essence with a real identity.

- Interspirituality

Interspirituality is a term that is occasionally used to connect religion with Panentheism. It teaches that divinity (God) is *in* all things and the presence of God is *in* all religions. Through meditation (*mysticism* - a direct experience with the supernatural realm) one may recognize this state of divinity.[17]

- Universalism

Universalism is also a fundamental belief of New Age Spirituality. Universalism teaches that all humanity has or will ultimately have a positive connection and relationship with God. Those with a belief in universalism believe that every human being will ultimately be reunited with God whether they believe in Jesus or do not. Universalism also embraces the idea that every human being has divinity or God within.[18]

New Age Spirituality in the church

In addition to spiritual formation, spiritual disciplines, and contemplative spirituality, there are several aspects of New Age Spirituality that have mutated into certain false but widely held beliefs and practices within certain quarters of the church.

- New Thought

New Thought is a movement that attempts to merge certain classic occult concepts with Christian terminology. Norman Vincent Peale's practical Christianity was a merger of humanistic psychology with occult beliefs and practices of the New Age. Both were intended to heal the soul of man—one through *self-realization* and the other through getting *in touch with the god within*. To these ministrations, Peale added a third ingredient to his practical Christianity—the introduction of church growth methodologies and practices.

- Dominion theology

Dominion theology was discussed in the last chapter, but its connection with New Age Spirituality is discussed in this section. Dominion theology is an odd mixture of several elements of New Age Spirituality's progressivism and self-help along with panentheism's "...all God's creation will be saved." *Dominionism* is the belief that God's people will rise up as overcomers and place Satan and his followers under their feet (not Christ's). Dominionists teach that Christ cannot return until this is accomplished. The rapture is dismissed as a myth. Christ will not return for his people because He is already in them. Therefore, there is no need for a physical return. The overcomers will deliver to Christ a perfect world over which He will then rule. *Kingdom Now and Latter Rain* theologies are similar and teach that Christians are to walk consistently in supernatural power while doing the work of establishing Christ's kingdom on earth.[19] In Dominion theology we see elements of pantheism and panentheism.

- Ecumenism (ecumenicalism)

The push for ecumenism (ecumenicalism) has been growing in the church for almost seventy-five years. But unity through ecumenism is not the same as the unity of the body of Christ about which Paul spoke in his letter to the Ephesians.

> As a prisoner for the Lord, then, I urge you to live a life worthy of the calling you have received…Make every effort to keep the unity of the Spirit through the bond of peace. There is one body and one Spirit, just as you were called to one hope when you were called; one Lord, one faith, one baptism; one God and Father of all, who is over all and through all and in all. [Ephesians 4:1, 3-6. NIV]

This verse is not meant to imply a pantheistic oneness or God-in-all theology which was refuted in a previous section of this chapter. In these verses Paul is talking to Christians who He described as prisoners of the Lord. The Holy Spirit resides in every Christian but not those who are not born-again and therefore cannot be in unity with the Lord or Christians.

Ecumenism as it has been promoted and practiced beginning near the middle of the twentieth century is far different from the unity Paul instructed the church to seek. Ecumenism has come to mean the merging of faiths or finding common ground among the various doctrinal persuasions of Protestant churches and also with the Catholic and Orthodox Churches, many of which have irreconcilable differences from a biblical perspective. In other words, ecumenically-inclined churches must focus on beliefs held in common and not the differences that divide, but it should not be surprising that this has led to great dilution of biblical faith. Whereas Paul spoke of unity of the Spirit and belief in the body of Christ (one body, one spirit, one Lord, one faith, and One God), modern ecumenicists seek unity by casting off of those biblical doctrines and teachings thought divisive and therefore stumbling blocks to modern sentiments of tolerance and unity. Ecumenism is now being pushed to the point of seeking common ground not only among Protestants and the Catholic Church but common ground with non-Christian religions such as Islam (e.g. The Yale Covenant and its signers such as Rick Warren and Bill Hybels).

- Emerging church

The *emerging church* will be examined extensively in the next chapter. It is mentioned here because the proponents of the emerging church are highly ecumenical and combine elements of the liberal church's social gospel, Catholic mysticism, and New Age Spirituality's practices of contemplative prayer, Eastern meditational techniques, and pagan religious practices. They are very postmodern in worldview and follow a loose set of doctrines that promotes a redefinition of Christianity. Emerging church leaders believe that a "new" reformation occurs every 500 years, and that one is now due. But they claim this new reformation will not be a breaking away from the Catholic Church that occurred five hundred years ago but a uniting of all belief systems through ecumenism. For those who have been paying attention, they will quickly recognize the striking similarities between the beliefs of the emerging church and those of New Age Spirituality.[20]

––––––––

This chapter has covered only a partial listing of the beliefs and practices of New Age Spirituality that are infiltrating vast numbers of pulpits, Sunday school classrooms, youth groups, Bible studies, prayer groups, seminaries, Bible colleges, and various Christian-based organizations. Every Christian leader and congregant down to the newest convert should with utmost seriousness take to heart the apostle John's warning previously quoted in this book.

> Dear friends, do not believe every spirit, but test the spirits to see whether they are from God, because many false prophets have gone out into the world. [1 John 4:1. NIV]

In the next chapter are examinations as to how and through whom New Age Spirituality entered a large segment of evangelicalism beginning in the latter half of the twentieth century.

13

The Emergent Church – Mystical Experiences Replace the Holy Spirit

The "Christian" purveyors of New Age Spirituality

As noted in a previous chapter, secular humanism captured the liberal Protestant churches over a sixty-year period (about 1870-1930). Although *secular* humanism was an abomination to conservative and evangelical churches, *spiritual* humanism under various names and disguises has found a friendly welcome and home among many of these churches and ministries following the end of World War II in 1945. Various facets of spiritual humanism are found under the broadly inclusive term "New Age Spirituality."

The invasion of the evangelical church by New Age Spirituality did not occur because of a sneak attack by Satan that occurred when the church wasn't paying attention or was preoccupied with other matters. To the contrary, over a period of seventy five years following the end of World War II, New Age Spirituality marched down the middle of Main Street America and into the homes and churches of evangelical Christians who expressed remarkably little concern or offered only token resistance at best. Not only was there little resistance, but a cursory examination of several major ministries and movements that dominated American evangelicalism since the 1950s have proven to be unequivocal champions and practitioners of many aspects of New Age Spirituality. The following is a brief overview of the principal tributary through which New Age Spirituality flowed into the evangelical church.

- Norman Vincent Peale – Practical Christianity

Peale's practical Christianity was unique in that it blended humanistic psychology with the occult beliefs and practices of the New Age. Both were intended to heal the soul of man—one through *self-realization* and the other through getting *in touch with the god within*. To these ministrations, Peale added a third ingredient to his practical Christianity—the introduction of church growth methodologies and practices focused on "…'discipling' rather than 'perfecting' members— that is, bringing them into the church in the anticipation that education would subsequently reveal to them the fuller implications of a richer, more self-conscious faith." Peale's practical Christianity served the god of "self" and has been adopted by many American evangelical churches pursuing the therapeutic, seeker-friendly ministry model since the 1970s. The focus of the Church Growth movement is to make unbelievers comfortable in the church as opposed to discipling believers.[1]

Peale's practical Christianity was a modernized and Christianized version of "New Thought" popularized by occult writer and teacher Florence Scovel Shinn (1871-1940).[2] In New Thought teachings, the human mind has extraordinary potential, material or physical events are shaped by mental and spiritual realities, and physical realities experienced by man originate in the mental and metaphysical (beyond what is perceptible to the senses). Through prayer and positive thinking, one can see the spark of divinity in one's self and bring it into alignment with God (the divine spirit of the universe) which makes possible healing and worldly wealth.[3] The origins and teachings of New Thought and positive thinking are deeply intertwined and indisputably New Age.

- Prosperity Gospel

Kenneth Hagin was the founder of Word of Faith movement. As a result of a spiritual vision he had in the 1950s, Hagin wrote *How To Write Your Own Ticket With God* which promotes a gospel based on positive confession.

> ...you can receive anything in the present tense, such as salvation, the baptism in the Holy Spirit, healing for your body, spiritual victory, or finances. Anything the Bible promises you now, you can receive now by taking these four steps...
>
> Step 1: Say it...In my vision, Jesus said, "Positive or negative, it is up to the individual. According to what the individual says, that shall he receive."...
>
> Step 2: Do it...Jesus dictated to me during my vision. "Your action defeats you or puts you over. According to your action, you receive or you are kept from receiving."...

Step 3: Receive it…It is like plugging into an electrical outlet. If we can learn to plug into this supernatural power, we can put it to work for us, and we can be healed…

Step 4: Tell it…Jesus said to me, "Tell it so others may believe."…

…In the vision, I said, "Lord, I can see that. I can see that anybody that would take these four steps, they would receive healing just like the woman did. But now You said if anybody anywhere would take these four steps they would receive from you *whatever they wanted.* Do You mean that they could receive the infilling of the Holy Spirit that way?" He said, "Most assuredly, yes."[4] [emphasis in original]

Although perhaps not intentional, his beliefs are only a short step to cross the line into what became derisively known as the prosperity gospel and whose false teachings, rightly or wrongly, misunderstood or not, originated with Hagin's book and its distorted presentation of the Gospel with regard to faith.

The principle teaching of positive confession is that there are both positive and negative aspects to confession. It is believed that the pleasant circumstances of life can be enjoyed through expressing positive statements that align with specific Scriptures. The unpleasant is avoided by refraining from negative statements. Effectively, what a person says is the determinant of what he will receive and what he will become. Therefore, positive confession is a tool with which one can banish poverty, disease, sickness, and other afflictions of life.[5] Such words easily resonate and have strong similarities with the teachings of many facets of New Age Spirituality.

This is not a condemnation of all who reside under the Word of Faith banner. Many follow sound biblical doctrine with regard to faith and its practice and have not succumbed to the seductive tenets of positive confession and the prosperity gospel. However, it appears that many in the evangelical churches of America have embraced and widely promote these unbiblical beliefs and practices, especially a large number of mega church pastors and high profile TV evangelists and pastors.

- Robert Schuller – Possibility Thinking

The essence of Robert Schuller's theology was centered on one's *self* and grossly deviated from sound biblical doctrines and teachings. Schuller's possibility thinking also mirrored the New Age propensities of Peale's practical Christianity. For Schuller, inborn sin is a *condition* to be dealt with therapeutically as opposed to an *action* requiring repentance and a turning from sin. Merely taking a step of faith itself absolves one's sin without the necessity of an ongoing faith walk—a daily dying to self and sin. The purpose for one's salvation is to do good works as opposed to having a right relationship with God. Therefore, hell is minimized or ignored altogether. Positivism emphasizes divine dreams in this life as opposed to man's eternal destination. Through reason, methods, techniques, and pandering to self, man can proactively overcome sin.[6]

On closer examination, Schuller's theology mimics many of the New Age terms and definitions listed in the previous chapter. Schuller's strong links to New Age Spirituality are undeniable given his long support of Gerald Jampolsky's "A Course in Miracles" theology and its New Age pantheistic teachings. Schuller's close connection with the New Age is also confirmed by his support of well-known surgeon Bernie Siegel, a New Age teacher who wrote *Love, Medicine, and Miracles.* Siegel claims that he has an "inner guide" named George who helped him with his work. George was a bearded, long-haired young man who Siegel claims to have met while in a session of directed meditation. Siegel was also on the board of Jampolsky's Attitudinal Healing Centers and endorsed "A Course in Miracles." The opening page of Schuller's 1995 *Prayer: My Soul's Adventure With God* included Siegel's warm endorsement of the book which he said "…reaches beyond religion and information to what we all need—spirituality, inspiration, and understanding."[7]

- Rick Warren and Bill Hybels – New Age Spirituality in the Church Growth movement

If Norman Vincent Peale and Robert Schuller can be called the first and second generations of the Church Growth movement, Rick Warren and Bill Hybels must certainly be considered its third generation beginning in the late 1970s. Like their forebears, Hybels and Warren and their ministries have been very comfortable and intertwined with New Age Spirituality's practices and beliefs such as contemplative prayer, ecumenism, dominion theology, and spiritual formation among others.

The Church Growth movement put down its roots in the heart of conservative evangelicalism in order to make the church more relevant to the modern and postmodern generations while claiming to do so without compromising the gospel. After four decades, the true colors of the Church Growth movement and the damage it has done to the church have been unmasked. A large number of evangelical Christian leaders are far less concerned with sound doctrine and faithfulness to New Testament Christianity and are now fully supportive of the emerging church. Rick Warren, frequently called "America's pastor," helped launch the emerging church. He gave it his unreserved blessing when writing the forward to Dan Kimball's book, *The Emerging Church*. According to Warren,

> This book is a wonderful, detailed example of what a purpose-driven church can look like in a postmodern world...Dan's book explains how to do it [reach the "emerging generation"] with the cultural-creatives who think and feel in postmodern terms. You need to pay attention to him [Kimball] because times are changing.[8]

The contents of Kimball's book remove any doubts about Warren and Kimball's close connection with New Age Spirituality and the direction of the purpose-driven church. Kimball and Warren are indisputably promoting New Age Spirituality through such contemplative prayer (including Lectio Divina, a form contemplative prayer that began with the Desert Fathers of the Catholic Church in the fourth century), practicing the silence, labyrinth walking, and chanting words or phrases (centering down).[9]

Warren unreservedly endorses spiritual formation and its associated disciples in his seminal book, *The Purpose Driven Church*. Warren attempts to separate spiritual growth from the mystical by making such growth a "matter of learning certain *spiritual* exercises and being disciplined to do them until they become habits...Often called spiritual disciplines, we use the term habits because it is less threatening to new believers."[10] [emphasis in original] But changing the labels from "spiritual formation" and "spiritual disciplines" to "spiritual exercises" does not change the essence or intent of these New Age based practices.

In the previous chapter we saw that spiritual formation and spiritual disciplines may contain several biblically sound practices such as fasting, good works, and prayer. But the spiritual disciplines associated with spiritual formation must *always* include *contemplative spirituality,* which at its center lays contemplative prayer. Ray Yungen in his book *A Time of Departing* sums up Warren's position on his connection with New Age Spirituality's spiritual reformation.

> ...Warren does indeed embrace the spiritual formation movement, of which he writes that this movement has a "valid message for the church" and has "given the body of Christ a wake-up call." What this means is that Warren, leader of this "New Reformation," has landed on the side of the contemplative prayer (i.e., spiritual formation) movement. In order to prove this to be true, it is essential to examine Warren and his ministry. In doing so, you may also come to the conclusion, as I have, that the Purpose Driven paradigm could very well be providing an avenue not for a new reformation and spiritual awakening from God but rather for a descent into spiritual apostasy.[11]

The American evangelical church's journey through the New Age teachings of Peale, Hagin, Schuller, Hybels, and Warren has led it to the doors of the emerging church.

The emerging church

Discernment of something unholy is often preceded by a sense of uneasiness or foreboding. Although many Christians could not quite put a finger on the things that were troubling evangelical Christianity during the 1970s and 1980s, there were a few voices, crying in the wilderness so to speak, warning of the storm of apostasy, heresy, cultism, and worldliness that was even then blowing through the church. These were men such as Francis Schaeffer (*The Great Evangelical Disaster*), David Wilkerson (*Set the Trumpet to Thy Mouth*), and Dave Hunt (*The Seduction of Christianity* and *Beyond Seduction*). Many in the church ridiculed and maligned these men and their prophetic contemporaries, but a few heeded their warnings.

This storm in the evangelical church was occurring at the same time as Western civilization was transitioning to a predominantly post-modern worldview. Many in the church now considered the biblical teachings and practices which sustained Christianity for two thousand years as being outmoded and insufficient to meet the challenges of the modern and postmodern era. Thus, for several decades the enlightened gurus of the Church Growth movement pointed the church in a new direction, one designed with new ways to "reach people."[12] Ministers following the Church Growth formula were told that their people must get on board with the new program or get out of the church. The new ways of doing church carried various labels (e.g., purpose-driven, seeker-friendly, ecumenical, New Reformation). But the Church Growth movement leaders were preparing and conditioning the evangelical church to accept a far more ominous level of entanglement with New Age Spirituality and departure from the Christian faith—the emerging church.

In 1984, Bob Buford was the owner of a successful cable television company in Texas. Receiving inspiration from the writings and philosophy of famed business/management expert Peter Drucker, Buford established Leadership Network, an organization to help connect leaders of "innovative churches." Leadership Network was the spark that initially caused the emerging church to come into being. Leadership Network eventually became the heart of the emerging church movement. The proponents of the emerging church received a major boost in 1994 when Buford's book *Halftime* was endorsed by Rick Warren. Warren called Buford a "rare individual" and his admiration was reciprocated by Buford who called Warren and Bill Hybels (Willow Creek Church) as "change makers" during the early days of Leadership Network. Hybels and Willow Creek have had a long-term partnership with Leadership Network which propelled many evangelicals to shift toward the emerging church theology. Warren called Leadership Network "the advance scout for the emerging church."[13]

Theological underpinnings of the emerging church

If there is one word that could be used to describe the emerging church it would be "amorphous." Several synonyms help our understanding: formless, shapeless, nebulous, vague, unstructured, and fluid. The difficulty in precisely defining the emerging church occurs because its components are continually shifting, merging, separating, and reconfiguring themselves to meet the ever-changing experiential needs of its followers. Put another way, to find a consistent and coherent definition of the emerging church is the equivalent of "nailing jello to the wall." But we can gain a clearer picture as we sort through and fit together the various pieces of the emerging church puzzle: its goals, beliefs, pronouncements, and practices. The following pieces are supplied by Roger Oakland.

- Scripture is no longer the ultimate authority as the basis for the Christian faith.
- The centrality of the Gospel of Jesus Christ is being replaced by humanistic methods promoting church growth and a social gospel.
- More and more emphasis is being placed on building the kingdom of God now and less and less on the warnings of Scripture about the imminent return of Jesus Christ and a coming judgment in the future.
- The teaching that Jesus Christ will rule and reign in a literal millennial period is considered unbiblical and heretical.
- The teaching that the church has taken the place of Israel and Israel has no prophetic significance is often embraced (often called "Replacement Theology").
- The teaching that the Book of Revelation does not refer to the future is promoted and presented as having been already fulfilled in the past.
- An experiential mystical form of Christianity begins to be promoted as a method to reach the postmodern generation.
- Ideas are promoted teaching that Christianity needs to be reinvented in order to provide meaning for this generation.
- The pastor may implement an idea called "ancient-future" or "vintage Christianity" claiming that in order to take the church forward, we need to go back in church history and find out what experiences were effective to get people to embrace Christianity (but not as far back as the apostles' and Jesus' teachings in the Bible).
- While the authority of the Word of God is undermined, images and sensual experiences are promoted as the key to experiencing and knowing God.
- These experiences include icons, candles, incense, liturgy, labyrinths, prayer stations, contemplative prayer, experiencing the sacraments, particularly the sacraments of the Eucharist.

- There seems to be a strong emphasis on ecumenism indicating a bridge is being established that leads in the direction of unity with the Roman Catholic Church.
- Some evangelical Protestant leaders are saying that the Reformation went too far. They are re-examining the claims of the "church fathers" saying that communion is more than a symbol and that Jesus actually becomes present in the wafer at communion.
- There is a growing trend towards ecumenical unity for the cause of world peace claiming the validity of other religions and that there are many ways to God (universalism).
- Members of churches who question or resist the new changes that the pastor is implementing are reprimanded and usually asked to leave.[14]

The emerging church – reinventing Christianity

The goal of emerging church leaders is nothing less than the reinvention of Christianity. We can find out what reinventing Christianity means by listening to the words of their leaders. We begin with Leith Anderson, President of the National Association of Evangelicals and signer of the Yale Covenant which calls for the Christian church to find common ground with Islam. In his 1992 book, *A Church for the 21st Century*, Anderson called for a paradigm shift in the church which is an integral element in becoming an emerging church.

> The only way to cope and be effective during this period of structural change in society is to change some of the ways we view our world and the church. It is what some call a paradigm shift—a new way of looking at something. Such a shift will allow us to view our changing world with new perspective.[15]

Doug Pagitt was one of the original leaders chosen by Bob Buford when he formed the Leadership Network. Pagitt's journey to reinvent Christianity culminated with his book, *Church Re-Imagined*.

> ...I needed to move into a Christianity that somehow fit better with the world I lived in, not an expression reconstituted from another time.

We also understand ourselves as part of a global community. We are required to live our local expressions of Christianity in harmony with those around the world. The beliefs and practices of our Western church must never override or negate the equally valid and righteous expressions of faith lived by Christians around the world. It is essential we recognize our own cultural version of Christianity and make ourselves open to the work of God's hand in the global community of faith.[16]

It is obvious that Pagitt has made several leaps in his faith journey to reinvent Christianity. First, it is clear that he rejects objective truth and fixed notions of Christianity from another time as he blithely brushes aside Christ's words that say, "Heaven and earth will pass away, but my words will never pass away." [Luke 21:33. NIV] Put another way, Pagitt requires that Christianity's fundamental beliefs should be subject to the winds of the current cultural dynamic. He also reduces Christianity to being an equal with other religions of the world. But Paul in his letter to Timothy said, "For there is one God and one mediator between God and mankind, the man Christ Jesus. [1 Timothy 2:5. NIV]

Brian McLaren is perhaps the preeminent leader of the emerging church movement and a strong proponent of reinventing Christianity. McLaren doesn't believe that "making disciples must equal making adherents to the Christian religion. It may be advisable in many (not all!) circumstances to help people become followers of Jesus and remain within their Buddhist, Hindu, or Jewish contexts."[17]

McLaren is considerably more forthright about what he is doing when many defenders of the emerging church naively claim that although the way the message is presented may have changed, the message itself remains unchanged. McLaren disagrees.

It has been fashionable among the innovative [emerging] pastors I know to say, "We're not changing the message; were only changing the medium." This claim is probably less than honest...in the new church we must realize how medium and message are intertwined. When we change the medium, the message that's received is changed, however subtly, as well. We might as well get beyond our naïveté or denial about this.[18]

McLaren's statement effectively debunks the title of Rick Warren's widely acclaimed book which falsely assures the reader that the message has not changed: *The Purpose Driven Church – Growth Without Compromising Your Message or Mission.*

A New Reformation – The path to reinventing Christianity

As noted in the previous chapter, the emerging church believes that a "new" reformation occurs every 500 years, and that one is now due. But the new reformation will not be a breaking away from the Catholic Church as had occurred five hundred years ago but a uniting of all belief systems through ecumenism. This is the hope of Rick Warren.

> I'm looking for a second reformation. The first reformation of the church 500 years ago was about beliefs. This one is going to be about behavior. The first one was about creeds. This one is going to be about deeds. It is not going to be about what does the church believe, but about what is the church doing.[19]

What will this new reformation look like? We get a glimpse from two leaders of the emerging church.

> You see, if we have a new world, we will need a new church. We won't need a new religion per se, but a new framework for our theology. Not a new Spirit, but a new spirituality. Not a new Christ, but a new Christian. Not a new denomination, but a new kind of church in every denomination. Brian McLaren.[20]

> A sea change of transitions and transformations is birthing a whole new world and a whole new set of ways of making our way in the world...It is time for a Postmodern Reformation. Reinvent yourself for the 21st century or die. Some would rather die than change. Leonard Sweet.[21]

One may characterize the emerging church as New Age Spirituality on steroids, and the thing it has become bears no resemblance to the true church of Jesus Christ and two thousand years of New Testament Christianity.

———

In Chapter 12 an examination was made of the conditions and forces that have allowed false revivals to flourish in the church through an invasion of the beliefs and practices of New Age Spirituality. In this chapter an examination has been made as to how and through whom New Age Spirituality entered large segments of evangelicalism beginning in the latter half of the twentieth century.

This book is about revival of the body of Christ in every generation. So why must Christians seeking true revival be concerned with New Age Spirituality? It is because this generation in Western civilization (predominantly the English speaking countries) is facing something that is relatively new to evangelicalism. For over two hundred fifty of the three hundred plus years of evangelical history, Britain and America were generally considered to be Christian friendly, but that is no longer the case. Over the last seventy-five years the evangelical church lost the battle for the secular culture and its voice in the public square. Now the enemy is in the camp. The West is bitterly divided and the forces of secularism, the apostate church, and New Age Spirituality are bent on destroying those remaining in the body of Christ who have not succumbed to the Great Apostasy.

The church is spiritually weak and in significant decline because of the advances of New Age Spirituality and its grip on much of evangelicalism which has led to a crescendo of wickedness and evil in every facet of culture. How is the church to effectively combat the flood of evil and prepare for and seek a revival of the church? It cannot without heeding Christ's words in Matthew's gospel, "I am sending you out like sheep among wolves. Therefore be as shrewd as snakes and as innocent as doves." [Matthew 10:1. NIV] Shrewdness comes from knowing the Word, understanding the times in which one is living, recognizing the enemy and his tactics, and being sensitive to the leading of the Holy Spirit.

God's Word and His plan for bringing revival and restoration to the nations never changes. Nevertheless, Christians must strap on the "whole armor of God" for it is sufficient to meet the unique challenges encountered by God's people in every generation, in every culture, and in every situation.

14

The American Church – R.I.P. or Revival?

The general thesis of this book stated in the first chapter is that America's only hope is the church and the only hope for the church is revival. In that chapter the tragic decline and disorder of the American church, the nation, and Western civilization in general was concisely exposed with laser-like precision by eight men writing or speaking at different times over seven decades. Based on their perceptive assessment of this pervasive spiritual and moral decline, the reader may have concluded that all hope was lost and that Christianity was caught in an irreversible death spiral as the world watched and prepared its obituary. This assessment is not a new phenomenon for the death of the church has been forecast during the entirety of its two-thousand year history. But nothing could be farther from the truth. As A. W. Tozer has written, "The church cannot die."[1] Tozer's words bring great comfort and assurance as to the future of the true church in these trying and troublesome times.

> We [the Church] are in real need of a reformation that will lead to *revival* among the churches, but the Church is not dead, neither is it dying. The Church cannot die. A local church can die. This happens when all the old saints in a given place fall asleep and no young saints arise to take their place. Sometimes under these circumstances the congregation ceases to be a church, or there is no congregation left and the doors of the chapel are nailed shut. But such a condition, however deplorable, should not discourage us. The true Church is the repository of the life of God among men, and if in one place the frail vessels fail, that life will break out somewhere else. Of this we may be sure.[2] [emphasis added]

It is no secret that the Western church is in its greatest time of spiritual weakness and is assailed within by much deception, apostasy, heresy, and worldliness. Some have said that the principal proof of her imminent doom is that she has failed "to provide leadership for the world just when it needs it the most."[3] Unquestionably the American church over the last seven decades has failed to defend the faith and speak truth and life into the various spheres of culture and the public square, but that was not a failure to provide leadership to the world. Rather, it was a failure to be salt and light throughout the earth.

> You are the salt of the earth. But if the salt loses its saltiness, how can it be made salty again? It is no longer good for anything, except to be thrown out and trampled underfoot. You are the light of the world. A town built on a hill cannot be hidden. Neither do people light a lamp and put it under a bowl. Instead they put it on its stand, and it gives light to everyone in the house. In the same way, let your light shine before others, that they may see your good deeds and glorify your Father in heaven. [Matthew 5:13-16. NIV]

To bring salt and light to the world, Christians must be "strong in the Lord and in his mighty power" by putting on the full armor of God so they can stand against the devil's schemes (see: Ephesians 6:10-20).

A revived church will be a bold and powerful witness to a spiritually lost world. This witness occurs when the power of the Holy Spirit works through the lives of Spirit-filled Christians and may lead to a general moral and spiritual awakening not only in the body of Christ but to the nations as well. This does not mean that the church should be viewed as a conquering Army commissioned to banish Satan and set the world aright as those promoting various dominion theologies would have us believe. The false doctrines of dominion theology are exposed by reading Matthew 14. Christ describes the terrible conditions in the world during the last days before the rapture in which the church will exist during its struggles against rulers, authorities, powers of this dark world, and the spiritual forces of evil in the heavenly realms.

- Increase of false prophets and religious compromise within the church (Matthew 24:4-5, 10-11, 24)
- Increase of crime and disregard of God's law (Matthew 24:12; 37-39)
- Increase of wars, famines, and earthquakes (Matthew 24:6-8)
- Decrease in love and family affection (Matthew 10:21; 24:12)

- More severe persecution of God's people (Matthew 10:22-23; 24:9-10)
- Those who stand firm will be saved (Matthew 24:13)
- Gospel will be preached to the whole world (Matthew 24:14)[4]

Revival – Prescription for an ailing church

Tozer's prescription for an ailing church is revival, and that is the great theme of this book. There is much in the Old and New Testaments that is both descriptive and prescriptive at the same time. When speaking of revival, there is no greater prescription than that which is found in 2 Chronicles 7:14, sometimes called the revival verse.

> …if my people, who are called by my name, will humble themselves and pray and seek my face and turn from their wicked ways, then I will hear from heaven, and I will forgive their sin and will heal their land. [2 Chronicles 7:14. NIV]

The back story of 2 Chronicles 7:14 is that God is speaking to Solomon who had built the First Temple in Jerusalem as a monument to God and as a permanent home for the Ark of the Covenant. God is responding to Solomon's prayer of consecration of the Temple.

Here it is very important that we understand to whom God is speaking. God required *His people*, not the culture at large, to do certain things in exchange for receiving his promises. Some may argue that 2 Chronicles 7:14 was a promise to ancient Israel and has nothing to do with the church today. However, the verse is both descriptive of God's dealings with Israel and also prescriptive for His people through successive generations. In other words, the verse was not only a promise to Israel but a biblical principle that when followed down through history has been proven to dramatically revive the church as well as change the destiny of cultures and mankind for the better. God was talking to His people called by His name at that time in Israel, but He was also talking to His people called by His name down through the centuries to the present day.

Conditions that must precede revival

During times of spiritual and moral decline within the church and nations, God will hear His people when the four conditions listed in verse 14 are met and will respond by fulfilling His three promises of spiritual revival, renewed purpose, and restored blessings.[5] In legal parlance, these conditions and promises are the equivalent of "If...then" clauses in a legal contract or agreement: "If my people will...then I will..."

- Humility

God's people must humble themselves. True humility is a brokenhearted expression of spiritual poverty and wretchedness. This humility comes from their shame and chastisement as their pride and sinful natures are exposed and for which they now express deep sorrow. True humility leads to a renewed commitment to follow God's commandments and seek direction for their lives. The supreme model of humility for every Christian is the life of Christ on the earth.

> In your relationships with one another, have the same mindset as Christ Jesus: Who, being in very nature God, did not consider equality with God something to be used to his own advantage; rather, he made himself nothing by taking the very nature of a servant, being made in human likeness. And being found in appearance as a man, he humbled himself by becoming obedient to death—even death on a cross! [Philippians 2:5-8. NIV]

- Intercessory Prayer

Recall that in an earlier chapter it was said that concerted, heart-felt intercessory prayer is the common and inextricable thread running through all spiritual revivals and awakenings throughout the history of the church. Thus, we see that intercessory prayer is a special kind of prayer and occurs when someone faithfully and continually pleads with God to take action with regard to another person, other people, or a situation. Intercessory prayer is born of a burden. Few have a better understanding of the inner workings of intercessory prayer for revival than Martyn Lloyd-Jones, the great British theologian of the mid-twentieth century, who called intercessory prayer "the very nerve and center of this whole question of revival."[6]

The precursor to all revivals is that one or more individuals begin to feel a growing disquiet in their souls. This may be accompanied by recognition of an unrelenting feeling of emptiness within, a deep hunger or yearning because the presence of God has departed from the midst of His people. This anguish of soul does not pass but grows into a burden that continually weighs on the hearts of one or more intercessors. It may even be said that intercessory prayer for revival is not only difficult but may be impossible without intercessors having a burden for that which they are praying.

In some circumstances the burden may spring suddenly from a long season of brooding discontent with the low spiritual state of the church, the moral and spiritual decline of a nation, or an intense consciousness of the vast number of lost souls streaming toward the abyss of death and an eternity in hell. When this burden is felt by Christians sensitive to the leading of the Holy Spirit, sometimes aided by anointed revival preaching, many will respond by crying out to God in prayer. Such travail often becomes an incessant and desperate plea for mercy and a casting of one's complete trust and dependence on God.

Intercessory prayer must come from the burdened heart of individual Christians, whether they pray in solitude or gather in groups, because intercessory prayer is an individual concern that must first deal with the condition of one's own heart. Lloyd-Jones has said that, "The first indication of a true and genuine concern is that we are aware of our unworthiness and uncleanness."[7] Intercessors must first lay their personal pride, rebellion, and lethargy on the altar of repentance for themselves and the spiritual conditions about which they are praying.

As intercessors recognize and deal with their own shortcomings and weaknesses, their attention inevitably turns to intercession for those people or situations that have created the burden—the church, the nation, or lost souls. However, true intercession for revival must never be about self or a matter of seeking excitement, blessings, happiness, experiencing manifestations, or having a good time.

- Seek my face

Seeking God's face is seeking his presence. This is the third requirement of 2 Chronicles 7:14. When God's presence is withdrawn, Christians feel it. The individual Christian and the body of Christ must turn back to God and seek his presence once again with passion born of an all-consuming desire to feel and see more clearly the nearness of His presence. This leads to a deeper and closer relationship with Him. As the Christian basks in His presence, there will be an increasing desire to please Him by obeying His commandments, plans, and purposes for his or her life.

To understand what it means when God says "seek my face," we must know whom we seek. Many people know about God, but knowing about someone does not mean that a person really knows that other person. To truly know someone one must have a relationship with that person. When God says "seek my face" He is telling the lost that they do not have eternal life with Him. Jesus said, "Now this is eternal life: that they know you, the only true God, and Jesus Christ, whom you have sent." [John 17:3. NIV] Conversely, to know God is to have eternal life. We have eternal life when we have a saving relationship with Jesus Christ, a personal relationship that far surpasses anything that can be imagined by the human mind.

- Turn from sinful ways

Christians must repent for their sins and turn from their own sinful ways and rebellion against God. This is a separation from evil influences while focusing on a life of purity and holiness.[8] The separateness of the church from worldliness and the wicked is a consistent theme which runs throughout the Bible, particularly in the New Testament. One of the clearest statements to the believer regarding God's command to be separate is found in Paul's second letter to the Corinthian church.

> Do not be yoked together with unbelievers. For what do righteousness and wickedness have in common? Or what fellowship can light have with darkness? What harmony is there between Christ and Belial? Or what does a believer have in common with an unbeliever? What agreement is there between the temple of God and idols? For we are the temple of the living God...Therefore come out from them and be separate says the Lord. [2 Corinthians 6:14-16a, 17a. NIV]

Life is a journey and the separateness of which Paul spoke is not achieved by a one-time inoculation of holiness. To be holy or set apart is both a singular event at salvation and a continuing process. We must contend for separateness which is the narrow path as described by Christ near the end of the Sermon on the Mount. "Enter through the narrow gate. For wide is the gate and broad is the road that leads to destruction, and many enter through it. But small is the gate and narrow the road that leads to life, and only a few find it." [Matthew 7:13-14. NIV]

The modern Laodicean church compared to the requirements of 2 Chronicles 7:14

Too often Christians seeking revival breeze through the four conditions of 2 Chronicles 7:14 without considering the depth of meaning and commitment that each condition requires before Christ will honor His promises.

To gain a better understanding of the meaning and level of commitment necessary to meet the conditions required for revival, let us look at each requirement through the lens of the modern-day equivalent of the Laodicean church. Jesus' seven letters to the seven churches dictated through the apostle John prophesied specifically about the future of His church throughout the centuries to the end of the age. Although there were many more churches than the seven located in Western Turkey, Jesus selected these churches to represent a type of church that would be predominant in each of the seven periods of church history since it was commissioned on the day of Pentecost. One type of church would dominate each period of church history, but each of the other types of churches would also be present.[9] It is the author's opinion that the Philadelphian period in church history began with the establishment of the church in America by the Pilgrims and Puritans during the early to mid-1600s and which lasted through the middle of the 1800s. During the Philadelphian period, the church would also greatly impact the British Isles and many other parts of the world through the outworking of the First and Second Great Awakenings. As the church succumbed to the humanistic forces of Enlightenment thought and secularism between 1870 and 1930, the Laodicean church became dominant in Western civilization. In both the first century and in the present period of church history, the Laodicean church is considered the worst of all.

> I know your deeds, that you are neither cold nor hot. I wish you were either one or the other! So, because you are lukewarm—neither hot nor cold—I am about to spit you out of my mouth. You say, 'I am rich; I have acquired wealth and do not need a thing.' But you do not

realize that you are wretched, pitiful, poor, blind and naked. I counsel you to buy from me gold refined in the fire, so you can become rich; and white clothes to wear, so you can cover your shameful nakedness; and salve to put on your eyes, so you can see. [Revelation 3:15-18. NIV]

The spiritual condition of the modern Laodicean church at the end of the age stands in stark contrast to the requirements of 2 Chronicles 7:14 necessary for spiritual revival, renewed purpose, and restored blessings.

- Pride vs. Humility

To understand humility, we must describe its opposite which is pride, the besetting sin of all mankind since Satan's seductive temptation caused Eve to imagine herself as being as an equal of the Creator. The modern Western church has drunk long and deeply at the well of humanism (in both its secular and spiritual forms) which pushes God from the throne and installs the god of self in His place. Arrogant pride is the outward expression of bowing to the humanistic god of self. The Western church is proud of her wealth and position in the world which has led to a Laodicean lukewarmness—a spiritual shallowness and indifference to the things of God. And it is this lukewarmness that is the breeding ground for pride which is responsible for much of what ails the modern church. While the body of Christ hungers for the rejuvenating special outpouring of the Holy Spirit, modern Laodicean church leaders offer worldly charms, diversions, and activities to distract their people from the absence of God in their midst.

> Satan's strategy is to defeat the church by subtly injecting the god of self into the church body. It is the little foxes that destroy the vine. At first he encourages a little compromise here and there. Mix in a bit of disunity. Allude to the harshness and inflexibility of the Bible. Question the relevancy of the Bible and the church in light of modern problems. Concentrate the churches' focus and efforts substantially if not exclusively on temporal problems and injustice in the world. Attempt to discredit the truth of the Bible through science and psychology. Finally, the church elevates self

above God. The new church is now consumer-oriented, and its patrons are clients to be pampered. The gospel is softened so as not to offend. Therapy replaces salvation in dealing with sin. Worship becomes entertainment. Commitment becomes optional as church attendance for many is limited to an hour or two on Sunday mornings a couple of times a month. The gospel of self-improvement is preached instead of the Word of God found in the Bible.[10]

Prideful Christians and churches stand in stark contrast to God's people who humble themselves before Him. Rather than forsake their pride, many churches and their leaders attempt to divert attention from their prideful nature by redefining humility as something different than that found in 2 Chronicles 7:14. Nowadays, "service" has become the "new humility" and has become the essential ingredient in constructing the "persuasive" paradigm for engaging culture. Larry Osborne, pastor of a California mega church, points to Daniel's humility during Israel's Babylonian captivity and calls it "service" to his wicked captors and masters.

> He [Daniel] served his captors and wicked masters so well and loyally that he kept getting promoted. And with every promotion, his influence in Babylon grew greater…Yet I'm afraid that a modern-day Daniel would be harshly criticized. Many Christians would see him as a spiritual compromiser…Instead of avoiding or attacking the godless leaders of our day, we'll need to begin to engage them in the same way Daniel did, humbly serving whomever God chooses to temporarily place into positions of authority.[11]

Osborne has erroneously redefined biblical humility as "…simply serving others by putting their needs and interest above our own. It's treating others the same way we'd treat them if they were someone 'important'."[12] However, there is a significant difference between being humble and being a servant. Those that are humble have the nature of a servant, but just being a servant does not make one humble. Osborne's definition of humility is not to be found in the Bible or the dictionary.

Noah Webster Dictionary of 1828: Humility: In *ethics*, freedom from pride and arrogance, humbleness of mind, a modest estimate of one's own worth. In *theology,* a lowliness of mind, a deep sense of one's own unworthiness in the sight of God. Self-abasement, penitence for sin, submission to the Divine will.[13]

Merriam-Webster Dictionary of 1963: Humility: Quality or state of being humble. Humble: Not proud or haughty. Spirit of deference, not arrogant or assertive, submission, ranking low in some hierarchy of scale.[14]

Osborne and many others in the modern-day lukewarm Laodicean church attempt to curry favor and acceptance of the world which has little more than contempt for the things of God. However, "service" to wicked captors and masters must never be confused with true humility and being salt and light to a spiritually dark world. These lukewarm Christians fail to see that they have become the Laodicean church and are "wretched, pitiful, poor, blind and naked."

- Prayerlessness vs. prayer

The Western church considers itself rich and not in need of anything. But prosperity leads to spiritual laziness and contentment. A. W. Tozer said that "contentment with earthly goods is the mark of a saint; contentment with our spiritual state is a mark of inward blindness."[15] One may add a corollary that contentment with one's spiritual state also leads to prayerlessness. The prophet Samuel believed that a failure to pray was a sin. In his farewell speech to the people of Israel he said, "As for me, far be it from me that I should sin against the LORD by failing to pray for you…" [1 Samuel 12:23. NIV]

Writing perhaps prophetically many years ago, R. A. Torrey painted a word picture of a prayerless church which bears a remarkable likeness to that of the modern-day Laodicean church. "We are too busy to pray, and so we are too busy to have power. We have a great deal of activity, but we accomplish little; many services but few conversions; much machinery but few results."[16]

- Seeking self vs. seeking God's face

The defining characteristic of the modern Laodicean church is *self* or *self-centeredness* which numbs the soul to things eternal. Its polar opposite is the overarching importance of *relationships* (man to God and man to man) which is the keystone of the Christianity. Those who know God continually seek Him as they rest in His presence in love and obedience. Those that don't know God must seek Him.

The modern-day Laodicean church, though materially rich and powerful by worldly standards, is blind to its separation from God and its eternal damnation. It practices a form of godliness, but in reality it is a self-absorbed religion that exists for the comfort, satisfaction, happiness, entertainment, and sensual religious experiences of its people. Describing the characteristics of the Laodicean church in his commentary, Donald Stamps captures the essence of its lukewarmness.

> The church's outward prosperity had made the people blind to their deep spiritual need…They were "blind" to their own spiritual condition and did not have the vison of how they could use their wealth and benefits to spread Christ's message. They were "naked" in that they were no longer clothed with the power and purity of God, unable to see that their prosperity was not evidence of God's blessing.[17]

"As the deer pants for streams of water, so my soul pants for you, my God." [Psalm 42:1. NIV] These words are often sung by churches, but in many of them there is little evidence that they mean it or even know that His presence has departed. God's command to "seek my face" in 2 Chronicles 7:14 seems to be particularly pertinent for the modern-day Laodicean church.

- Compromise and accommodation vs. turning from sin

Failure of a church or an individual Christian to turn from sin and worldliness often begins with compromise of the faith and accommodation of the world in their midst. They have failed to separate themselves from the evil influences of the world as they cast off their garments of righteousness and holiness.

David Wilkerson (1931-2011) was the author of the best-selling *The Cross and Switchblade* and the founding pastor of Times Square Church in New York City. In 1998, Wilkerson preached a sermon titled

"The Dangers of the Gospel of Accommodation" in which he described the seduction of the modern church in the United States.

> A gospel of accommodation is creeping into the United States. It's an American cultural invention to appease the lifestyle of luxury and pleasure. Primarily a Caucasian, suburban gospel, it's also in our major cities and is sweeping the nation, influencing ministers of every denomination, and giving birth to megachurches with thousands who come to hear a *non-confronting* message. It's an adaptable gospel that is spoon-fed through humorous skits, drama, and short, nonabrasive sermonettes on how to cope—called a seeker-friendly or sinner-friendly gospel...The gospel of Jesus Christ has always been confronting—there is no such thing as a friendly gospel but a friendly grace.[18] [emphasis added]

Wilkerson's description perfectly defines the modern-day Laodicean church and its gospel of accommodation and compromise.

———

While many in the church are dabbling with other gospels and seeking other Jesuses just as they did in the time of the apostles, there is a faithful remnant that is hungering for revival of the church in America. But God's power and presence will not return until all four of His requirements for revival are met. Those sincerely seeking revival are compelled to pray that sin residing in the camp will be recognized, exposed, and expelled through the work of the Holy Spirit. To do so the church must have bold preachers and lay men and women full of the Holy Spirit and wisdom who have humbled themselves, are praying for revival, are seeking the face of God, and who are not afraid to confront sin and preach the uncompromised message of Jesus Christ to a hurting, lost, and hell-bound world.

The only hope for America is the church, and the only home for the church is revival. Let us pray once again that there will be a special outpouring of the Holy Spirit in the churches of America to bring spiritual revival, renewed purpose, and restored blessings to His people and the nation.

Book II

History of
Evangelical Revivals
and
Awakenings

1

Purifying the Reformation – England and America

To understand the nature and origins of the great awakenings and revivals beginning in the early eighteenth century, we must first look at the history of God's people in England and the American colonies following the Reformation. Much of their history presented in this chapter is drawn from Chapters 6 through 9 in *Evangelical Winter-Restoring New Testament Christianity*.[1]

Although the reformers readily affirmed their allegiance to "the Scriptures alone" as the final authority for the church and living the Christian life, it was a far more difficult matter to shed centuries of teachings and practices of the Catholic Church. Therefore, implementation of reforms in the new Protestant churches often carried with it many of the old Roman Catholic doctrines and practices that conflicted with or undermined faithful adherence to the Scriptures.

By 1550, the church in the West had settled into three main branches of state religion: papal Catholicism, Lutheranism (Christianity subordinated to the state), and Calvinism (theocracy).[2] The Protestant branches were similar in that each was a compulsory religion, had strong ties with the state in one way or another, retained certain extra-biblical elements of Catholic orthodoxy, and attempted to use the state to impose a religious monopoly. The false teachings and practices carried over from the Catholic Church would not be effectively challenged on a broad scale within the Protestant churches until the birth of the evangelical arm of the church in the great revivals that arose in England and the American colonies in the early eighteenth century.

Protestant Reformation – 1517

The Church of Jesus Christ had traveled a tortuous path through 1500 years of persecution, victories, corruption, triumphs, and tragedies. Along the way the universal church had accumulated an inordinate amount of wealth, excess doctrinal baggage, and a large measure of worldliness. But in spite of the faults and corruptions within the church, the sustaining inerrant truth of the New Testament and its doctrines were the church's life preserver to which a faithful remnant clung, however tenuously, for a millennium and a half. The Reformation was a time of casting off of much of the church's excesses, failures, and worldliness, but it would be a painful and imperfect parting for both Catholic and Protestant churches.

When Luther nailed the ninety-five theses to the door of the Wittenberg Church on October 31, 1517, he called into question certain practices of the church and sought to change them. Initially his actions were not meant to divide the church but to rid it of the practices that many in the church felt were contrary to the tenets of the New Testament. What many define as the beginning of the Protestant Reformation in 1517 may be more correctly viewed as a step (although the last major one) in a centuries-long process that eventually led to the irrevocable separation of the Protestants from the Roman Catholic Church.[3]

Following the break from the Catholic Church, the years between 1520 and 1562 were a time of bloody martyrdom for the Protestants. But the worst was to come between 1562 and 1648 when Protestants fought for their very survival.[4] In a belated and half-hearted effort to reunite the Roman Catholic Church and the Protestants, Pope Paul III called for a council to consider reforms within the Catholic Church in the little town of Trent in the mountains of northern Italy. With two interruptions of several years each, the Council of Trent lasted from 1545 until 1563. The council developed a creed and a new catechism (religious instruction) for the church. The religious abuses that had caused much of the trouble for the church were corrected, and provisions were made to better educate the clergy. Although significant reforms had been accomplished within the Catholic Church, the essential character of the church remained unchanged which was considered a triumph for the preservation of the papacy.[5]

The efforts of the Catholics at Trent revitalized the church following the shock of the Reformation and spurred its efforts to stamp out Protestantism. Between 1562 and 1618, the Calvinistic Protestants suffered their greatest martyrdom. In 1618, the Lutherans were also dragged into the conflict with the Catholics. The Catholic-Protestant wars throughout the European continent eventually ended in 1648 with the Peace of Westphalia which had the effect of substantially fixing the boundaries of Catholicism, Lutheranism, and Calvinism in Europe to the present day.[6]

England – 1517 -1688

The progress of the Reformation and rejection of papal authority generally was a grass roots affair in every country as most rulers were aligned with the Catholic hierarchy. But the Reformation in England was unique in that it became the first nation-state to reject papal authority but *not* the church's doctrines or forms of worship.

Henry VIII was eighteen when he became king of England in 1509 and ruled for thirty-eight years until his death in 1547. Henry became embroiled in a controversy with the papacy because of his desire to divorce his long-time first wife and marry Ann Boleyn (second of six marriages) with the hope of producing a male heir to inherit the throne. Failing to receive a timely reply from the Pope that Henry be allowed to divorce his wife, the powerful monarch took matters into his own hands. He pushed the Parliament to rubber-stamp the necessary legislation which decreed that the King was the supreme head of the Church of England. His actions were not meant to be a rejection of Catholicism for he had previously rejected Luther's concept of the church. But Henry's proclamation of royal supremacy over the church effectively separated the English church from Rome and led to the dissolution of monasteries and the confiscation of church property which Henry sold to the aristocracy and gentry. Henry's view of the Church of England (also called the Anglican or Episcopal Church) was that it was still Catholic in doctrine but now rested on the supremacy of the king and his descendants.[7] Although Henry thought Luther a heretic, many Protestants believed Henry's rejection of papal authority was a step, however feeble, in reformation of the church.[8]

From Henry's death in 1547 until 1688, the quest for domination of the religious order in England was a free-for-all among Henry's heirs, competing challengers for the throne, and Parliament, all of whom chose sides in championing the cause of Catholicism or the Church of England. Other dissenting Protestant groups felt the wrath of both as they defied the Roman church and the Church of England, depending on who was in power at the moment. These religious wars came to an end when William III and Mary came from Holland in 1688 and drove James II from the throne in what became known as the Glorious Revolution. Church historian B. K. Kuiper states that, "William had saved England, Holland, and America for Protestantism and liberty against the Catholicism and despotism of Louis XIV of France and James II of England." Although the Episcopal Church of England remained the established and endowed church of the land, religious toleration was granted in 1689 to religious dissenters including Presbyterians, Congregationalists, Baptists, and Quakers. The only exceptions were Roman Catholics and those denying the Trinity.[9]

As we have seen, the English Reformation was the result of royal intrigues and politics of kings, queens, and Parliament. Therefore, reformation is perhaps too strong a word for what had occurred in England. The Church of England considered itself neither Protestant nor fully Catholic for the changes were more political and organizational than religious and doctrinal. As a result, unrest and desire for freedom from the strictures of the Church of England continued for a long time after the Reformation had run its course and become settled in other countries. Those members of the Church of England who pushed for a more thoroughly purified church were called Puritans. They objected to the rites, ceremonies, and episcopal form of government of the Church of England, but they wanted to remain in the church and work for reform from within. Separatists were those who believed the process of reforming the Church of England was hopeless and chose to separate from the church altogether. Separatists were called Congregationalists or Independents. These were the Pilgrims who eventually founded the Plymouth Colony in 1620. Nine years later the Puritans followed and established a reform-minded outpost of the Church of England in the Massachusetts Bay Colony.[10]

America – 1620-1640

It all began as a tiny ship approached the shores of a primitive continent called America. Historian Paul Johnson in his massive *A History of the American People* called the Pilgrims' arrival on an old wine ship at New Plymouth on December 11, 1620, "…the single most important formative event in early American history." The *Mayflower* contained a mixture of thirty-five English Calvinist Christians including some who had lived in exile in Holland to escape religious persecution in England. All were going to America for religious freedom. They were Separatist Puritans who had despaired of reforming the Church of England, its episcopal form of government, and the heavy influence of Catholic teaching. They were accompanied by sixty-six non-Puritans. The two groups contained forty-one families.[11]

The men and women who came to the American colonies at the beginning still considered themselves Englishmen and were in agreement with much of English law, politics, and social customs. Yet, the major motivating force that caused them to leave England was their differences concerning the nature of the Christian. The notion of consulting the Scriptures as opposed to the dictates of the English clergy was followed by this small group of Separatists that had come from the north of England. The Separatists who joined themselves together in voluntary fashion believed in the authority of the congregation in the choice of ministers and other matters, i.e., self-government.[12]

The Separatists disdained the papacy, the Church of England, and also the Puritans of southern England (whom they believed had compromised their faith). In attempting to separate themselves from the world, they defied the efforts of King James I to make all worshipers conform to the practices of the Church of England. The Pilgrim Separatists were a humble people and often viewed as radicals because of their desire to separate from the Church of England as opposed to most Puritans who wanted to stay in the church and reform it from within.[13]

While crossing the Atlantic on the tiny Mayflower and fearing anarchy because of the larger number of non-Separatists aboard, they formed themselves into a political body. The Mayflower Compact established a government by consent, similar to their church covenant, with governing authority lying in the entire adult male body with no distinctions as to class, wealth, or church membership. Thus, the compact representing one-third Separatists and two-thirds of the voyagers from London with other motives was signed by all adult male members including four servants. The Separatists landed at Plymouth, Massachusetts, in November, far north of their Virginia destination, and became known as the Pilgrims. Years of harsh existence lay before them, but they were free to "establish once more on earth the Church of Christ in its pristine purity."[14]

We must distinguish between the separatist band of outlawed Pilgrims that fled across the Atlantic on the Mayflower and the influential Puritans who would soon follow. The English Puritans had arisen about 1560 within the Anglican Church and sought reforms to bring about "a pure and stainless religion."[15] But almost seventy years had passed since their beginning, and the Church of England had repeatedly rejected their efforts to reform the church. If the Puritans could not reform the church in England, they would bring the church to America and change it to their liking. Their departure was not intended to be a separation from the Church of England but a separation from its corruption. This second group formed the great migration of English Puritans that began in 1628 upon establishment of the Massachusetts Bay Colony. Many were able men with wealth and social position. By 1640, an astounding twenty thousand made the harrowing voyage across the Atlantic and settled in the Salem area.[16]

Sherwood Eddy called those early years when colonial Puritanism was at its highest "…the finest expression of spiritual life that Britain or America or Continental Europe had at that time."[17]

2

The British Great Awakening

Conditions in England 1688-1739

As discussed in the previous chapter, the Catholic Church and the various branches of the Protestant Church were in great turmoil from the beginning of the Reformation in 1517 until 1648 when the peace agreement at Westphalia substantially ended the Catholic-Protestant wars on the continent of Europe. However, the conflict would not end in Great Britain until the Glorious Revolution of 1688 and the triumph of Protestantism under William III.

All wars invariably lead to post-war periods in which the Christian faith is neglected and leads to a general decay of national morality. This was the condition in which the British people found themselves at the end of the seventeenth century. Not only had the opposing camps of Christianity fought among themselves, but England had been involved in almost constant civil and international warfare for almost two centuries by the end of the 1600s. As a consequence there existed a significant decline of morality and general religious impulse within the nation. This decline was deepened by the ascendance of Enlightenment philosophies and deism in the late 1600s and all of the 1700s throughout Europe and Great Britain. By the time the British Great Awaking began in 1739, England, Scotland, and Wales were in a deplorable state. Mathew Backholer described the depths to which the moral breakdown of English society had sunk just prior to the awakening.

> Across Britain, before the Great Awakening, there was a rise in deism, a decline of Christian observances, a massive rise in gin consumption and other alcoholic beverages which led to poverty and abuses within families. Every sixth house in London was a grogshop (where spirits were sold, gin, rum, etc.) and you could get drunk for a pence and dead drunk for two pence...In 1714, two million gallons of spirits were distilled; by 1742, it was seven million gallons, and by 1750, it was more than eleven million...Only four or five members of Parliament were regular attendants at church.

This was the land and age of highwaymen in the countryside, burglars in the cities, profanity, bear-baiting, bull-baiting, prize-fighting, cock-fighting – the amusements of all classes were calculated to create a cruel disposition. It was the age of mobs and riots and the state of the criminal law was cruel in the extremes. There were no fewer than one hundred and sixty crimes for which a man, woman, or child could be hanged!

In 1736, Archbishop Secker, the Bishop of Oxford, said, "That an open and professed disregard to religion is become...the distinguishing character of the present age; that this evil is grown to a great height of the nation and is daily spreading through every part of it."

Parliamentary life was rotten through and through...There was a growing neglect of Sunday observance among the ruling elite. Cabinet dinners and even cabinet councils were constantly being held on that day. Sunday concerts and card parties were common. Drunkenness was almost universal, and the drunkards walked unashamed.

In the higher ranks the young "Bloods" (nobility) often banded themselves together and paraded the streets in search of victims for what they were pleased to call their wit. Many a man and many a woman died in their hands, in consequence of their ferocious treatment.[1]

Great moves of God within a nation generally start with small beginnings, and so it was with the British Great Awakening. In 1728, a student at Oxford University started a Holy Club. That student was Charles Wesley who became a preacher but is better known as one of the greatest hymn writers of all time. Because of his methodical habits in study, Charles was called a "Methodist." Leadership of the Holy Club would soon pass into the hands of John Wesley, Charles' older brother.[2]

By 1733, Charles was a junior tutor of Christ Church at Oxford University. He and the other members of Holy Club had noticed a thin young man's attendance at a weekday church service which was most unusual behavior for a lowly and poor freshman. It was through a chain of events that eventually led Charles Wesley to send word to the eighteen-year-old student at Oxford's Pembroke College to visit him. It was to be a providential meeting that October morning between the twenty-six year old Master of Arts tutor and George Whitefield who came to Wesley's rooms at Christ Church. Charles fed him coffee and breakfast as he coaxed Whitefield's life story from him. He had come from Gloucester the year before. Being from a very poor family, Whitfield earned his way at Pembroke by becoming a servitor to the gentlemen students in the upper social strata. Servitors were the lowest rank of undergraduate and at the opposite end of the scale to those noblemen who resided at the top.[3]

But the members of the Holy Club were being observed by Whitefield long before the club members had noticed him. At the start of the term Whitefield had watched and admired the members of the Holy Club as they passed through a crowd of hostile mocking hecklers when attending Holy Communion at the University Church. Being poor and lacking any form of social status, Whitefield stood afar off, fearing public rejection by associating himself with the Holy Club's members. Whitefield confessed his cowardice to Wesley at their first meeting, but Wesley comforted Whitefield with good advice, kindly encouragement in his spiritual journey, and extended an invitation to the next meeting of the Holy Club. As he walked back to Pembroke College Whitefield was "happier than he had been since coming to Oxford."[4] This meeting eventually would have an incalculable impact on both England and America.

The British Great Awakening 1739

The British Great Awakening is also known by several other titles: Evangelical Revival, the Methodist Revival, and the Wesleyan Revival. Just over five years after that fateful first meeting between Charles Wesley and George Whitefield, the Methodist Revival was birthed by a powerful move of the Holy Spirit which is the definitive event in all true revivals. The incontrovertible fact of the powerful presence of the Holy Spirit is confirmed by a reading of excerpts from the January 1, 1739 entry in John Wesley's *Journal*.

> Mr. Hall, Kinchin, Ingham, Whitefield, Hutchins, and my brother Charles, were present at our love-fest in Fetters Lane, with about sixty of our brethren. About three in the morning, as we were continuing instant in

prayer, the power of God came mightily upon us, in so much that many cried out for exceeding joy, and many fell to the ground. As soon as we recovered a little from that awe and amazement at the presence of His Majesty, we broke out with one voice, "We praise thee, O God, we acknowledge thee to be the Lord."[5]

George Whitefield also wrote of the events of that evening at Fetter's Lane in London and other meetings to follow that led to the beginning of the British Great Awakening on February 17, 1739.

It was a Pentecostal season indeed, sometimes whole nights were spent in prayer. Often we have been filled as with new wine, and often I have seen them overwhelmed with the Divine Presence, and cry out, "Will God, indeed, dwell with men on earth? How dreadful is this place! This is none other than the house of God, and the gate of heaven!"[6]

On January 14th, Whitefield was ordained a priest in the Church of England. Apart from his meeting with fellow Methodists, all was not heavenly for Whitefield before the revival broke forth on February 17th. Strong opposition to the message preached by Whitefield and the two Wesleys soon developed among some members of the clergy. Some clergymen argued against the "despised Methodists'" understanding of the "new birth" which their critics believed was a "pretending to special effusions of the Holy Ghost." The essence of the arguments was that those opposed to the Methodist message believed only in an outward Christ and denied that Christ must be "inwardly formed in our hearts also." These clergymen began to influence others to close their pulpits to Whitefield and the Wesleys. False accusations about Whitefield were spread among the clergy.[7]

Having been refused the pulpit in Bath on February 14th, he stayed with his sister and her husband in Bristol. Following two more rejections for permission to preach at Bristol churches, Whitefield knew of one place he would be allowed to preach. The Corporation of Bristol had a jail chapel but not a chaplain. The jailer had become a convert through Whitefield's preaching two years earlier and wholeheartedly welcomed his request to preach to the prisoners that Saturday morning. Following the chapel service, an aged Dissenter invited Whitefield to lunch at his home in Kingswood, just two miles or less from the closed walls surrounding Bristol and near the forest coal mines. It was here that an impoverished and shunned people lived in a world far more distant from the respectable people of Bristol than a mere two miles might suggest.[8] Whitefield's biographer John Pollock described the plight of the coal miners and their families.

> Respectable citizens were afraid of them; they caused violent affrays and had shocked even the hard-bitten sailors by digging up the corpse of a murderer whose suicide had cheated them of a public execution to hold high festival round it. They were totally illiterate. Their shacks, like the mines lay on the far boundaries of four different parishes so they were ignored by the clergy of all. Gin-devils, wife beaters, sodomites – the Bristol world had not a good word for the colliers (coal miners) of Kingswood, and considered that they illustrated perfectly the dictum of Thomas Hobbes: "No arts; no letters; no society; and which is worst of all, continual fear and danger of violent death; and the life of man, solitary, poor, nasty, brutish and short."[9]

Over dinner Whitefield talked to his host of how, "My bowels have long yearned towards the poor colliers, who are very numerous and are as sheep having no shepherd." They could only be reached in the open air for no church would welcome them. To preach in the open air was an idea that he once mentioned to John Wesley who called it a "mad notion." To do so was to defy church law and risk being prosecuted or at least shunned by the clergy and gentry for disorderly conduct.[10]

Whitefield, the two friends, and his host went out for a walk about the time the coal miners left the pits. The four men had climbed a little hill about a hundred yards from a group of miners walking toward them. Whitefield called out to them in clear voice, "Blessed are the poor in spirit, for they shall see the kingdom of heaven!" The miners immediately stopped and stared at the strange spectacle before them – a young "parson in a cassock, gown, and bands holding a book and audible at a hundred yards." Pollock vividly described the scene.[11]

> The crowd grew until perhaps two hundred were clustered around Hannam Mount. George Whitefield spoke of hell, black as a pit, about "Jesus, who was a friend of publicans and sinners and came not to call the

177

righteous, but sinners to repentance." He spoke of the cross, and the love of God, and brushed tears from his eyes. On and on he went, in dead silence except for his own voice and the slight stirring of wind through the bare trees behind him.

Suddenly he noticed pale streaks forming on grimy faces, on that of a young man on his right, and on an old bent miner on his left, and two scarred, depraved faces in front: more and more of them. Whitefield, still preaching, saw the "white gutters made by their tears down their black cheeks."[12]

Sunday morning Whitefield was reluctantly invited to preach at a local church. However, on the following Tuesday Whitefield was summoned to appear before the Chancellor of the diocese who threatened to excommunicate him if he continued to preach false doctrine. The Chancellor further prohibited Whitefield from preaching anywhere in the diocese without a license. But a little over twenty-four hours later a young coal miner called upon Whitefield and asked the young preacher to come and preach to the coal miners at a set time. He did not hesitate, and on a relatively warm February day at Kingswood, Whitefield preached for an hour to a crowd of two thousand coal miners, their families, and a number of townspeople. He would preach in open spaces to the coal miners on three additional occasions. On March 25th Whitefield preached at Hannam Mount to the largest crowd yet. Twenty three thousand reverent and tear-stained faces listen as Whitefield for nearly an hour delivered Jesus' message that "...except a man be born again, he cannot see the kingdom of God!"[13]

Whitefield called on his friend John Wesley to come to Bristol to preach and shepherd the converts with organizing skills that Whitefield did not possess. But Wesley would have to abandon his reluctance to preach in places other than Church of England pulpits. On April 1, 1739, Wesley joined Whitefield at Bristol's Bowling Green, at Rose Green in Kingswood, and at Hannam Mount. As a result Wesley was also banned from many Church of England pulpits. His great offense was not just that he preached outside the sanctioned churches but that his fiery sermons preached "justification by faith." Wesley continued to preach elsewhere. In June he preached at Blackheath to a crowd estimated to be between twelve and fourteen thousand, Upper Moorefield to six or seven thousand, and to fifteen thousand at Kennington Common.[14]

As he rode around the countryside, revivals broke out. Wesley began traveling four or five thousand miles per year throughout England, sometimes preaching at 5 AM to crowds exceeding twenty thousand. Wesley's work eventually established one hundred preaching circuits attended by three hundred ministers and thousands of local lay preachers. Both Whitefield and Wesley took Methodism's message to North America where the ideas of religious independence from the Church of England merged easily with the North Americans' growing ideas of political independence from England.[15]

The British Great Awakening began on Hannam Mount in Kingsford on February 17, 1739, not as a revival but an evangelistic meeting. The Holy Spirit's stirring in the hearts of those lost men would soon stir and revive the hearts of the British Christians and change the course of a nation. The British revivals that sparked the Great Awakening would subside as all revivals eventually do. However, the blessings that flowed from the "awakening" in the church and society in general in England, Scotland, and Wales would continue for decades.

From 1739 to 1791, it is estimated that the British Great Awakening had caused one-fourth of the population, about 1.25 million, to be converted to Christ. Over the course of time many towns, villages, and other places were so completely transformed that the character of the nation was changed. Some historians credit the awakening for preventing a revolution in Britain similar to the bloody French Revolution of 1789.[16]

This remarkable transformation of these nations by the effects of the Great Awakening was attested by many. Isaac Taylor said, "No such harvest of souls is recorded to have been gathered by any body of contemporary men since the first century."[17] C. Grant Robertson wrote,

> Wesley swept the dead air with an irresistible cleansing ozone. To thousands of men and women his preaching and gospel revealed a new heaven and a new earth; it brought religion into soulless lives and reconstituted it as a comforter, an inspiration and a judge…Aloof alike from politics and the speculations of the schools, Wesley wrestled with the evil of his day and proclaimed the infinite power of the Christian faith based on personal conviction, eternally renewed from within, to battle sin, misery and vice in all its forms. The social service that he accomplished was not the least of his triumphs.[18]

In 1922 British Prime Minster David Lloyd George said that the Methodist Movement was "probably the greatest religious movement in the past 250 years at least. Its influence, just like that of the Reformation – its indirect influence was probably greater than even its direct influence. That is the story of all great religious reformations." In 1887, E. Paxton Hood in *Vignettes of the Great Revival* wrote, "There was a deeper upheaving of religious life...A change passed over the whole of English society...In the course of fifty years...a sense of religious decorum, and some idea of religious duty, took possession of homes and minds...[19]

———

Both Whitefield and Wesley took Methodism's message of "justification by faith" to North America colonists in spiritual decline. It is to the colonists and the work of these two transplanted English preachers to which we turn our attention in the next three chapters.

3

Spiritual Conditions in America 1620-1720

What occurred among the New England Puritans between 1620 and 1660 is a remarkable story that began with a rag-tag band of beleaguered Separatist Puritans (Pilgrims) that landed on the shores of a vast wilderness in 1620. By the end of that decade many of the prosperous, well-educated members of the Church of England also began immigrating to New England. Unlike the Pilgrims, they still considered themselves to be members of the Church of England, although separated from their corrupt brethren that remained in their homeland. Known as Puritans, they formed the great migration to the Massachusetts Bay Colony which by 1640 had grown to a population of twenty-six thousand. For these Protestant Puritans who strongly followed the teachings of John Calvin, religion was the beginning, center, and end of all social and political life. The Puritans' adventure in their New England colony began as a theocracy, but the Massachusetts Puritans were not alone in their religious affections. Religion and religious liberty were the fundamental reasons for the founding of most of the original thirteen colonies, and nearly all were founded upon various social and religious experiments.[1]

However, none were so well organized or advanced in their religious practices as the New England colonies, particularly the Puritans of Massachusetts. New England was the foremost center of revivalist activity prior to and at the beginning of The Great Awakening. As early as the 1670s, Puritan leaders recognized the need for an outpouring of the Holy Spirit because churches and towns were spiritually languishing and in need of corporate renewal.[2]

The seeds of the Puritans' early spiritual decline were found in both the Catholic and Reformed churches' practice of infant baptism. If one had not been baptized and confirmed or had been excommunicated, they were excluded from the Lord's Table. In early New England, excommunication meant the loss of certain civil rights (e.g., voting and holding office) and could lead to punishment by the civil government. "Under such laws, the Lord's Table must be open to all who have been baptized, who have learned the creed and catechism, and have not committed any crime which a civil court would judge 'scandalous'." Although the bishop could require additional evidence of regeneration, this practice was rarely followed. Subject to the foregoing conditions, all young people and adults baptized as infants were considered to be members of the church in full communion.[3]

Clergymen were reluctant if not loathed to withhold participation in the Lord's Supper for to do so would inflict civil injury. Claims of wrongful denial of church membership or participation in the Lord's Supper made the clergymen liable for prosecution and, if found guilty, subject to punishment.[4] The only safe option for clergymen was to treat every one as a real convert and hope that regeneration had occurred even if no apparent change was present in the life of the professing Christian. Because of such a mindset within the clergy, their preaching was greatly restricted and diminished. As to the unconverted, they could only hope that somehow the heretofore undetected regeneration would mysteriously occur through participation in the Lord's Table.[5]

But New England Puritans would have none of this. Irrespective of their baptism of infants, they still believed that if a man was "born again," a change occurred which was observable by both the person and others. There was a difference in the unregenerate and regenerate in which the latter would exhibit good qualities through their thought, feeling, and conduct. All who did not give evidence of Christian piety would be considered unregenerate, and they would admit none to their communion unless considered regenerate. These beliefs were very different from those of their English cousins. So strong were these beliefs and practices that they were set forth in the preface to the Puritans' Cambridge Platform published in 1648.[6]

Puritan church records of that time contained a list of those considered to be on the road to heaven and therefore *full participants* in the ordinances of the church. It also contained a list of those names who by common consent were "...to be regarded and addressed as persons in the road to hell." Consequently, the New England clergy were not hesitant to assail their listeners with argument and entreaty aimed at prompting regeneration of those in the church known to be in a spiritually lost condition.[7]

But erosion of the high standards of the Puritan churches of New England began at the Puritans' Synod of 1662. It was decided that the children of parents who were *avowedly unregenerate* and excluded from the Lord's Table could be baptized if the parents were otherwise qualified. Those other qualifications and requirements were that the parents had to have been baptized in infancy, understood the doctrine of faith and publicly confessed their assent thereunto, did not lead a scandalous life, agreed to give themselves and their children to the Lord, and submitted themselves to the government of Christ in the Church.

This practice was immediately adopted over vehement protests and became the new standard for many churches.[8] This new practice was called the Halfway Covenant of 1662 and allowed New England churches to be filled with "substantial numbers of pseudo-members waiting for their conversion."[9] Sherwood Eddy described the inevitable outcome of this fateful decision.

> There was a gradual loss of the sense of sin, and the idea of God's sovereignty became a means of oppression by the ecclesiastical oligarchy...The children of the hardy pioneers became softer and more worldly. The unregenerate second generation was allowed to remain in the church as members though not in full communion. Thus originated the *halfway covenant* with a mixed membership of a more *all-inclusive church* that had lost the purity of a separated regenerate sect. The genteel churches turned from the difficult gospel of election and regeneration to "societies of Christians by mutual agreement" who avoided "scandalous sin."[10] [emphasis added]

Other compromises followed. Solomon Stoddard, the pastor of the Northampton church, published a sermon in 1707 whose message stated that sanctification (to set apart, make holy) was *not* a necessary qualification for participation in the Lord's Supper and that "the Lord's Supper is a *converting* ordinance." [emphasis added] In other words, those desiring the full advantages of church membership, even though they did not have "a Saving Work of God's spirit on their hearts," were eligible to partake of the Lord's Supper. This practice at Stoddard's Northampton Church was vigorously opposed by some, but given the general high esteem in which the prominent pastor was held and the general desire of many halfway covenanters to enjoy the benefits of church membership, the practice was adopted and spread extensively to churches in other parts of New England.[11]

The outworking of these practices adopted by the New England churches tended to destroy church discipline. Why should the unconverted be concerned with conversion when they are not held accountable by the church for their unregenerate heart and disobedient ways?[12] These beliefs and practices must inevitably lead to confusion as to the true meaning of conversion and thus undermine the redemptive work of the Holy Spirit in the hearts and minds of the lost. Writing over one hundred and seventy-five years ago, historian Joseph Tracey in his book *The Great Awakening-A History of the Revival of Religion in the Time of Edwards and Whitefield* described the eventual course that the resulting confusion would take after the loss of a biblical understanding of conversion.

> What must it teach the unconverted church member to think of himself, and of his prospects for eternity?...And what must he suppose conversion to be? Not a change by which a man begins to obey God; for he had already begun to obey him, as he supposed, and yet was unconverted. Not a change righteously required of him at every moment; for God had given him something to do before conversion, and he was doing it. He must have thought it some mysterious benefit, which God would, in his own good time, bestow on those for whom it was appointed...Being thus deceived with respect to the very nature of conversion, all his desires and prayers and labors for it would be misdirected.[13]

Stoddard and other New England pastors hoped to counteract the dangers of their beliefs on conversion and sanctification by faithfully and forcefully preaching the Word so as to compel conversion. But as Tracey so ably points out, "...in the end, the doctrines on which a church is seen to act, will prevail over those which are only uttered; and the state of feeling among the members, and ultimately the preaching itself, will conform to the theory on which the church is governed and the ordinances are administered."[14] Put another way, doctrines which are observed and practiced will inevitably prevail over those that are merely preached.

There were a number of revivals that occurred before the recognized beginning of The Great Awakening in America. One of the first to preach the essence of true revival was Samuel Torrey, pastor of the Weymouth, Massachusetts church. Torrey may be considered the first evangelical in New England for by 1674 he had begun preaching the need for revival among pastors and congregations. Torrey emphasized the "Work of Reformation." He believed that the churches would not be revived through moral efforts but only an outpouring of the Holy Spirit. This would occur only when each person experienced a "Heart-reformation, or making of a new heart." This would occur when God would pour "out [an] abundance of converting grace, and so revive and renew the work of conversion." Torrey preached his greatest sermon on revival in 1695. In "Mans Extremity, Gods Opportunity," Torrey preached that the sin of New Englanders had grown to such an extent that an ordinary reformation was not possible. God must unilaterally intercede, but that "We must follow God mourning…Such a mourning is the certain effect of the saving dispensation of the Spirit and converting grace."[15]

Covenant renewals had begun occurring in the late 1600s. Typically, in covenant renewal ceremonies, pastors reminded all church members of their promises to God and to each other. Full covenant members could consider if their relationship with God was truly right. Halfway members could seek conversion and admission into full membership in the church. These ceremonies were generally followed by preaching on salvation for a period of several weeks. Samuel Willard led a covenant renewal in 1680 at Boston's Old South Church. Early in the renewal, several children publicly embraced the responsibilities of their baptismal covenant. This sparked the whole church to go through renewal and recognition of their baptismal covenant with many becoming members in full communion.[16]

A covenant ceremony was led by Samuel Danforth Jr. in 1705 at Taunton, Massachusetts. Thomas Kidd in his book *The Great Awakening – The Roots of Evangelical Christianity in Colonial America* gave an account of the events that occurred.

> Danforth reported in February 1705 that "we are much encouraged by an unusual and amazing Impression, made by GOD'S SPIRIT on all Sorts among us, especially on the young Men and Women." The young people had become sober as a result of the meetings and some "awful Deaths and amazing Providences." He hoped that their sobriety was not temporary and asked for "Prayer that these Strivings of the SPIRIT, may have a saving Issue."…"We gave Liberty to all Men and Women Kind, from sixteen Years old and upwards to act with us," and three hundred people added their names to a list forsaking sin." Later that month Danforth reported that he had no time for his regular pastoral duties because of his constant visits from young people seeking salvation.[17] [emphasis in original]

There were many such outpourings of the Holy Spirit in the late 1600s and early 1700s, and the frequency of these revivals grew in New England during the 1710s and 1720s. Out of these early stirrings came a renewal movement called *evangelicalism* that fundamentally changed many churches and denominations and helped birth the First Great Awakening. Those churches that embraced evangelicalism emphasized a revivalist style of preaching, personal conversion, personal devotion and holiness, and individual access to God which de-emphasized the importance and authority of church government.[18]

Heretofore, our emphasis has been on Puritan revivals that preceded The Great Awakening. However, in addition to the English stream of evangelicalism there were two other streams that fed the rising river of revival fervor: Scots-Irish Presbyterianism and German and Dutch Pietism.[19][19]

> Pietism contributed an intense focus on the heart, often in conflict with the decayed state of formal, established religion. Scots-Irish Presbyterianism supplied legions of pious immigrants, who often came expecting revival to occur…The Pietists and Presbyterians of those colonies had begun striving for awakenings well before the Grand Itinerant George Whitefield came on the scene.[20]

Pietism stressed Bible study and personal religious experience and was a reaction to formalism and intellectualism. Reformed Pietism primarily focused on heart religion and Christian practice whereas Puritanism focused on doctrinal and ecclesiastical purity.[21]

———

We have examined the dire circumstances and conditions that led to the various revivals throughout the American colonies prior to the beginning of The American Great Awakening during the 1720s. In the next chapter we shall examine the outpouring of the Holy Spirit in various revivals that comprised The Great American Awakening, the course of those revivals, and the long-term consequences for the colonies and future nation and the churches therein after the revival fires had subsided.

4

The Great Awakening in America – The Early Years

The dates of the beginning of the Great Awakening in America and its conclusion are a matter of supposition. If the long view is taken and includes the revivals in the early 1720s and concludes with the waning of the Awakening's long-term effects on society, then The Great Awakening can be said to span from about 1720 to the conclusion of the American Revolution in 1783.[1] Other historians date the Awakening as beginning with the 1735 revival in Northampton, Massachusetts, under the ministry of Jonathan Edwards and ending with the conclusion of the powerful and unprecedented season of revivals that occurred during 1740-1743.[2] A third view dates the Awakening as occurring between 1735 and 1760 which is considered by many to be the period of greatest frequency and intensity of revivals in eighteenth century America.[3]

The Great Awakening is a massive subject that covers decades and involves a host of revivals, participants, and consequences which are far beyond the scope of this book. Our purpose is to obtain a general understanding of these revivals, how they came about, what occurred during those revivals, and the long-term consequences after the revival fires had subsided. To do so we shall briefly look at some of the major revivalists of The Great Awakening, the conflicts and issues that arose between revivalists and anti-revivalists and between moderate and radical evangelicals, and the long-term consequences for the Protestant churches and the colonies both before and during the fight for independence from British rule.

Renowned revival historian J. Edwin Orr believed that The Great Awakening actually began with a revival among the Pietists in New Jersey. This revival occurred eight years earlier than the general consensus that the Awakening began in Jonathan Edward's Puritan church at Northampton, Massachusetts, in the latter part of December 1734. The 1727 Pietist revival in New Jersey sprang from the preaching of a Dutch Reformed minister named Theodorus Frelinghuysen who arrived in New York City in the early 1720s. Through Frelinghuysen's influence, revival spread to Scots-Irish Presbyterians under the leadership of Gilbert Tennent and then to the Baptists in Virginia.[4]

However, Thomas Kidd points to the beginning as an extraordinary series of revivals in towns along the Connecticut and Thames Rivers from 1720 to 1722. The Connecticut revival was "the first major event of the evangelical era in New England" which "...touched congregations in Windham, Preston, Franklin, Norwich, and Windsor." One of the largest of the Connecticut revivals occurred in the Windham church during 1721 with eighty people joining the church in six months. Over the three-year course of the revivals, several hundred new members and possibly more conversions were reported. The significance of this revival has been generally forgotten because of its lack of publicity through print media which may also account for the revival not spreading beyond its regional borders.[5]

The Tennent Brothers – Gilbert, William, Jr., John, and Charles

William Tennent, Sr. and his family left Ireland in 1718 and arrived in Philadelphia where he joined the Presbyterian Synod of that city and soon established the Log College in which he trained candidates for the ministry. The Log College became the well-known forerunner of the College of New Jersey which later became Princeton University. His four sons followed their father into the ministry. Gilbert and William, Jr. along with the graduates of the Log College became a powerful revivalist force in the Scots-Irish Philadelphia Presbyterian Synod based predominantly in Northeast Pennsylvania and east New Jersey.[6]

While at New Brunswick, Gilbert's work was described as one of steady success that resulted in a considerable number of conversions. At one revival on Staten Island in 1728, the Holy Spirit was "suddenly poured down upon the Assembly." The congregation was initially passive or complacent, but after a while several fell to their knees and prayed for mercy. Others "cried out 'both under the Impressions of Terror and Love,' depending on their stage of conversion." John Tennent, the third son, showed great promise as a powerful revivalist but died at a young age in 1732. William Jr. recalled that as a result of his brother John's preaching at Freehold, several congregants began "sobbing as if their Hearts would break, but without any public Out-cry; and some have been carry'd out of the Assembly (being overcome) as if they had been dead."[7]

During the 1730s there began a debate among the Presbyterian ministers of the Philadelphia Synod with regard to itinerancy and licensing. Disagreements arose between the pro-revivalists ("New Side") and the anti-revivalists ("Old Side) Presbyterians. The conflict escalated in 1738-1739 over the appointment of John Rowland, a graduate of the Tennents' Log College, by the New Brunswick Presbytery which was controlled by the Tennent camp. The Philadelphia Synod revoked Rowland's license because of "disorderly" and "divisive" conduct. Some believed that Rowland's preaching encouraged emotional outbreaks which "led not to solid piety but to dangerous enthusiasm."[8]

In March 1740, the division between the two sides intensified with the publication of Gilbert Tennent's controversial sermon, *The Danger of an Unconverted Ministry*, in which "he called supposedly unconverted 'hireling' ministers just about every bad name he could use in religious company." Tennent believed that as a result of their un-renewed Nature they preached "easy, human-centered doctrines."[9] The conflict between the New Side and Old Side Presbyterians was a preview of the deep divisions to come between evangelicals and the leaders of the more formal, institutional wings within other Protestant denominations. Those festering divisions eventually resulted in several denominational separations at various times during the awakening and which continued to periodically occur over the next two hundred and fifty years.

Irrespective of the conflicts between the New Side and Old Side Presbyterians, the Tennents became the "single most influential family of the revivalist movement in the Middle Colonies,"[10] generally considered to be the mid-Atlantic colonies (Pennsylvania, Delaware, New Jersey, and New York) that lay between the New England and Southern colonies.

Jonathan Edwards

Although not the first, largest, or most widespread revival of the Great Awakening, the revival led by Jonathan Edwards at Northampton in 1734-1735 is perhaps the best known and most influential revival of the Awakening. Edwards had an impressive background. He was the grandson of the venerable Solomon Stoddard who led the Northampton congregation for sixty years until his death in 1729. Born in 1703, Edwards had a brilliant mind. At Yale University he earned his B.A. in 1720 and M.A. in 1723. Already an assistant in his grandfather's church, the twenty-six year old became the pastor of Northampton Church in 1729 upon the death of his grandfather.[11]

The young Edwards was no stranger to revivals and was taught to expect seasons of revival characterized by special outpourings of the Holy Spirit. Timothy Edwards, Jonathan's father, pastored the East Windsor Church and had led four or five revivals before 1734-1735. Two

189

of these revivals occurred in the 1710s and had a great influence on the young Edwards. The Northampton Church had experienced six significant "harvests" as the revivals were called under Stoddard's tenure (1679, 1683, 1687, 1690, 1712, 1718, and 1727). The 1727 revival occurred on the occasion of a major New England earthquake. This was the first revival to be highly publicized.[12]

When Edwards took the pulpit of Northampton in 1729, the spiritual state of the young people of the congregation was a cause for concern since they would not abandon their "carousing for the holy ways of the Lord."[13] Thomas Kidd described Edwards' efforts to curtail the continued waywardness of the young people at the Northampton Church.

> In 1733 Edwards began to notice the congregation's young people had adopted a new "flexibleness" in their attitudes toward his preaching. He insisted that they give up their "mirth and company-keeping" on Sunday evenings, and he began to see in them a willingness to comply. At the time Edwards also organized neighborhood meetings (the settlements encompassed by the Northampton congregation were far-flung) of fathers concerning the governance of their children. Surprisingly, the fathers reported that their children needed no extra chastening to get them to remain faithful to the Sabbath. The youths themselves were convinced by Edwards' preaching.[14]

It was the occurrence of two untimely deaths of young people that broke the complacency with regard to the young Northampton congregants' dismal spiritual state. In Pascommuck, three miles from Northampton but in Edward's parish, a young man had fallen ill with pleurisy and died in two days. Soon thereafter a young married woman fell ill and died but only after assuring those around her of her salvation. Edwards used the shock of those deaths to encourage the distraught young people to gather into small groups for "social religion."[15]

But preaching and gatherings for "social religion" were not the primary impetus by which the Holy Spirit was poured out on the Northampton congregation. For several years Edwards and his wife had prayed day and night for revival of their church. In the latter part of December 1734, there were five or six people who were wonderfully converted which created considerable excitement in the congregation. On the evening preceding the day the revival broke out several "Christians met and spent the whole night in prayer."[16] Prayer was the kindling that set ablaze the Northampton revival of 1734-1735. Edwards reported the events that caused the revival to break forth.

> ...the Spirit of God began extraordinarily to set in and wonderfully to work among us; and there were very suddenly, one after another, five or six persons, who were, to all appearance, savingly converted, and some of them wrought upon in a very remarkable manner.

> One of these converts was a young woman who had been notorious as a leader in scenes of gayety and rustic dissipation. Edwards was surprised at the account which she gave of her religious exercises, of which he had heard no report till she came to converse with him, apparently humble and penitent.[17]

Edwards was at first concerned that the conversion experience of a person with such questionable character would hinder the progress of the conversion of others. However, he was happily surprised when the news of her conversion became a great encouragement to other young people who went to talk with her and observed her remarkable transformation.[18]

Many miraculous and ecstatic manifestations of the Holy Spirit were present during the Northampton revival. These manifestations included emotional ecstasies and mysterious signs and wonders such as visions and healings. This was not unusual for these manifestations accompanied most of the major revivals that occurred during the eighteenth century. Edwards approved of emotional expressions in revivals, but he also knew the importance of balance because too much spiritual passion could lead to excess. Even though he did not understand some of the mystical experiences that occurred, Edwards did not condemn them when they were accompanied by "a great sense of the spiritual excellency of divine things." Edwards believed that such ecstatic expressions in worship could be tested: "...did they lead the worshipper to a greater appreciation of God's glory? Or did they encourage self-glorification?" If it was a greater appreciation of God's glory, then "the expressions were likely to be incidental operations of the Holy Spirit in persons receptive to them because of their particular mental constitution." He cautioned that worshippers must not "mistake the vain and imaginary for the truly spiritual."[19] Within five years these manifestations would become the source of great conflict between the revivalists and anti-revivalists and between the moderate and more radical evangelicals.

Three hundred people were saved during the first six months of the Northampton revival including children, adults, and the elderly. Eventually, 220 families totaling 620 people were entitled to take communion at Edwards' church which included almost all adults in the town. At the revival's peak in March and April of 1735, an average of thirty souls were saved each week. During 1735 Edwards wrote, "The town seemed to be full of the presence of God…There were remarkable tokens of God's presence in almost every house."[20] The revival that began at Northampton in late December 1734 spread to the north and south along the Connecticut River to thirty-two communities that were about evenly divided between Massachusetts and Connecticut.[21]

By mid-1735, the revival at Northampton was coming to an end, but the effects of the awakening would reverberate for centuries afterward through the medium of print. Edwards' account of the Northampton revival was published under the title *Faithful Narrative*. The publisher printed an abridged version in 1736 and a full edition appeared in London in 1737. Although the Northampton revival was just one in a series of earlier revivals that began in the 1720s, Edwards account of the revival "became the model revival of evangelicalism. It dramatically heightened expectations in Britain and America for new awakenings, and it provided a framework for local pastors to use to promote revival in their own congregations."[22]

As the revival in Northampton and the other communities to which it spread began to subside, the effects would continue on as churches remained strong in numbers and piety. In 1739, the instances of revival once again began to increase in other parts of the country and also at Northampton. The church at Newark was originally established by New Englanders. Religious life in Newark was in a low state and exhibited little evidence of godliness among its people during the 1730s. This began to change in August 1739 when a revival began among the young people and spread to the whole church body by March 1740. The church at Harvard, Massachusetts, followed the same pattern. In September 1739 there began a spiritual stirring among the people who exhibited a noticeable increase of seriousness about spiritual matters, church attendance, and attentiveness to the preaching of the Word and sanctity of the Sabbath. From that beginning until June 1741 over a hundred came into communion through a steady procession of conversions.[23]

The effects of the Northampton revival had a lasting beneficial effect on the religious and community life of its citizens. However, compared to the conditions at the close of the revival in 1735, Edwards later wrote that there had been "...a very lamentable decay of religious affections, and eagerness for prayer and social religion." But this began to change in the spring of 1740 as the church moved toward a renewed seriousness with regard to matters concerning religion and spiritual life, especially among the young people. This move of the Holy Spirit continued until October 1741 when George Whitefield arrived at Northampton.[24]

Theology of salvation: Debating who and how one may be "born again"

Much of the theology of conversion held by Solomon Stoddard was held by his grandson Jonathan Edwards. Stoddard believed that it was through the Holy Spirit that God drew sinners to salvation. Without the Holy Spirit conversions would not take place. He also considered powerful preaching as a tool used by God to draw sinners to God. The power in this preaching was a result of the Spirit who allowed ministers to effectively preach God's judgment. Like other revivalists, Edwards believed there would be seasons of revival in which there would be special outpourings of the Holy Spirit.[25]

Although Solomon Stoddard and his grandson held similar views on revival and the theology of conversion, Edwards would significantly differ on two points embraced by his grandfather. Recall that in the previous chapter the half-way covenant emerged from the Synod of 1662 which allowed the children of parents who were *avowedly unregenerate* and excluded from the Lord's Table to be baptized if the parents were otherwise qualified. Stoddard agreed with the halfway covenant. In 1707, Stoddard also began preaching that sanctification (to set apart, make holy) was *not* a necessary qualification for participation in the Lord's Supper and that "the Lord's Supper is a *converting* ordinance." However, during his tenure at the Northampton Church, Edwards opposed these all-inclusive policies of his grandfather and preached that only the children of parents who were full communicant members of the church should be allowed to be baptized. This doctrinal stance was very unpopular compared to the beliefs preached by his grandfather. Edwards' stance eventually led to his dismissal as pastor of the Northampton Church in 1750 and "signaled his own church's bitter repudiation of his evangelical ideal of a pure church of converted saints."[26]

The "heart religion" of evangelicalism

In Chapter 3 it was noted that first generation New England Puritans believed that a man must be "born again," and this transformation was observable by both the person and others. They also believed there was a difference between the unregenerate and regenerate in which the latter would exhibit good qualities through their thought, feeling, and conduct. But these desired qualities are not a matter of works but flowed from a *heart change* which must invariably testify to the transformative power of true salvation. This was the central issue of the Reformation: justification by faith alone. And it was this same justification by faith alone that was at the core of evangelicalism's "heart religion" which propelled the Great Awakening in America. However, with regard to the meaning of salvation and its related doctrines, there would continue to be differences among the revivalists of The Great Awakening and thereafter as will be seen in the next chapter.

Before we leave the early history of The Great Awakening, we must once again clarify and better understand the core elements that precipitated the revivals. As previously discussed, revivals are necessary when the spiritual and moral conditions of the church and society at large are in various stages of decline or decay. However, it must be remembered that revival of the culture can *never* precede revival of the church. Revival of the culture is made possible only through the influence of a revived church (individual Christians who comprise the body of Christ). Therefore, revival is ultimately a matter of renewal of the hearts of individuals—both renewal of the hearts of the spiritually languishing Christians and the dead hearts of lost sinners.

5

The Great Awakening in America – The Later Years

The beginnings of revivalism in New England occurred during the late 1600s to about 1720. The early years of The Great Awakening are generally considered to encompass the years from about 1720 to 1740. During both of these periods the characteristics and practices of religious revivals and revivalism grew in importance and frequency and gave birth to *evangelicalism* with its (1) dramatic and powerful style of preaching, (2) emphasis on personal conversion called the "new birth" often accompanied by outward physical manifestations, (3) personal devotion and holiness, and (4) justification by faith alone (individual access to God) which de-emphasized the importance and authority of church government and its leaders. In many ways the characteristics of the newly-born evangelicalism can be said to mirror many elements found in the early Reformation.

The Great Awakening matures amidst opportunities and challenges

By the end of the 1730s, revivalism in The Great Awakening was beginning to emerge from its youth, strengthen, and expand throughout the colonies. Revivalism's developing maturity introduced many new and unforeseen opportunities and challenges to churches in the colonies. The essence of this flowering revivalism was best exemplified by the Northampton revival guided by Jonathan Edwards and the other New England revivals that arose from it. In this chapter we shall examine various facets of The Great Awakening that ultimately defined revivalism and established evangelicalism as a dominant force in America to the present day.

As discussed in Chapter 3, the call for revival in the colonies began in 1674 when Samuel Torrey, pastor of the church at Weymouth, Massachusetts, began preaching the need for revival among pastors and congregations because of the perceived general spiritual decline and loss of religious vigor among the Puritans. Torrey emphasized the "Work of Reformation." He believed that churches would not be revived through moral efforts alone but only through an outpouring of the Holy Spirit.[1]

Torrey's work of reformation easily resonated in the minds of the Puritans of New England as a result of their very presence in their new colonial homeland. This occurred because of their efforts to revive the church and continue the work of purifying the Reformation in America. They believed that purification could not be accomplished among the corrupted brethren in England. So revival and revivalism was a natural fit with a mindset that already existed among most colonists who sought religious freedom from the strictures of authoritarian churches and kings.

In spite of their quest for religious freedom, the colonists still considered themselves English men and women and retained much of the English social order including many of the same ecclesiastical doctrines and practices brought from their former homeland. What the religious colonists sought was spiritual reformation, not extra-biblical innovation. But as every generation of the church must realize, the outworking of reformation and revival, to varying degrees, produce both the good and the bad. In every revival, the church body and individual Christians must distinguish between the Holy Spirit's wheat and the tares of sinful human nature and demonic influence.

Historian Thomas Kidd wrote that, "The Puritan colonies had once been godly showcases for the Reformation but had forgotten their first love."[2] And it was Torrey and other early Puritan church leaders who saw revival as the necessary path for a return to that first love. Prior to 1720, revivals generally occurred in the more formal confines of established local churches. Revivals spread as pastors heeded the example of other churches experiencing revival and began preaching and encouraging revival in their own churches. This was generally the accepted pattern for most revivals prior to 1740. But that pattern was beginning to change even before the arrival of the "Great Itinerant" George Whitefield.

Over the course of his life Whitefield made seven trips across the dangerous and often storm-tossed North Atlantic until his death in 1770. The first voyage in 1738 resulted in a stay in Georgia of less than four months and which was consumed mostly with efforts to establish an orphanage in Savannah. Whitefield was a larger than life figure whose cultural and religious impact on England and America and the course of their histories is incalculable. Even before he landed in America for the second time, Whitefield's reputation as an "evangelical superstar" preceded him. Whitefield's powerful preaching style, outreach to various denominations, focus on the new birth, and effective use of the media would energize the growing revivalist movement throughout the colonies.[3] Whitefield did not invent revivalism or evangelicalism or cause The Great Awakening in America. However, his ministry would eventually personify their essential elements as he energized and hastened their ascendance on the American scene.

"New Light" Revivalists and "Old Light" Anti-revivalists in America

There were elements of the established American churches that opposed revivalism from its very beginning. Opposition centered on several issues including the operation of the Holy Spirit, especially concerning physical manifestations that occurred during revivals. Jonathan Edwards was the foremost apologist for the "New Lights" and favored increased numbers of converts through revivals. "Old Lights" such as Rev. Charles Chauncy of Boston's First Church thought revivalists to be misguided sensationalists who promoted powerful, passionate preaching and demonstrative conversion experiences to the detriment of true religious growth.[4]

The essence of the divide between evangelicals and traditional clergy was a disagreement as to the path to conversion or how one receives divine grace. For evangelicals conversion was an immediate personal experience that occurred through repentance and acceptance of God's grace which brought one into personal relationship with Him. For the traditional clergy, the path to conversion was gradual, progressive, and subtle which occurred within the "stabilizing" influence of the local church through "rational guidance of learned ministers." Revival preaching was acceptable to the traditionalists and established clergy, but revivalism as practiced by Whitefield and the New Lights was in their view "the great abandoning" of the true path to divine grace.[5]

Although the conflict between the Old and New Lights revolved around the theology of conversion, three subsidiary issues would enlarge the battlefield: the growth of unrestrained itinerancy, the subject of unconverted ministry, and disagreement over bodily manifestations resulting from revival fervor. Within the New Light wing, disagreement on these issues eventually led to Separatism between the moderate and more radical elements of revivalism.[6]

Calvinist and Arminian differences among the Revivalists

Even though Solomon Stoddard and his grandson Jonathan Edwards were staunch Calvinists, there were many aspects in their Reformed theology that were compatible with the beliefs of many

197

emerging evangelicals who held or at least were in sympathy with an Arminian understanding of salvation. However, there were certain fundamental doctrines developed by the leaders of the Reformed churches after Calvin's death that continued to provoke conflict with those who held Arminian beliefs.

Briefly, the two camps' points of agreement were: humankind is in need of salvation, God alone can provide that salvation, and Christ is God's provision for man's need. The principle differences between Reformed and Arminian believers dealt with the role of God and humans in salvation. Those of the Arminian view disagreed with the Reformed churches' beliefs of *unconditional election* by God of those he will save, *limited atonement* in which Christ paid the price only for the sins of the elect, *irresistible grace* which meant that those whom God has determined to save will inevitably come to saving faith, and *perseverance of the saints*, that is, all who have been chosen by God (the "elect") will continue in the faith (once saved, always saved).[7] To summarize, Arminians agree with Calvinists on the need for repentance and the new birth but could not accept Calvinist predestination and its other accoutrements.

It was those differences that would ultimately cause a break in the relationship of the Wesley brothers and George Whitefield. Although the Wesleys' Methodist theology generally mirrored that of orthodox Protestantism as practiced by the Anglican Church, John Wesley rejected and openly opposed the Calvinist doctrine of predestination and election which he believed would hinder the call to repentance and conversion. In its place Wesley embraced the Arminian doctrine of freewill or freedom of choice as the means whereby people accepted Christ.[8]

The break came in 1740 when Whitefield was in America and Wesley was preaching in England. While at Bristol, Wesley was offended by certain teachings of pointedly Calvinist doctrines which Wesley assumed represented Whitefield's view that "God arbitrarily predestined (or 'elected') some to salvation and some to damnation (or "reprobation") by an irreversible decree." Wesley struck back against this teaching by preaching on "Free Grace." All through 1740 Wesley and Whitefield exchanged letters across the Atlantic regarding their differences. The conflict remained unresolved, and Wesley eventually published his sermon on "Free Grace." Whitefield received a copy and sent his reply which he saw as an attack by Wesley on the New Testament doctrines of God's sovereign grace, foreknowledge, and electing love. In late 1740 Whitefield's reply was sent to London to be published on Christmas Eve.[9]

By March 1741, Whitefield was back in London and went to hear Wesley preach, having heard of many unkind remarks made by Whitefield since his return from Georgia. Wesley wrote of the disagreement in his *Journal*, "He (Whitefield) told me, he and I preach two different gospels; and therefore, he not only would not join with, or give me the right hand of fellowship, but was resolved to publicly preach against me and my brother, wheresoever he preached at all." There were efforts to bring the two together, a meeting was held, and other exchanges made. Over time there was a softening of the hostilities between the men, but it would be a decade before Whitefield and the Wesleys were restored to their former unity. In January 1750, Wesley wrote, "I read prayers and Mr. Whitefield preached. How wise is God in giving different talents to different preachers." Upon the death of Whitefield in 1770 and at the request of his executors, Wesley preached a memorial sermon in London.[10]

The public break damaged the ministries of both men and diminished the cause of Christ. Wesley was a brilliant organizer and better theologian, but Whitefield was a much better preacher. Whitefield's biographer John Pollock wrote of the consequence of the separation of once close friends and laborers in the Christ. "Two streams would therefore flow from the evangelical revival, often crossing and coalescing, instead of one mighty river watering the land."[11]

Moderate and Radical Revivalists

Division was also occurring between the revivalists' moderate and more radical wings. As early as 1741, some members of the clergy in Connecticut called on civil government to prevent disorders and punish offenders without trial. This was an attempt by anti-revivalists and some moderate evangelicals to stop ministers and itinerant preachers from preaching and administering the seals of the covenant "without the consent of, or in opposition to, the settled minister of the parish." To do so would cause disorder and require punishment. In May 1742, the legislature passed "An act for regulating abuses and correcting disorders in ecclesiastical affairs." Soon arrests were made and fines imposed on those deemed to have violated the ordinance.[12]

Almost immediately a serious riff developed between the radical itinerants and most of the established powers in Connecticut and Massachusetts including moderate evangelicals. Radical itinerant James Davenport conducted a revival at Groton, Connecticut, in the winter of 1741-1742 and then went to Long Island where he led significant revivals at two churches. With concerns about growing complaints of excess in the revivalist movement, the moderates latched onto accounts of Davenport's "wild enthusiasm" as being "beyond legitimate evangelical limits." They saw Davenport as a sacrificial lamb that could separate the moderates from the perceived excesses of radical itinerants. In May, Davenport returned to Connecticut where he was promptly arrested and brought to court. He was summarily banished from Connecticut for violating the newly passed provincial law that prohibited itinerants from preaching in churches without the resident pastor's permission and outlawed all non-Connecticut itinerants.[13]

As these excesses and extremes played out, a point was reached in March 1743 when even Davenport's most devoted supporters began to question his tactics and extreme actions. As a result Davenport fell into a "repentant despondency."[14] In 1744, the chastened ex-radical made a public apology for his excesses.[15] Davenport continued in the ministry but abandoned his extreme radicalism. He and his less radical colleagues would play an important role in the revivals of the 1750s and 1760s preceding the Revolutionary War.

Revivals continued to increase in number in spite of the growing conflict between the Anti-revivalists, moderate evangelicals, and radicals regarding the legitimacy and manifestations of revivals. Between 1740 and 1742 there were enormous numbers of revivals and conversions throughout New England. By the time the great numbers and intensity of revivals began to decline following 1743, evangelicalism had become a powerful movement in its own right.[16] No longer would the evangelical spirit rise and fall with revivals. The revivalist style of preaching, emphasis on immediate and recognizable personal conversion, personal devotion and holiness, and individual access to God that characterized evangelicalism during revivals would now sustain the church in those times between periodic revivals. Originally birthed by revivalism, evangelicalism had become the incubator from which revivalism would be encouraged over the years to come.

Evangelicalism's divergent paths

Largely due to the aggravating effects of Davenport's abrasive tactics in confronting non-radical revivalists, the evangelical movement in New England and the Middle colonies had publicly split by March 1743. But the radicals would continue to be a serious presence through the remainder of The Great Awakening as many New Englanders eventually believed that fulfillment of radical awakenings could only be achieved by starting separate illegal congregations.[17]

New England was the epicenter of church separations during the middle and late eighteenth century. Hundreds of Separate or Separate Baptist congregations were formed, and the rallying cry for radical evangelicals was liberty of conscience. In spite of numerous laws to curtail the activities of radical itinerants and the congregations formed by them, the energy generated by the continuing radical evangelical revivals was difficult to contain.[18]

The split between the Separates and established churches aggravated the split between the moderate and radical evangelicals. However, not all radicals left their churches and became Separates, and not all Separates became Baptists. Issues that united the Separates were commitments to immediate and discernable conversions and the right of uneducated laypeople to become involved in ministry (exhortation, itineration, and ordination). Baptists rejected both infant baptism and the halfway covenant. Both Baptists and Separates would challenge the legalized monopoly of religious life held by the established Congregational churches of New England.[19]

In time only a few of the hundreds of Separatist churches that began in New England survived, and many that did survive would become Baptist. Although the New England Baptist churches had great influence on the northern colonies, their most enduring achievement was exportation of the Separate Baptist movement to the middle and southern colonies. Eventually, the Baptists along with the Methodists and Presbyterians would utterly dominate the South.[20]

Following the public break between the moderate and radical evangelicals in 1743, revivals continued to occur throughout the colonies in the 1750s, 1760s, and during the revolutionary war years. During this era the radical evangelicals were the most vigorous and productive arm of revivalism. Its maturation in the 1760s was reflected by their efforts to articulate a radical definition of revivalism in the public square. The key tenets of this narrative were freedom of private judgement and power to establish independent churches free from the dictates of competing ecclesiastical and legislative authorities. The revivals of 1762-1765 were particularly important in continuing the radical tendencies of the evangelical movement, furthering evangelical populism, and aligning the movement with the Patriot cause in separating from Great Britain.[21]

The conflict between moderate and radical evangelicals that emerged in the 1740s continued into the 1780s. The greatest area of disagreement was with regard to manifestations of the Spirit during revivals. Thus, evangelicalism remained deeply divided between moderates and radicals at the conclusion of the Great Awakening and foreshadowed the eventual abyss separating the liberal churches and conservative evangelicals of the nineteenth and twentieth centuries. Evangelicalism grew in spite of the conflicts between moderates and radicals which, according to Thomas Kidd, "hinted toward the contemporary global evangelical expansion that remains split between Pentecostal and non-charismatic believers."[22]

Perhaps one of the best and most succinct descriptions of the broad panoply of The Great Awakening was written by American historian Paul Johnson.

> It crossed all religious and sectarian boundaries, made light of them indeed, and turned what had been a series of European-style churches into American ones. It began the process which created an ecumenical and American type of religious devotion which affected all groups, and gave a distinctive American flavor to a wide range of denominations. This might be summed up under the following five heads: evangelical vigor, a tendency to downgrade the clergy, little stress on liturgical correctness, even less on parish boundaries, and above all an emphasis on individual experience. Its key was Revelations 21:5: "Behold, I make all things new"—which was also the text for the American experience as a whole.[23]

The influence of The Great Awakening on America's war for independence

How do we determine the extent to which The Great Awakening influenced the character and worldview of the colonists leading up to America's war for independence? Here we turn to the words of two distinguished American historians. Sherwood Eddy in his 1941 *The Kingdom of God and the American Dream*, wrote, "No country on earth was ever founded on deeper religious foundations. This was America's priceless heritage."[24] Eddy captured the importance of the eighteenth century American religious awakening on the Revolution and later writing of the Constitution.

Throughout the Revolution and the framing of the Constitution, the religious and the secular life of America could not be separated. The very ideals of political freedom had grown out of the principle of religious liberty of the Reformation and out of the experience of the Pilgrims, Puritans, and protesting colonists. It was in the churches of Boston and Virginia that revolutionary meetings were held. The clergy of the free, dissenting, and popular churches were preaching liberty as a religious principle. The pulpit inspired the Revolution and summoned the faithful to patriotic service and to the realization of the American Dream.[25]

In *A History of the American People*, Paul Johnson again distills the essence of The Great Awakening and its importance in the founding of America.

...There was a spiritual event in the first half of the 18th century in America, and it proved to be of vast significance, both in religion and politics...The Great Awakening was the proto-revolutionary event, the formative moment in American history, preceding the political drive for independence and making it possible...The Revolution could not have taken place without this religious background. The essential difference between the American Revolution and the French Revolution is that the American Revolution, in its origins, was a religious event, whereas the French Revolution was an anti-religious event."[26]

Following the American Revolution (1775-1783) and efforts to form a new nation, there was a second ebb-tide of religious fervor and an increase in secularism and irreligion, especially in the decade of 1790s. America's spiritual and moral decline threatened the survival of the new republic. The conditions that preceded this decline will be examined in the next chapter as we move toward the Second Great Awakening at the beginning of the nineteenth century.

6

Spiritual Conditions in America 1760-1790

Religious Revivals amid political turmoil and war

To properly understand revivals that occurred during the later years of The Great Awakening, it is important to have knowledge of the contemporary events that impacted those revivals and religious life in general from the 1760s through the end of the Revolutionary War and establishment of the nation.

During the 1750s the British had awakened to the importance to the British Empire of the few American colonies that clung to the eastern edge of a vast wilderness thousands of miles across the Atlantic. This new found interest was kindled by the French and Indian War being fought on the American continent (1754-1763). Britain's interest and involvement in the affairs of the American colonists significantly increased following the war and ended decades of salutary neglect the colonists had come to expect and enjoy. The war left the British with massive debt, high taxes at home, and a permanent army of paid soldiers in the colonies that was costly to maintain. Accordingly, the British Parliament passed a series of revenue-generating measures which unilaterally imposed on the colonies many very burdensome taxes, duties, and tariffs, the most troublesome of which was the Stamp Act of 1765.[1]

Colonial unrest aggravated by British intransigence continued over the course of the next ten years and culminated with hostilities at Lexington and Concord in April 1775 and marked the beginning of the colonists' eight-year struggle for independence. The war officially ended in January 1783 with the signing of the Articles of Peace.[2]

Even in war life goes on and so did the colonial revivals. Of particular note was a series of revivals from 1778 to 1782 which are called the "New Light Stir." Although several evangelical denominations were successful during the Stir, the Baptists led the way with thirty six new churches planted in New England between 1778 and 1782. Isaac Backus had been involved in revivalism since the 1740s and knew well its history. He estimated that two thousand New Englanders received believer's baptism in 1780 alone. Regarding the New Light Stir, Backus believed that the outpouring of the Holy Spirit "spread the most extensively and the most powerfully through New England than any revival had done for near forty years," and it "was undoubtedly a great means of saving this land from foreign invasion, and from ruin by internal corruption."[3]

In spite of the widespread success of the revivals, tensions between the rival moderate and radical camps of evangelicalism continued as it had for forty years. One of the most pronounced developments of revivalism's New Light Stir was the growing abandonment of Calvinism among the radicals, and this abandonment would become even more common in the early years of the nineteenth century. Although Congregationalism began to decline during the late eighteenth century, it would remain a significant force in northern religious life and reform movements through the end of the Civil War. Moderate Baptist and radical evangelical growth continued during the war, but the bulk of the Methodists' amazing growth would occur after the war.[4]

Revolutionary Revival

Irrespective of the abundance of primary historical evidence to the contrary, many if not most all early historians gave little to no credit to religion's role in fostering the American Revolution. Most present-day historians of the American Revolution generally believe that religion was substantially displaced by politics as lawyers replaced the clergy as leaders which effectively "...transformed and secularized the intellectual character of the culture."[5] They often point to declines in church attendance, fewer publications devoted to religious matters, and other such statistics regarding the health of the church. However, a thoughtful response easily brings one to the natural conclusion that these declines resulted from dislocations caused by the war. Based on the *appearance* of a decline of religion *in the public arena* during the revolution, historians have leaped to the erroneous conclusion that the American people were significantly less religious. This is a blatant misreading of the mood and character of Americans during the Revolutionary period. Protestantism in whatever form it took remained the principle means by which Americans perceived and explained the world and ordered their lives.[6]

A brief look at the growth in the number of revivals and growth in the number of churches during 1760-1790 refute the historians' assertions that concern for religious matters and religious fervor had declined during the Revolutionary period. The number of church congregations doubled between 1760 and 1790. It is true that the older churches that dominated colonial society (Anglican, Congregational, and Presbyterian) declined or failed to grow relative to other groups. The Church of England which dominated the South and the powerful Puritan churches of New England accounted for more than forty percent of all American congregations in 1760 but declined to less than twenty-five percent by 1790. However, new denominations spawned by the Great Awakening were alive, well, and growing. The Baptists grew from 94 in 1760 to 858 by 1790. During the same time period the Methodists grew from no adherents to over seven hundred congregations which nationally rivaled the numbers of the older Congregationalist and Presbyterian churches. American historian Gordon Wood wrote that, "The revolution released more religious energy and fragmented Christendom to a greater degree than had been seen since the upheavals of seventeenth century England or perhaps since the Reformation." Stephen A. Marini (quoted by Wood) wrote that the extent of the profound changes in religious life and substantial religious growth in America between 1760 and 1790 can be described as nothing less than a "…Revolutionary Revival."[7]

Spiritual and moral decline in America

History has proven that significant spiritual and moral decline occur during the years of war and for protracted periods thereafter. Even as revivals flourished during the Revolutionary War years, there was a simultaneous beginning of spiritual and moral decline among the general population. This decline continued following the end of the war in 1783 and especially during the last decade of the eighteenth century. Following eight years of war, all denominations and the new nation as a whole began to feel the effects of spiritual and moral decay. Revival historian J. Edwin Orr described the conditions in America.

> The Methodists were losing more members than they were gaining. The Baptists said that they had their most wintry season. The Presbyterians in general assembly deplored the nation's ungodliness. In a typical Congregational church, the Rev. Samuel Shepherd of Lennos (Lenox), Massachusetts, in sixteen years had not taken one young person in fellowship. The Lutherans were so languishing that they discussed uniting with Episcopalians who were even worse off. The Protestant Episcopal Bishop of New York…quit functioning; he had confirmed no one for so long that he decided he was

207

out of work, so he took up other employment. The Chief Justice of the United States, John Marshall, wrote to the Bishop of Virginia, James Madison, that the Church "was too far gone ever to be redeemed."…Tom Paine echoed, "Christianity will be forgotten in thirty years."[8]

The churches had become almost totally irrelevant in curbing the nation's downward spiral into immorality. During the last decade of the century, out of a population of five million Americans, six percent were confirmed drunkards. Crime had grown to such an extent that bank robberies were a daily occurrence and women did not go out at night for fear of assault.[9]

Christianity at the universities was just as destitute. Students at Harvard were polled, and not one Christian was found. Two admitted to being Christians at Princeton while only five members of the student body were *not* members of the filthy speech movement of the times. Few if any campuses escaped the denigration of Christianity and general mayhem. Anti-Christian plays were presented at Dartmouth, a Bible taken from a local church was burned in a public bonfire, students burned Nassau Hall at Princeton, and students forced the resignation of Harvard's president. Christians on college campuses in the 1790s were so few "…that they met in secret, like a communist cell, and kept their minutes in code so that no one would know."[10]

But America was not alone in her misery. Although the founding Americans had relied on an order that rested upon a respect for prescriptive rights and customs, the egalitarian notions of French philosophers fueled the bonfires of the French Revolution (1789-1799). The aberrant humanistic philosophies emerging from the late Renaissance and Enlightenment during the seventeenth and eighteenth centuries nurtured the egalitarian notions of the French philosophers. These Enlightenment philosophies supplied the framework for the French revolutionists as they fostered societal changes based on the ethereal, imaginary, or invented "rights of man" as well as imposition of an ever increasing number of laws to address the failings of human nature. In spite of the French Revolution's high-minded chorus of "Liberty! Equality! Fraternity!", the French reality was "monarchy, anarchy, dictatorship" all occurring in a little more than a decade.

However, across the English Channel the course of Western civilization was taking a different turn throughout the British Isles. As noted in Chapter 2, the British Great Awakening over the course of five decades beginning in 1739 had so completely transformed the character of the nation by 1791 that some historians credit the British Awakening for preventing a revolution in Britain similar to the bloody French Revolution of 1789.[11]

In the last two decades of the eighteenth century, immense social upheavals and change throughout the Western world began to occur during the initial stages of the Industrial Revolution. However, the seeds destined to flower as the Second Worldwide Awakening were being sown by Christians in Great Britain. Recall that it was the providential publication in England during 1737 of Jonathan Edwards' account of the revivals in American that greatly influenced two key figures of the approaching First British Great Awakening—John Wesley in England and Howell Harris in Wales.[12] Forty-five years later the powerful influence of Edwards' writings would again impact the people of the British Isles.

Influence of the Second British Great Awakening

Jonathan Edwards believed that concerted prayers of Christians would release the power of the Holy Spirit and result in converts which would be followed by worldwide revival. In 1745 Edwards had heard of a prayer movement for revival that had begun among several Scottish evangelical ministers. This information may have come from John Erskine, a Scottish Presbyterian minister who began corresponding with Edwards in the mid-1740s. Edwards was inspired by the information he had received and felt led to write his own thoughts on the matter and in 1746 published *An Humble Attempt to Promote Explicit Agreement and Visible Union of God's People in Extraordinary Prayer for the Revival of Religion and the Advancement of Christ's Kingdom on Earth, pursuant to Scripture Promises and Prophecies concerning the last Time.*[13]

John Sutcliffe (1752-1814) attended Bristol Baptist College from 1772 to May 1774. He became pastor of the Baptist church in Olney, Buckinghamshire, England, in 1775 where he began to earnestly study the writings of Jonathan Edwards. In the spring of 1784 John Ryland, Jr., a pastor friend of Sutcliffe, had received a copy of Edwards' *An Humble Attempt* from John Erskine, the Scottish Presbyterian minister who had corresponded with Edwards forty years earlier. Ryland shared Edwards' book with Sutcliffe. The book had a profound impact on Sutcliffe, Ryland, and Andrew Fuller, another pastor friend. They soon enlisted sixteen other Baptist pastors to "establish monthly prayer meetings for the outpouring of God's Holy Spirit and the consequent revival of the churches of Great Britain." By 1789 the prayer meetings among the Calvinist Baptist churches had grown considerably. Sutcliffe decided to reprint Edwards' An *Humble Attempt.* By 1790 the prayer movement for revival had spread beyond the Calvinistic Baptist denomination and led to "copious showers of blessing" which later historians would mark as the beginning of the Second Evangelical Awakening (1790-1830).[14]

But the story does not end there. The providential series of events beginning with Edwards'1746 treatise on praying for revival, the calls for concerted prayer beginning in 1784 by Scottish pastors, and the unfolding of the Second Great Awakening in Britain in 1790 also influenced an American pastor and allowed the new British Awakening to traverse the Atlantic to America in the late 1790s.

Isaac Backus – God's agent for revival

Isaac Backus (1724-1806) was born into a "pure" Congregational church by which was meant that it was not part of an association of Congregational churches adhering to the Saybrook Platform. This association linked individual Connecticut congregations and provided for church discipline. Backus' mother raised him to understand the necessity of conviction and conversion which was later reinforced by the preaching of Eleazar Wheelock and James Davenport (mentioned in Chapter 5). While "mowing alone in the field," the young seventeen-year-old Backus experienced both conviction and conversion. He joined the Norwich, Connecticut, Congregational Church but later left in the summer of 1745 with about thirty men and a large number of women to become part of the "New Light" revivalist movement.[15] It appears that the principal dividing issues causing their departure were the relaxed standards for full membership as allowed by the Saybrook Platform and a de-emphasis on personal conversion testimonies for full membership. In other words, the Norwich church received people "to Communion who could not testify to a work of gracious conversion."[16]

On September 27, 1746, Backus sensed a call to preach and did so the next day by "exercising the right of exhortation." In 1748, after fourteen months of itinerant preaching in a style similar to George Whitefield, Backus was called to pastor a congregation in Middleborough, Massachusetts.[17] Backus was twenty-four when the original sixteen members signed the new church's covenant in February. By year's end, membership had grown to sixty-one. However, Backus continued to struggle with the issue of baptism, and by July 1751 he began preaching that he could find no scriptural basis for infant baptism.

In August, he and six other members of his congregation were baptized by immersion to demonstrate their commitment to the requirement of believer's baptism for full communion. Backus' action threw the church into turmoil because the majority of members were opposed to believer's baptism. Backus agreed to continue as pastor of the church under a mixed-communion plan that accepted either infant or believer's baptism.[18]

The church struggled along for another five years, but Backus finally became convinced that infant baptism was not compatible with the requirement that a congregant must be saved by grace. In 1756, Backus and several other congregation members re-constituted the Middleborough church under a Baptist covenant of freedom of conscience and that the Lord's Supper was only to be taken by those after profession of their faith and having been baptized by immersion. Backus eventually became the principle agent for the Massachusetts Baptists' quest for religious liberty in their struggle against power of the Congregationalists' legalized religious monopoly. For decades after fully embracing the Baptist covenant, Backus was a tireless writer, spokesman, and defender of religious liberty through separation of church and state.[19] Here the reader must understand that the separation of church and state sought by Backus was that which would eventually be expressed in the First Amendment to the U.S. Constitution and not the aberrant modern interpretation of separation of church and state as expressed by humanistic and liberal political orthodoxy.

Isaac Backus was an enormously important figure in The Great American Awakening. His career spanned six decades beginning in the great revivals of the early 1740s. He joined the Congregationalists, became a Separatist, and then founded a Baptist church, all during the moderate and radical conflicts of the 1740s and 1750s. He was a strong advocate of revivalism and participated in numerous revivals from the 1750s through the end of the American Revolution and then into the Second Great Awakening. He was an itinerant evangelist; pastor of one church for fifty-eight years; revival historian; political activist; denominational speaker, debater, and essayist; Revolutionary War Patriot; and perhaps the most important Baptist figure of the entire Awakening.[20] However, Backus' most important work for the kingdom of God may have occurred after these events and during the last twelve years of his life.

In 1794, Backus and other New England ministers met in Connecticut and reread Edwards' *Humble Attempt* which inspired Backus to write to Christian churches throughout the spiritually

211

struggling new nation. Backus called them to join the Union of Prayer and pray for revival in America.[21] These prayers eventually ignited the Second Great Awakening in America and changed the course of history.

7

The Second Great Awakening in America – The Early Years – 1794-1812

Revival historian J. Edwin Orr marks the beginning of the Second Great Awakening in America with Isaac Backus' call to the churches to pray for revival in 1794.[1] Soon thereafter, a period of almost continuous revival existed in the United States until 1842 except for a decade beginning with the War of 1812. The early years of revival (1794-1812) occurred in the colleges and churches in the East followed by revival in the wilderness churches and camp meetings of the West. The early years produced many young leaders, but there was no dominant personality that led the revivals. Orr dated the second half of the Second Great Awakening as beginning in 1822 and lasting until 1842. Unlike the early years, this era produced one dominant figure in evangelical revivals during the middle third of the nineteenth century— Charles Grandison Finney.[2] This second period of the Second Great Awakening will be discussed in the next chapter.

Changes in the American Protestant landscape

Before we proceed further in our discussion, it is important to step back and once again summarize the forces that preceded and later shaped the Second Great Awakening in the nineteenth century. Thomas Kidd identified several key factors that defined the flourishing American evangelicalism during the last half of The Great Awakening. These changes in the American Protestant landscape greatly influenced the shape and character of the Second Great Awakening at the beginning of the nineteenth century.

The first influence was the disestablishment of the dominant moderate evangelical churches of the 1740s-1750s, primarily the Congregational, Presbyterian, and Episcopalian (Anglican) churches. As noted in the last chapter, these three denominations accounted for more than forty percent of all American congregations in 1760 but declined to less than twenty-five percent by 1790. However, the number of populist evangelical churches grew dramatically. The Baptists grew from forty-nine churches in 1760 to 858 by 1790. The Methodists went from having no churches to over 700 congregations during the same thirty year period.[3]

The revivals of the 1760s proved to be a key moment of transition by the former radical revivalists. Much of the leadership of the radicals from the revivals in the 1740s remained in place and had become prominent players in the revivals of the 1760s. These seasoned revival leaders now saw themselves in a somewhat different, less-radical light. One reason was that by the 1760s the influence of George Whitefield on the radicals had waned. As new churches were birthed from the revivals, the once radical leaders found that they must not only stir the revival fires but also pastor the new congregants between revivals. A second reason was that the former radicals sought to carry their populist and egalitarian ideas into mainstream American Christianity. Although liberty of conscience and separation from the established churches continued to be of central importance, the former radicals saw the necessity of presenting new revivals as both "reasonable *and* enthusiastic."[4] [emphasis in original]

A second influence on the America Protestant denominations was a decline in Calvinistic theology. To many in the new populist Protestant denominations during the last half of the eighteenth century, the Calvinist beliefs about predestination seemed doctrinally incompatible with the emerging individualistic nature of evangelicalism. The rejection of Calvinism was found among many North American evangelical denominations such as the Baptists and Methodists. The abandonment of Calvinism by the former radical evangelicals was a frequent occurrence in the revivals of the New Light Stir during the Revolutionary War.[5]

A third influence on American Protestantism was the "new birth" which became permanently identified as the most significant feature of evangelical Christianity. For the individual, conversion by the grace of Christ became the most important and spiritually significant moment of one's life. Whether radical or moderate, emphasizing salvation by faith in the atoning death of Jesus Christ through personal conversion had forever become the heart of evangelical churches' reason for being.[6]

Anti-evangelicalism, deism, Unitarianism, Universalism

As a result of disagreement with certain aspects of The Great Awakening in the 1740s and thereafter, many churches become inclined toward formalism and rejected evangelicalism. As the influence of the anti-evangelical churches declined during 1760-1790, these churches eventually became powerful allies of those professing deism. Together, they would counter what they perceived to be the growing threat of evangelicalism. Deism had once again began to grow and expand during the last quarter of the eighteenth century as it had done for a season during the first quarter of the century before being displaced by revivals and the birth of evangelicalism. However, the new deism of the late eighteenth century was of a much more poisonous variety for it embraced a large measure of French rationalism which championed human reason over religious teachings. Although deists would not deny God, worship, or Christian ethics as the Enlightenment humanists did, the new deism directly attacked revivalism and its emphasis on a personalized heart religion. As a result, the growing influence of deistic rationalism on Protestant thought "had numbed conviction and cooled enthusiasm" in many Protestant churches. The latent deism that had crept into anti-evangelical New England churches in decline after 1760 paved the way for the even greater heretical philosophies of Unitarianism and Universalism. Proponents of these philosophies were able to gain control of many strategic and influential Congregational churches which eventually split over these false philosophies. Over time, many churches captured by Unitarian and Universalist philosophies completely abandoned evangelical Christianity as they drifted toward outright humanism.[7]

The influence of these anti-evangelical forces in the last quarter of the eighteenth century coupled with the spiritual and moral decline as a result of the debilitating effects of eight years of war quickly became a disastrous setback for evangelicals and the Christian cause in general. This general decline was evident in 1796 near the end of George Washington's second term as president. A friend wrote to Washington of his concerns for the survival of the young nation.

> "Our affairs seem to lead to some crisis, some revolution; something that I can not foresee or conjecture. I am more uneasy than during the war."

> And George Washington replied: "Your sentiment... accords with mine. What will be is beyond my foresight."[8]

A call for a "concert of prayer" in the midst of desperate times

Given the dominance of Christianity and revivalism in much of American culture during the middle years of the eighteenth century, many modern Americans appear baffled by the new nation's sudden poverty of Christian spiritual and moral fiber. But for Christians who are familiar with the biblical accounts of God's people through the ages, great victories invariably lead to strong opposition by Satan. But Christians also know that when conditions are bleak and defeat is imminent, they must seek God's face and pray the prayers of desperate men and women for they know that only divine intervention can save the day. Arthur Skevington Wood said that when such dire situations were of a national scale it meant "nothing less than a revival could effectively deal with the situation."[9] And so it was in 1794 America.

A brief synopsis of Isaac Backus' life and ministry was presented in the previous chapter. He was a great man of faith and had pastored the Middleborough, Massachusetts, Baptist congregation for forty-six years. But by 1794 Backus and other pastors were discouraged because of the resurgence of widespread personal impiety and blatant corruption of public morals in the new nation. The churches in America appeared to be powerless in stopping the abandonment of religious principles and consequent decline of the moral state of the nation. Although many had given up hope, Backus still wavered between hope and despair. In his desperation Backus recruited Stephen Gano, a long-time friend and Baptist pastor, and twenty New England pastors to issue a call for a nation-wide "Concert of Prayer." The call for prayer for revival went to pastors of every Christian denomination throughout the United States, and the prayer network almost universally adopted and followed the pattern of the British Union of Prayer which set aside the first Monday of each month for prayer.[10]

Whisperings of revival

Soon revival began in the most unlikely of places—the colleges in the longest settled parts of the nation. Although these schools had been founded by godly men for godly purposes, they had become known as brazen centers of infidelity and immorality. Revival began almost imperceptibly among a handful of students who assembled unobtrusively to pray at various colleges. A few students at Virginia's Hampden-Sydney College, none professing to be Christians, attempted to conduct a prayer meeting, but ungodly students sought to disrupt the meeting. The president of the college quelled the disturbance and chastised the unruly students. Thereafter he invited the students wanting to pray to meet in his study. Very soon more than half of the students attending professed to have been converted and become Christians. Local churches also began to be roused from their spiritual lethargy by the students' conversions.[11]

Timothy Dwight, grandson of Jonathan Edwards, became the president of Yale College in 1795. Dwight soon encouraged his students to attack without hesitation the truth of the Bible. He then answered their attacks in chapel with a series of powerful sermons such as "The nature and danger of Infidel Philosophy" and "Is the Bible the Word of God?" He then challenged the students with plain expository preaching regarding the problems of materialism and deism. Interest in religion grew to such an extent that by 1802, one-third of the entire student body had made public confessions of faith in Christ. Several new revivals at Yale College would occur in the years to come.[12]

During the summer of 1806, five students at Williams College in Massachusetts met for prayer in a grove of maples as they were accustomed. Caught in the open by a brief thunderstorm, they sought shelter beneath a haystack. There they prayed about evangelizing the heathen for Christ and determined to devise a plan to do so. The small band of five organized a society, met in secret, and recorded their minutes in code. Soon they recruited at least twenty other students who shared their burden. In 1810, the burden for lost souls still burned in the hearts of the students. Samuel J. Mills, one of the original haystack group at Williams College, and three of his closest friends were attending Andover Seminary. The four seminarians met with six ministers of their denomination in the parlor of an interested professor. The students presented their plan to reach lost souls, but it was met with skepticism by several of the ministers who pointed to various obstacles that would hinder their mission. The ministers eventually gave their blessing to the young men after being warned by one minister against trying to stop God's purposes. From its humble origins under a New England haystack during a thunderstorm in 1806, the "whole modern missionary movement" was birthed.[13]

Small though they may have been, these initial college prayer meetings at several American campuses in the early years of the Second Great Awakening eventually led to revivals of religion in a multitude of colleges and subsequently spread to the churches. J. Edwin Orr described these revivals as beginning "...quietly and without fanaticism of any kind. There was undoubtedly an appeal to the hearts of the students, but first their minds and consciences were moved." By the turn of the century the awakenings on the college campuses had produced many powerful revivals from Maine to the southern states and most areas between. This was providential for at that very time there were enormous numbers of people that sought to establish new lives in the unsettled regions west of the Allegheny Mountains. The college campus revivals eventually produced "a generation of evangelistic ministers to serve the opening western states." But in 1798, the illiterate frontiers west of the Allegheny Mountains would not wait for revival to be brought by these future ministers.[14]

Fourteen states had been admitted to the Union by 1791. In the space of a single generation, ten more states were added by 1821, all west of the Allegheny/Appalachian Mountains. Such was the vast migration of people surging into these new states that Ohio soon had a greater population than all but four of the original states in the Union.[15]

Rogues' Harbour and Cane Ridge Revivals

The revivals in the East were soon surpassed by revivals in the wilderness regions. Two legendary revivals occurred in Kentucky and set the tone for what was to come. By 1800, revival had reached the western extremities of civilization in Logan County in southern Kentucky. Perhaps civilized is too strong a word for Rogues' Harbour, an area known for its wild and irreligious people including escaped murderers, counterfeiters, highwaymen, and horse thieves. Lawlessness was so rampant that local citizens formed themselves into regiments of vigilantes to fight the outlaws, often unsuccessfully, to establish a measure of law and order for the settlements. It was here that Presbyterian minister James McCready settled in 1797 and became pastor of three small churches. All through the winter of 1799, McCready and several of his congregants joined the national monthly Monday meetings to pray for revival as well as holding weekly Saturday evening to Sunday morning prayer meetings.[16]

Following months of prayer, revival came in the summer of 1800. Toward the end of a sacramental service at the Red River congregation, Presbyterian McCready allowed Methodist preacher John McGee to address his congregation. This was an unusual occurrence, but McGee was the brother of one of McCready's Presbyterian colleagues. McGee's preaching so stirred the audience that "Suddenly persons began to fall as he passed through the crowd—some as dead." McCready and his fellow Presbyterians were so stunned by the bodily manifestations they "acquiesced and stood in astonishment, admiring the wonderful work of God." McCready soon began preaching in the Methodist-style at his other two congregations.[17] The spiritual hunger was so great that eleven thousand came to a communion service. Overwhelmed, McCready called for help from all denominations.[18]

The religious gathering in August 1801 at Cane Ridge, Kentucky, is considered to be one of the most famous religious events in American history. Cane Ridge was located a few miles northeast of Lexington in central Kentucky which at that time had a population of 2,000 that made it the largest city in the state. The unique feature of the Cane Ridge revival was that people came prepared to camp at the site of the revival meeting which allowed a new intensity and level of religious experience. Although camp meetings were a part of several earlier localized revivals, the Cane Ridge revival was different in that people came from great distances and included rich, poor, black, and white who joined in prayer together.[19] Drawing from many recorded accounts of eyewitnesses, historian Ellen Eslinger pieced together a picture of the historic outpouring of the Spirit of God that lasted for almost a week in the Kentucky wilderness.

> For more than half a mile, I could see people on their knees before God in humble prayer …Individuals, suddenly struck by their spiritual plight, began falling to the ground "as if dead." At times the effect was awesome, with several hundred people "swept down like the trees of the forest under the blast of the wild tornado…Religion has got to such a height here, that people attended from great distances; on this occasion I doubt not but there will be 10,000 people, and perhaps 500 wagons."…The meeting was presided over by the Cane Ridge pastor and 18 other Presbyterian ministers, at least four Methodists, plus several Baptist elders…Cane Ridge offered spectators a chaotic scene. When individuals were spiritually stricken and fell, a circle of curious onlookers gathered around them. The huge, unwieldy scale of the event necessitated parallel activities. Several ministers often preached at the same time in different sections of the grounds, and the only event that had been previously scheduled was the sacrament on Sunday afternoon.[20]

The fame of the Cane Ridge camp meeting revival was a pivotal event in evangelism and served as a pattern for other revivals in the early years of the Second Great Awakening much as Jonathan Edwards' widely published descriptions of the Northampton revival had done sixty years earlier during the First Great Awakening.

Revival spreads

Soon the Kentucky revivals had swept south into Tennessee, the western Carolinas, and Georgia and then north into Ohio Territory. The revival movement increased dramatically, and sometimes crowds of thirty or forty thousand illiterate pioneer settlers gathered. Preachers from Baptist, Methodist, and Presbyterian churches would preach in different parts of the campground. As always, Satan sowed tares in the revivals through extraordinary emotional excesses beyond the true work of the Holy Spirit. However, in spite of the bad, far greater good for the kingdom of God was accomplished and was remarkably evident in the general religious awe that pervaded the country as "drunkards, swearers, liars, and the quarrelsome were remarkably reformed." The college awakenings eventually provided a flood of well-educated Bible scholars for ministry in the western reaches of America.[21]

The decade beginning with the War of 1812 slowed the waves of evangelism and revival, but during the years 1822-1842, thousands were added to the churches which far surpassed the results of the early years of the Second Great Awakening. The primary beneficiaries were those churches who were most evangelistic in word and action, primarily the Baptists and Methodists who evangelized the unchurched masses.[22]

8

The Second Great Awakening in America – The Later Years – 1822-1842

The ripening fruit of the Second Great Awakening

During the first half of the Second Great Awakening from 1794 to the beginning of the second half in 1822, the expansion of Christianity rested on two pillars: revival and the evangelical organizations growing out of them, especially in the United States and Great Britain. It was in the first half of the Second Awakening that these Christian organizations were birthed and nurtured, but it was in the second half that they matured and spread Christianity's evangelical mandate to a waiting world. Here we note just a few of the Christian organizations brought about by the Second Great Awakening.

Baptist Missionary Society was founded in England by William Carey in May 1792 and is generally regarded as the beginning of modern Protestant missionary endeavors.

Wesleyan Missionary Society formed in 1817-1818 arose from the work of Thomas Coke's Methodist mission to the West Indies during the 1780s-1790s.

Anglican evangelical Thomas Haweis led in founding the interdenominational London Missionary Society in 1795.

Church Missionary Society was founded in 1799 based on an idea conceived by Charles Simeon and sponsored by the Church of England.

The Scottish and Glasgow Missionary Societies were formed in 1796 but did not send out missionaries until 1824 because of opposition from the General Assembly of the Church of Scotland.

The interdenominational British and Foreign Bible Society was established in 1804 for the purpose of dissemination of the Scriptures. The American Bible Society was founded in 1816.

Religious and Tract Society was established in 1799 at the urging of George Burder, a Congregational minister who had been influenced by George Whitefield. In 1825, the American Tract Society was founded to provide Christian literature to the religiously destitute.

The interdenominational Sunday School Union was formed in 1803 and was a direct result of the earlier work of Robert Raikes of Gloucester, England, who in 1780 organized a Sunday school to give religious and moral training to the poor children of his city.[1]

These organizations and many others supplied great energy and motivation to evangelicalism in America and Great Britain during 1822-1842 as well as to the churches' other missionary endeavors around the world.

During the second half of the Second Great Awakening, almost all denominations experienced revival. However, none were more involved in American revivalism during this period than the Methodists. In 1822, the Methodists participated in over a thousand camp meetings. But as the radical evangelicals had discovered during the First Great Awakening, the real work in all denominations began with the discipling of new converts after the revival fires died down, and none did it better than the methodical Methodists. A Methodist bishop of the time told his preachers: "We must attend camp-meetings; they make our harvest time."[2] But in the larger picture, the harvest must be understood as being that brief season that stands between the enormous preparation, prayer, and effort that must precede a bountiful harvest of souls and the great work of discipleship and training of the newly redeemed that must follow.

Even though revival fires burned hot in the years 1822-1842, there were still divisions among the denominations. The Baptists were divided not so much by doctrine or practice but of necessity due to reasons of geographical dispersion. An extensive network of small Baptist Associations comprised of local churches joined together in voluntary cooperation. These churches were usually guided by farmer-preachers with little formal education. The Presbyterians and Congregationalists were divided over the methods and manifestations of revival. Anglicans divided into Anglo-Catholic and Evangelical branches. Likewise, Lutherans were split between confessional orthodoxy and tolerant evangelism. Whatever their internal divisions, the Reformed, Anglican, and Lutheran churches were cautiously supportive of revival but to a degree far less than their enthusiastic evangelical counterparts.[3]

Charles Grandison Finney

As previously noted, revival was widespread among the American churches in 1822-1842. At the center of this great outpouring of the Holy Spirit was Charles Grandison Finney, born in Connecticut in 1792. He studied law in western New York. As a law student, Finney began studying the Mosaic legal code. His interest and study of the Bible grew to the point that he believed in the authority of the Word. Remarkably, but not surprising, Finney's conversion came not from evangelism by others but from his private study and prayer. Revival historian J. Edwin Orr described young Finney and his path to the pulpit.

> His conversion caused a great stir in his community, for he was already (at 29 years of age) a brilliant fellow, a splendid pagan, impressive in personality, and proudly conscious of his intellectual as well as his physical superiority.

> Self-taught, but well-disciplined in theology, Finney rebelled against the rigid Calvinism of his Presbyterian fellows, yet he was ordained by a lenient presbytery in western New York. To the end of his days, he pursued his own way in theology, and adopted methods of evangelism which brought him into conflict with many leaders of the Calvinistic churches.[4]

Finney's ministry virtually spanned the whole of the second half of the Second Great Awakening and extended well into the Third Great Awakening.

Finney began his ministry in 1824 at the age of thirty-two. He conducted a series of meetings in Evans Mills, Oneida County, New York, where he preached at a Congregationalist church without a pastor.

Although the congregation seemed pleased with his sermons, Finney became distressed after several weeks of preaching without any conversions. Finally, Finney confronted the people with regard to their seeming obstinacy in not responding to the message of the gospel. Frustrated with their complacency, he challenged the congregation. "You who have made up your minds to become Christians, and will give your pledge to make peace with God *immediately*, should rise up." [emphasis added] This challenge would be a milestone at the very beginning of Finney's evangelical career for it was the first time he had asked for an immediate response. He then instructed those that had not risen and therefore had "no interest in Christ" to "sit still." When no one stood, Finney pronounced judgement, "You have taken your stand. You have rejected Christ and His gospel." He promised to preach just once more the following night. Finney spent the next day in fasting and prayer. That night the school house was packed "almost to suffocation" with "deists, nominal believers, infidels, Universalists, tavern keepers, respectable citizens, and a husband so angry with the evangelist for upsetting his wife that he would 'kill Finney'." Finney preached with all his might and the power of God fell. "Conversions began to occur, some accompanied with falling, groaning, and bellowing. Many inhabitants made 'heart-broken confessions' and 'professed a hope' of salvation…"[5]

At one meeting while at Evans Mills, Finney closed his sermon with an invitation to all that would give their hearts to the Lord to come forward and take the front seats. In later years this became a standard practice in all of his meetings and was called the "mourner's bench" or "anxious seat."[6]

Following the breakthrough at Evans Mills, Finney perfected his preaching style over the next six years in local awakenings in western New York State.[7] Finney described his evangelistic preaching style as "…simply preaching, prayer and conference meetings, and much private prayer, much personal conversation, and meetings for instruction of earnest inquirers." Finney also served as his own song leader, but singing was never an important component at his revival meetings.[8]

The completion of the Erie Canal linked Lake Erie with the deep waters of the Hudson River near Albany which flowed into the Atlantic Ocean. As a result of this new pathway to the sea, the towns along and near the canal's route boomed and grew rapidly. In this setting Finney's ministry eventually transitioned to more urban settings in western New York.[9] Finney and his wife moved to Utica, New York, in October 1825; to Wilmington, Delaware, in December 1827; and then to other areas in the metropolitan East.[10]

224

In 1830, against the advice of friends, the Finneys chose to go to Rochester in western New York where they stayed from September 1830 to mid-June 1831. Although Rochester was the fastest growing city in the United States during the 1820s due to the completion of the Erie Canal, for ministry purposes it was still considered a smaller and more provincial town when compared to the opportunity to preach in the largest urban areas of the nation.[11]

The pulpit to which he was called to fill was located at the Third Presbyterian Church. The building housing the church had severe structural damage caused by dampness from the nearby canal and was dangerously near collapse. As a result, the doors of several local churches were opened to Finney's message. A significant aid to furthering the Rochester revival was its alliance with the local temperance movement in the city. The symbiotic relationship between revival and the temperance movement "united evangelical Protestants like no other social movement had, and it would continue to do so for almost a hundred years."[12] It was estimated that in Rochester alone, one-tenth of the city's ten thousand residents were converted and twelve hundred admitted to membership in local churches during the revival of 1830.[13]

Finney wrote that the Rochester revival "spread like waves in every direction." Without doubt Finney's assessment was accurate. The revival spread throughout the Northeast with estimates of new church members ranging from 100,000 to as high as 200,000. Finney wrote in his *Memoirs* that "the very fame of it was an efficient instrument in the hands of the Spirit of God."[14] Here again we see that the fame of certain revivals within a broad spiritual awakening tends to identify those revivals as the signature event of the era: Jonathan Edwards and the Northampton revival of the 1730s during the First Great Awakening, the Cane Ridge revival of 1801 during the first half of the Second Great Awakening, and now the Rochester revival that gave rise to the 1830-1831 revivals during the second half of the Second Great Awakening.

Dr. Lyman Beecher expressed his opinion of this remarkable work of the Holy Spirit that spread from Rochester to virtually all states in the nation.

> That was the greatest work of God and the greatest revival of religion that the world has ever seen, in so short a time. One hundred thousand were reported as having connected themselves to the churches as a result

of that great revival. This is unparalleled in the history of the church.[15]

As a result of the Rochester revival, Finney became nationally known and soon preached revival meetings to large crowds in Philadelphia, Boston, New York, and other large cities. He became professor of theology at Oberlin College in 1836 and the college's president in 1851 where he remained until 1866. Over the years following the Rochester revival, Finney's theology evolved from a Presbyterian-Congregationalist Calvinism to a middle path between Arminianism and Calvinism. By the end of his life he was a strong supporter of the doctrine of perfectionism.[16] Christian perfectionism was at the heart of John Wesley's preaching. The essence of this doctrine is that the Christian pursues a life of sanctification or holiness in which one has been separated from a past life of sin and continues to live a life separated from sin and dedicated to God.

Charles Finney was and remains a controversial figure as are almost all who preach revival for to do so is to incur the wrath of Satan and the forces of the reigning world system. One of Finney's most controversial beliefs dealt with how revivals begin. In his 1831 "Lectures on Revivals of Religion," Finney wrote:

> A revival is not a miracle, nor dependent on a miracle, in any sense. It is a purely philosophical result of the right use of the constituted means as much so as any other effect produced by the application of means...
>
> I said that a revival is the result of the right use of the appropriate means. The means which God has enjoined [ordered] for the production of a revival, doubtless have a natural tendency to produce a revival. Otherwise God would not have enjoined them. *But means will not produce a revival, we all know, without the blessing of God.* No more will grain, when it is sown, produce a crop without the blessing of God. It is impossible for us to say that there is not as direct an influence or agency from God, to produce a crop of grain, as there is to produce a revival.[17] [emphasis added]

Throughout his entire life Finney believed that "regeneration is always induced and effected by the personal agency of the Holy Spirit."

He also believed the Spirit works through natural means and human agency.[18] Unfortunately, and as is often the case in spiritual matters, this reasonable understanding of the centrality and manner of working of the Holy Spirit was frequently reduced to conversational shorthand devoid of Finney's intent and true meaning of his position. Thus, in the minds of many, "revivals of religion" amount to little more than human manipulation or fabrication resulting in salvation by emotion rather than salvation by faith. Dr. J. Edwin Orr described the consequences of this misunderstanding and misuse of Finney's path to revival by many ministers and evangelists, both friend and foe.

> [Finney's] theory of revivals encouraged a brash school of revivalists and evangelists who thought that they could promote genuine revival by use of means chosen by themselves. The use of means was patently successful in the case of so many other Spirit-filled men. In the case of the less spiritual promoters, the theory gave rise to a brand of promotional evangelism, one full of sensationalism and commercialism...[19]

Although Finney fully embraced the religious enthusiasm of the common people, he was steadfastly opposed to fanaticism which damaged the prospects of spiritual renewal by "ranting irresponsible preachers."[20] In spite of the objections to and misunderstandings of his methods and message, Charles Finney stands alone as the most brilliant evangelist of the nineteenth century. Although Finney was a master revival tactician and the undisputed revivalist leader between 1822 and 1842, the footprint of the later years of the Second Great Awakening was far larger than Finney's and included many other well-known revivals and evangelists of the era.

The decline of religious life in America 1842-1857

Religious life in the United States began a serious decline during the latter half of the 1840s and much of the 1850s as a result of the confluence of several religious, social, and political conditions.

One well-meaning but misguided evangelist of the 1830s and early 1840s brought reproach on the cause of Christ which helped cool the religious fervor of the Awakening. William Miller was a New England farmer, a sincere man, and a zealous leader of many evangelists. In 1831, Miller began preaching a message that the Lord was coming on

March 21, 1843. In the dozen years leading up to the projected date, Miller had gathered a following variously estimated to be between 100,000 and one million. As the date approached, many of the Millerites, as they were known, sold their possessions, camped out in fields, or waited in white garments on nearby hilltops for Christ's return. The date came and went as did two new dates in March and October of 1844 which were predicted for Christ's return. As a consequence many of the Millerites became embittered and left the church as a result of their misplaced faith. In 1846, a remnant of the Millerites established the Seventh-Day Adventists. The denomination developed several new doctrines to explain the Millerite disaster. Many of these doctrines were blatantly heretical including the assertion that Christ had already come secretly. These doctrines and other beliefs effectively isolated the Seventh-Day Adventists from the rest of evangelical Protestantism.[21] As a result of the Millerite debacle, the Protestant church as a whole was diminished and frequently ridiculed. During the period 1845-1855, faith in religion was greatly declined, and the church experienced severe losses.[22]

In the social realm, financial and commercial prosperity abounded to the point that the zeal for the material far outweighed the zeal for things religious. "Boom times caught the public fancy, and turned men's hearts from God."[23]

However, it was in the arena of politics that propelled the ship of state into uncharted and dangerous waters. The myths of Andrew Jackson as the hero of the common man and Jacksonian democracy as a watershed event in democratic processes is better described as a hypocritical reform movement steeped in corruption, spoils, and patronage. Elected in 1828, Jackson and his successors' actions "...ensured the dominance of a proslavery party in national politics..." which continued to exacerbate the problem of slavery until the beginning of the Civil War in 1861.[24]

Slavery was an issue that had been a great cause of concern among evangelicals and an institution upon which they had expended great energy in hopes of bringing it to an end. The efforts to abolish slavery in America began even before the nation's founding as a result of the moral suasion of Christian people who saw slavery as morally unacceptable within the biblical worldview. The case against slavery had been building among many evangelicals since the eighteenth century. By the 1830s, it was an issue whose time had come, and none were better positioned to press the cause of liberation than Charles Finney and Oberlin College. Finney spoke strongly against slavery in his *Lectures on*

Revivals. He told ministers that "their testimony must be given on this subject" and that failure to speak out implied "that they do not consider slavery a sin." Finney believed that it would take a national spiritual revival to end slavery and warned that the ideological struggle over the issue of slavery was quickly driving the nation to the brink of civil war.[25]

Each of the three Great Awakenings played a decisive role in the history of the nation. The Great Awakening was the *formative* moment in American history preceding the political drive for independence and making it possible. The Second Great Awakening was the *stabilizing* moment whose effects lasted until the 1840s and saved the new nation from political and moral destruction. The Third Great Awakening was the *sustaining* moment that prepared the nation to endure the national conflagration of the Civil War and made possible its reunification and survival in the war's aftermath. The revival of the late 1850s caused men and women, in both the North and South, to be spiritually prepared for the coming struggle in which the nation would exorcize the demon of slavery and recover its national unity.

9

The Third Great Awakening in America 1857-1858

Revival begins at a Canadian farm 1853

The first stirrings of revival that preceded the Third Great Awakening in the United States and Canada began on a Canadian farm in the province of Ontario. Dr. Walter Palmer was a wealthy physician who had become an evangelist. Both Palmer and his wife Phoebe held evangelistic meetings mostly in the United States but occasionally traveled to Canada. In August 1853, the Palmers preached at a camp meeting on a farm in an eastern township near Nappanee where over five hundred people were converted. They returned to Nappanee in 1854 and saw another great harvest of souls in which hundreds were converted. They returned to Barrie in 1855 and once again saw hundreds converted.[1]

Hamilton was a bustling Ontario community of 23,000 in October 1857. The Palmers were merely passing through Hamilton on their way back to Albany, New York, from Georgetown, Ontario, where three thousand were in attendance. The Palmers had planned to stay only one night but were forced to stay longer with friends because of the loss of their luggage. Two ministers soon discovered the couple's presence in Hamilton and invited them to tea at which they were encouraged to speak at the Thursday prayer meeting. The three downtown Methodist churches joined together for prayer in the basement of one of the churches. Sixty-five people came to the meeting and were challenged to pray for a revival. Thirty raised their hands in agreement not only to commit to "fervent, personal prayer" for revival but to bring their fellow townspeople with them to church. The first revival meeting was held the next day and twenty-one were converted. Saturday's meeting yielded another twenty, and Sunday saw an additional seventy conversions. After ten days conversions totaled four hundred. Soon the revival spread to Ancaster. The revivals lasted well into November of 1857.[2]

On October 28th, *The Christian Guardian* was the first Canadian newspaper to report the unusual events that had been occurring in Hamilton. A week later a New York newspaper, *The Christian Advocate*, gave the following report on the revival taking place in Hamilton, Ontario.

> The work is taking within its range...persons of all classes. Men from low degree and men of high estate for wealth and position, all men and maidens, and even little children are seen humbly kneeling together pleading for grace. The Mayor of the city with other persons of like position is not ashamed to be seen bowed at the altar of prayer beside their humble servants.[3]

Unfortunately, the Hamilton revival was to be almost exclusively a Methodist affair. Hesitant over the "Methodist enthusiasm," the Baptists and the Presbyterians were generally unaffected and the Anglicans remained indifferent.[4]

Revival stirrings were also happening in the United States well before the Hamilton revival began. On October 1, 1856, the Holy Spirit began to be "especially manifest" at the Stanton Street Baptist Church in New York City. At least five or six persons each week "presented themselves as inquirers to the Christian faith." Interest increased in December 1856 and January 1857 to such an extent that revival meetings began to be held nightly in February. Sixty persons were baptized in March and April. Following a summer lull, revival fervor increased again in the fall and winter months.[5]

The Revival of 1857-1858 (aka The Third Great Awakening)

The Third Great Awakening began in 1857 and has been called by many names including the Businessman's Revival, the Layman's Revival, and the Union Prayer Meeting. But it is most widely known as the Revival of 1857-1858. Much like the central theme of the Protestant Reformation, this revival was about *personal religious transformation* from which society greatly benefited. As noted at the end of the last chapter, the Third Great Awakening was the *sustaining* moment that prepared the nation to endure the national conflagration of the Civil War and made possible its reunification and survival in the war's aftermath.

On July 1, 1857, Jeremiah Lamphier was appointed a City Missionary in downtown New York. Converted fifteen years earlier in the Broadway Tabernacle built by Charles Finney, Lamphier was a quiet businessman. He was described as personable, capable, intelligent, and very ardent in his faith. He had been appointed to his lay position by the

North Church of the Dutch Reformed denomination which was losing membership in downtown New York because many members had moved away to better residential neighborhoods. As a layman City Missionary, his task was to visit the immediate neighborhoods and encourage church attendance.[6]

The spiritual lethargy of his fellow businessmen weighed heavily on Lamphier's mind and heart. He believed a weekly noonday prayer meeting would allow various merchants, businessmen, mechanics, clerks, and strangers "an opportunity to stop and call upon God amid the perplexities incident to their respective avocations." Accordingly, Lamphier distributed a handbill setting the weekly prayer meeting on Wednesdays from 12 to 1 o'clock at the North Dutch Church located at the corner of Fulton and William Streets in what today is lower Manhattan. At that first meeting on the 23rd of September, Lamphier anxiously awaited, but no one joined him until about 12:30 PM when in succession six persons quietly arrived. Two weeks later on October 7th, there were forty in attendance and it was decided to hold prayer meetings on a daily rather than weekly basis. In that *same week*, Walter and Phoebe Palmer began preaching revival meetings in Hamilton (noted above) that resulted in extraordinary numbers of converts, but reports of the Hamilton revival would not reach New York until November 5th.[7] But God had an additional means of arresting the attention of a wayward nation consumed with things other than religion.

Financial and commercial prosperity had been building at a dizzying pace for over a decade as the nation rapidly expanded with the addition of new states to the Union. New cities sprang up, and cheap land became available as the frontier was pushed farther and farther to the west. But in 1856 and 1857, there were disturbing signs of financial instability. By fall of 1857, various events coalesced to bring about the third great panic in American history. Much of the speculative wealth of the nation was swept away as banks failed and railroads went into bankruptcy. Factories were shut down, merchants went out of business, and thousands were thrown out of work including thirty thousand in New York City alone.[8] The panic was triggered when a bank holiday was declared on October 14th to prevent a run on the banks. By the time the banks were reopened on December 14th, recession had spread over the nation and to other parts of the world. As a result of the panic, the noon prayer meetings received a significant boost in attendance from those working in nearby Wall Street and others who were unemployed. Some sought salvation while others killed time.[9]

By the end of March 1858 every church and public hall was filled to capacity in downtown New York City as ten thousand business men were gathering daily for prayer. Soon revival was occurring in Brooklyn, Yonkers, and in New Jersey towns across the Hudson River. By February the national press began covering the story.[10] With mass unemployment during the winter of 1857-1858, one would have expected the crime rate to increase, but it actually dropped as the wealthy looked after the physical needs of many of their less fortunate brothers and sisters in Christ.[11] J. Edwin Orr described the impact of the revival throughout the United States.

> The national press from coast to coast carried news of the great awakening in the metropolis, and citizens everywhere were challenged by the movement. The "showers of blessing" in New York had caused a flood which suddenly burst its bounds and swept over New England, engulfed the Ohio Valley cities and states, rolled over the newly settled West, lapped the edges of the mountains in the South, and covered the United States of America and Canada with divine favour.

> The influence of the awakening was felt everywhere in the nation. It first moved the great cities, but it also spread through every town and village and country hamlet, swamping school and college. It affected all classes without respect to their condition. A divine influence seemed to pervade the land, and men's hearts were strangely warmed by a Power that was outpoured in unusual ways. There was no fanaticism. There was remarkable unanimity of approval among religious and secular observers alike, with scarcely one critical voice heard anywhere.[12]

After careful research, noted revival historian Dr. J. Edwin Orr estimated that approximately one million people were converted in the nation during 1858-1859. In other words, conversions amounted to over three percent of the population which was less than thirty million at that time. This seems a reasonable estimate given that some historians have estimated that conversions were occurring at the rate of fifty thousand per week at the height of the revival.[13]

The two revivals originating almost simultaneously in the United States and Canada also had a worldwide impact including many men and women across Great Britain. This influence led to revivals in Wales (1858-1860), Ireland and Scotland (1859-1860), and England (1859-1860). In 1858, two hundred thousand converts were recorded in Sweden in the first year of a two-year revival. The India Awakening began in late 1859 with the greatest revivals occurring in the south of India.[14]

The long-term consequences in America of the Revival of 1857-1858

The Revival of 1857-1858 influenced many young men who would later spark many revivals among troops on both sides of the Civil War. Large and widespread revivals in both Union and Confederate armies occurred between 1862 and 1865. Conversions during the war were estimated to be between 100,000 and 200,000 among Union troops and as many as 150,000 in the Confederate Army.[15]

One may ask how this can be—brothers fighting and killing each other while both called on God for protection and to save their immortal souls. To answer, we must remember that slavery was an institutional cancer on the national body. Regardless of slavery's origins and protectors, it was slavery that was being cut from the body, not the Southern soldier and citizen. God was just as concerned for the individual Southerner as he was for those in the North.

As previously mentioned, the efforts to abolish slavery in America began early in the nation's history as a result of the moral suasion of Christian people who saw slavery as morally unacceptable within the biblical worldview. It was a matter of right and wrong and not a matter of "rights" or equality. However, breaking the chains of injustice sometimes requires the hammer of state in the cause of brotherhood and fraternity. The Civil War cost 600,000 lives, billions of dollars, and loss of unity as the nation was tragically divided with few thoughts of Christian brotherhood on either side of the chasm filled with distrust.

The war years and the years following the draconian Reconstruction Act of 1867 left the South lying prostrate and ravaged. Called the Tragic Era, Sherwood Eddy paints a picture of the dozen years of life in the South following the end of the Civil War.

> Often with flagrant disregard of civil liberties, Southern
> officials, courts, customs, and organizations were
> removed or swept away, and a government by Northern

Carpetbaggers and Negroes was substituted under military tribunals. A Northern army of occupation of twenty thousand was aided by an irritating force of colored militia...The state administrations under Northern carpetbaggers were extravagant, corrupt, and vulgar. The state treasuries were systematically looted...The majority of the legislature and most of the important officers were Negroes and many of the rest were rascally whites from the North, or unsavory characters from the South. Taxes were levied by the Negroes, of whom 80 percent were illiterate, and were paid by the disfranchised whites...the future of the Negro was sadly prejudiced by these disreputable adventures in self-government.[16]

The post-war *product* of the hammer of state that broke the chains of injustice was dis-unifying, absent Christian principles and brotherhood, and was anything but moral. Should Abraham Lincoln have avoided the assassin's bullet, his post-war efforts at reconciliation of the divided nation could have forestalled much of the tragedy and anguish experienced during the Reconstruction period. Richard Weaver described the precipice upon which the nation teetered following Lincoln's death at the end of the Civil War.

There was a critical period when, if things had been managed a little worse, the South might have turned into a Poland or an Ireland, which is to say a hopelessly alienated and embittered province, willing to carry on a struggle for decades or even centuries to achieve a final self-determination...As it was, things were done which produced only rancor and made it difficult for either side to believe in the good faith of the other. It is unfortunate but it is true that the Negro was forced to pay a large part of the bill for the follies of Reconstruction.[17]

Therefore, we must ask how it was possible for the nation to survive the cataclysmic events of the Civil War and the subsequent Tragic Era in the midst of moral degradation and dashed hopes for brotherhood and unity. Once again we must look for the answer in the actions of Christians who originally provided the motivation and drive to end slavery and who, following the Civil War, would provide the motivation for the restoration and unification of the nation.

Restoration and unity would not come easily, and it would be decades before signs of healing were evident. The Northern and Southern churches continued to have different interpretations of the war and its outcome. Northerners viewed theirs as a righteous victory and themselves as guardians of the ideals embodied in the Constitution which were based on the same principles as found in Christianity.[18] Following the war main-stream Northern churches tended toward rectifying other ills of society through a social gospel with a consequent loss of focus as it switched its emphasis from perfecting the inner man to social justice.[19]

Faced with loss of the war, Southern evangelicals comforted themselves with the thought that their goals were spiritual and not temporal which resulted in the rise of an other-worldly mood within Southern Christianity. Thus, Christianity allowed the Southern culture to focus on spiritual victory in the midst of earthly defeat. Religion in the South became the bulwark of Southern culture and "…never appeared stronger than it did at the end of the nineteenth century." From this détente between Northern and Southern churches during the remainder of the century, old animosities began to wane as reconciliation became a common political, literary and religious theme in both the North and South. "Religion which once played a role in breaking the nation apart, now aided the reunification of the South with the North."[20]

In spite of differing views of the war and the rampant corruption and immorality that plagued both the North and South for decades after the Civil war, many of the faithful Civil War veterans who embraced Christianity during the war-time revivals returned to their homes with their religious fervor intact. They filled the pews, spurred post-war revivals (particularly in the South), and brought healing to the nation.[21] As a result, the unifying common ground of Christianity and faithfulness of individual Christians sheltered the flame of brotherhood amidst the winds of secularism and materialism of the Gilded Age in the latter part of the nineteenth century. Without this unifying Christian faith, the rebirth of national unity would have been still-born which could have easily and likely led to a permanent balkanization of much of the South. Because of the Revival of 1857 and 1858 and its legacy of Christian revivals among the soldiers during the Civil War, the Republic was saved.

The nature of the Revival of 1857-1858 in America

Historians have debated the impact of the Revival of 1857-1858 as it related to nineteenth century social reform efforts. Some historians such as Kathryn Teresa Long point to the revival prayer meeting practice of avoiding any discussion of controversial topics such as slavery and abolitionism as evidence of little direct social impact caused by the revival.[22]

> From this perspective, the 1857-1858 revival marked a *shift in the public role of revivals in American life*. It signaled a rejection of the combination of religious conversion and community moral reform that had been a part of the New England Calvinist tradition since the colonial revivals. Instead, a more limited, pietistic image of revivals emerged, one focused on prayer and evangelism and in which community meant experiences of shared feeling among middle class people. This *shift of urban revivalism in a more inward direction* reflected the changing nature of community in a rapidly industrializing society and promised northern evangelicals spiritual harmony in the midst of an increasingly complex society.[23] [emphasis added]

But there was *not* a shift in the public role of revivals to a more inward direction. The reality was that the 1857-1858 Revival was about *personal religious transformation but with which society greatly benefited*. It must be remembered that the ordering of society and the addressing of its social ills must begin with the individual through an ordering of his soul in right relationship with God. This is certainly the greatest impact of the Revival of 1857-1858 as the nation was soon to be immersed in its greatest struggle for survival. As noted at the close of the last chapter, it was the Revival of 1857-1858 that caused men and women, in both the North and South, to be spiritually prepared for the coming struggle in which the nation would exorcize the demon of slavery and recover its national unity.

After the Revival of 1757-1758, the real shift away from revivals as an instrument through which religious, moral, and social reformation of society was periodically accomplished was caused by the rise of increasingly liberal elements within the Protestant church. This was not a retreat to an inward spirituality but an *abandonment* of the *irreplaceable* renewing power of revival by much of the liberal Protestant establishment in America. During the last third of the nineteenth century, the Protestant churches came under assault by a rapid secularization of the culture and the emergence of powerful new humanistic forces that sought to replace Christianity as the measure of cultural norms and authority. All of these factors led to a dramatic loss of cultural power by the once preeminent Protestant church in America. This transition will be discussed in the next chapter.

10

America Embraces Babylon 1870-1930

America succumbs to mammon

J. M. Roberts in his definitive *The New History of the World* stated that the magnitude of societal change produced by industrialization was the "most striking in European history since the barbarian invasions"…and perhaps the "…biggest change in human history since the coming of agriculture, iron, or the wheel." By 1850 Great Britain was the only country in the world that had established a mature industrial society. Yet, most industrial workers in England were found at businesses employing fewer than fifty people and those that worked in larger factories were concentrated at the large Lancashire cotton mills with their distinctive urban appearance and character. However, a significant increase in the number of large factories would soon occur because of the trend toward greater centralization, specialization of function, economies of scale and transport, and regimentation of labor. By 1870, France, Switzerland, Belgium, Germany, and the United States had joined Britain in the race for self-sustained economic growth through industrialization.[1]

In "Shame of the Cities," American historians Larry Schweikart and Michael Allen gave a vivid description of American life in the cities during the late 1800s.

> …immigrants flooded into the seaport cities in search of a new life. Occasionally, they were fleeced by local politicians when they arrived. Often they melted in the American pot by starting businesses, shaping the culture, and transforming the urban scene. In the process the cities lost their antebellum identities, becoming true centers of commerce, arts, and the economy, as well as hotbeds of crime, corruption and degeneracy…in 1873, within three miles of New York's city hall, one survey counted more than four hundred brothels housing ten times that number of prostitutes. Such illicit behavior coincided with the highest alcohol consumption levels since the turn of the century, or a quart of whiskey a week for every adult American. Some level of social and

political pathology was inevitable in any population, but it was exacerbated by the gigantic size of the cities.[2]

The social gospel

Compassion was the premier Christian innovation in all of history and an example of Christ's concern for the hurting and sick. Therefore, the church did not quietly cede Western civilization to the flood waters of industrialization throughout the nineteenth century. From the earliest days of the Industrial Revolution, Christianity invaded the cities to not only save the soul but provide for earthly needs and address societal ills afflicting the hurting masses. The social impact of the mid-nineteenth century evangelical awakenings fostered tremendous efforts for the betterment of social conditions including the issues of the working man, the protection of women and children, poverty, education, slum housing, and racial strife. Changes came through sharing the gospel message, the transforming of individual lives by the power of Jesus Christ, evangelism, and initiating reforms through the work of tireless individuals and societies.[3]

But out of Christian compassion and its concern for a hurting humanity eventually arose a liberal social gospel found within many Protestant churches that had become less concerned with saving the soul than fixing the ills of society by works of men and government. However well-intentioned the liberal church's social gospel was, it was soon subjugated by the powerful forces of Enlightenment liberalism which quickly rolled over the nineteenth century Protestant establishment and the nation between 1870 and 1930.

Following the Civil War a perfect storm of societal dysfunction and pagan philosophies caused much of America to forget her Christian heritage and the blessings that flowed therefrom. The humanistic spirit of the age became a cultural force that inundated the Western world during the last half nineteenth century. Karl Marx in politics, Charles Darwin in biology, Christopher Langdell in law, and John Dewey in education and psychology were among the principle players of the nineteenth century vying to introduce within society a "new way" to solve its seemingly inextricable problems. The end result was devastating to the American Protestant church.

The enormous changes that occurred in the six decades between 1870 and 1930 profoundly transformed the way Americans thought and acted in all spheres of American life. By 1870 the nation had been guided for 250 years by a central cultural vision infused with the collective Judeo-Christian worldviews of the great majority of Americans since the Pilgrims undertook to establish a colony...Although Protestant cultural authority was at its peak in 1870, a brief sixty years later it had been relegated to the shadows within every institution of American life, despairing of approval and hoping only for an occasional hint of recognition from the new masters of American culture. The once prevailing Christian Protestant dominion had surrendered substantially all of its social power, institutional influence, and cultural authority and did so without much of a whimper. For the first time in American history a vast schism had developed between the religious and secular.[4]

The Gilded Age in America 1870-1930

The Gilded Age is generally considered to be the American era from about 1870 to 1900. It was a time of immense growth and change in America which did not bode well for all Americans. Not long after the beginning of the disaster known as Reconstruction Act of 1867 following the Civil War, concern for the plight of the former slaves was supplanted by other issues which began to occupy the attention of the nation: the often chaotic westward expansion, the rise of big business, rampant political corruption, and community fragmentation and moral decline caused by the rapid growth of large cities.

The tentacles of the monumental graft and corruption within Ulysses Grant's administration (1869-1877) spread over the whole nation—from the rural areas of the devastated Southern states to the cities of the north. In the first year of Grant's two terms in office, the notorious stock promoters Jay Gould and Jim Fisk almost succeeded in cornering the gold market after lavishly entertaining Grant and bribing his brother-in-law. The cities were no less corrupt. New York City was robbed of seventy-five million dollars by the Tweed Ring, and Philadelphia's city debt grew by three million dollars a year through the collusions of the Gas Ring.[5] In May 1869, the immensity of fraud and corruption in the world of government and business was epitomized by the Credit Mobilizer scandal which was a complicated scheme that involved using massive public funding for the benefit of transcontinental railroads (Union Pacific and Central Pacific). To keep government land grants and federal loans flowing to the railroads, a number of congressmen, senators, Grant administration officials, and even Vice President Schuyler Colfax were given generous Credit Mobilizer holdings.[6] These examples of corruption stand at the apex of a labyrinthine web of business and government graft, bribery, fraud, dishonesty, and greed that had infected almost all levels of American life during the Gilded Age.

The Great Divide – modernists and liberals v. fundamentalists and evangelicals

The American Protestant church, already divided by region, denomination, race, ethnicity, and class, would split again into fundamentalist and modernist factions between the late nineteenth century and the mid-1920s. Amid rising skepticism, positivism, and Darwinism emanating from Enlightenment liberalism, the new liberal and modernist Protestant leaders chose survival through accommodation by embracing their adversary's doctrines of Science, Progress, Reason, and Liberation. But this compromise would only forestall the approaching "...final dominance of Enlightenment moral order in the public square and the relegation of Christian and other religious concerns to private life" that has gained increasing momentum since the 1930s.[7]

As modernism and liberalism ascended in many Protestant churches, many members began to feel uncomfortable with the growing formalism among the wealthier and more prosperous segments of the congregations. Of greatest concern was the disappearance of a heart religion that was the defining symbol of evangelicalism since its birth in the early 1700s. As a result, these concerns over the question of "holiness" became a topic of great importance. This was especially true for the Methodists because Christian perfection as taught by John Wesley was no longer a goal of most Methodists in the late 1800s. As a result, a large measure of worldliness had crept into the church. Holiness groups began forming within these churches to defend Wesley's doctrines and ideals. Because the pastors and leading men of the most influential churches were opposed to Holiness groups and their concerns, the more orthodox and less powerful Holiness groups began to withdraw and form their own denominations.[8]

New Holiness denominations came from many churches and were mostly found in the rural districts of the Middle West. However, most Holiness denominations came out of Methodist churches. Between

1880 and 1926, twenty-five or more Holiness and Pentecostal denominations were formed in protest against the increasing modernism and liberalism they saw in the larger churches of America.[9] The new denominations included the Church of the Nazarene (formed in 1894 when eight smaller holiness groups combined), Christian and Missionary Alliance (1897), Church of God, Anderson, Indiana (1881), Church of God, Cleveland, Tennessee (1896), the Pilgrim Holiness Church, Cincinnati, Ohio (1897), and the Assemblies of God (1914).[10]

Dwight Lyman Moody

As previously noted, Charles Grandison Finney dominated the middle third of the nineteenth century. The man who would dominate the last third during the Gilded Age was Dwight Lyman Moody (1837-1899). The contrasts between the two men could hardly have been greater. Compared to the well-educated, articulate, and polished Finney, Moody was born in poverty and had little formal education. He was one of nine children whose father died when Moody was only four. Moody was converted at eighteen and a year later moved to Chicago where he was profoundly affected by the Revival of 1857-1858. Moody quickly developed a passion for winning young people for Christ through Sunday school and the Young Men's Christian Association. Moody's Sunday school soon became a church, and in 1860 Moody devoted himself to full time ministry.[11]

In 1867, Moody traveled to Britain to seek out leaders of the evangelical movement such as of Charles Spurgeon, George Muller, and Harry Morehouse. Moody listen to Morehouse preach for a week on the love of God and was so profoundly affected that Moody's preaching was forever changed. In 1872 Moody again traveled to England, and his preaching brought a local awakening to a church in North London. Other invitations followed, but the great breakthrough in his ministry came at Edinburgh, Scotland, where his meetings filled even the largest arenas. Moody continued holding meetings throughout Scotland, Ireland, and England. Attendance was enormous. Twenty thousand each night listened to Moody preach in London's Islington Agricultural Hall. The London campaign lasted twenty weeks at which two and a half million people attended.[12]

Moody spent three years in Britain before returning to the United States in August 1875. As in Britain, vast crowds flocked to hear Moody preach all across the United States. Another trip to England was made in October 1881. Beginning in 1884, Moody began devoting much of his time to promotion of education at his institutes in Chicago and Northfield, Massachusetts, as well as conducting a number of evangelistic campaigns in smaller cities. In 1893, approximately two million visitors attended evangelistic services held by Moody during the World's Fair, the Columbian Exposition in Chicago. With the help of Moody's Bible Institute, three centers of preaching were established on the north, west, and south sides of Chicago. On Sundays, Moody preached in a large circus tent at the city's lakefront on the east side. In November 1899, Moody preached his last campaign in Kansas City, Missouri. Exhausted, he withdrew from the campaign and returned home. He passed away December 22, 1899, after forty years of ministry.[13]

D. L. Moody's success did not depend on his earthly attributes. He did not have a commanding physical appearance, was not a renowned theologian, and certainly was not a great orator. His theology and convictions were strongly conservative. His preaching was very simple but strong on Scripture which he illustrated with homely stories presented in everyday language.[14]

The inspiration that led to Moody's great contributions to the Kingdom of God occurred when Moody visited England for the first time in 1868. There he met Henry Varley, one of the great British evangelists, who said to him, "Moody, the world has yet to see what God will do with a man fully consecrated to Him." Over thirty years later, the world had seen and heard Dwight Lyman Moody and now knew what God could do with a man fully consecrated to Him.[15]

Revival or evangelism?

Although the words "revival" and "evangelism" are often used interchangeably, Dr. J. Edwin Orr in his book *The Light of the Nations* explained that there is a difference. In English-speaking countries outside of North America, revival is generally used to identify a great outpouring of the Holy Spirit upon the churches resulting in a renewed interest in religion after a period of indifference or decline. Although this is the correct meaning when the term "revival" is used in the United States, it is often used interchangeably to describe an organized campaign of evangelism or a series of evangelistic meetings.[16] Dr. Orr points out the differences.

> It often happens that there are elements of revival in an evangelistic campaign, and effects of evangelism in a

246

revival movement. Evangelism is what dedicated men do for God, but revival is what God does to earnest men to bring them to fuller dedication.[17]

Orr described Moody as an evangelist and not a revivalist in the historic sense whereas Orr used revivalist as the correct term to describe the works of George Whitefield, John Wesley, Charles Finney, and Evan Roberts of Wales. Nevertheless, there are almost always elements of revival in evangelism and elements of evangelism in revivals.[18]

Revival and religion in the Gilded Age 1870-1900

Timothy L. Smith in his book *Revivalism and Social Reform* stated the primary feature distinguishing American religion after 1865 was "The rapid growth of concern with purely social issues such as poverty, working men's rights, the liquor traffic, slum housing, and racial bitterness." The Christian imperative of this concern eventually divided into two avenues. The first avenue was "militant modernism" in theology of the liberal branch which focused its energies on socialism, preaching a social gospel, and establishing a pre-millennial "Kingdom of Heaven on Earth." On the second avenue were found the footprints of Moody and other conservative evangelicals and revivalists who advocated social service and the post-millennial hope of the Kingdom of God while distancing themselves from the social gospel which abandoned the soul in its quest for humanistic answers to individual and societal pathologies.[19]

The Revival of 1857-1858 in America was often called the Layman's Revival because of the broad inter-denominational support, absence of clerical leadership, and focus on prayer. According to Dr. Orr, the greatest achievements of the nineteenth century were brought about by dedicated lay men and women nurtured in the faith and worship of evangelical fellowships. Because of the Great Awakenings, it was individual Christian lay people who persuaded church leaders and parliaments to address the great issues of the century: "abolition of the slave trade, reform of prisons, emancipation of slaves, care of the sick, education of the young, protection of workers and the like..."[20]

Dr. Orr closed his remarkable book, *The Light of the Nations*, by giving a final summation of the impact of the evangelical awakenings throughout the nineteen century.

247

The nineteenth century proved to be a time of evangelical renewal and advance, in which shone widely the Light of the Nations. The phenomena of the Great Awakenings brought blessing untold to the Christian believer, to the congregation, to the Christian community, to the Church at Large, to the laboring man, to the world of women, to the welfare of children, to the care of the sick, to the shelter of the insane, to the protection of the unfortunate, to the education of the young, to the guaranteeing of liberty, to the granting of freedom, to the administration of justice, to the evolution of self-government, to the crusade for peace among nations—in fact, in the nineteenth century, the Evangelical Awakenings may be shown to be the foremost method of an almighty God to promote the betterment of all mankind and His chiefest instrument to win men to transforming faith in Himself.[21]

In the next chapter we will examine two great revivals in the first decade of the twentieth century which were followed by a gradual but prolonged decline of revival and revivalism in America, Great Britain, and continental Europe. All former strongholds of evangelicalism, they are now in decline because of the absence of revival.

11

Revival in the Twentieth Century – Part I

The Welsh Revival of 1905

Wales is a country that is part of the United Kingdom on the island of Great Britain. It borders England to the east, the Irish Sea to the north and west, and the Bristol Channel to the South. Wales has been called the "land of Revivals." No less than sixteen remarkable revivals occurred in Wales between 1762 and 1862.[1]

In spite of its great history of revivals throughout the land, the church in Wales was in decline during the last decade of the nineteen century. According to revival historian Dr. J. Edwin Orr, the church suffered from a "loss of power in the pulpits and a worldly spirit in the pews." Church attendance was low for Sunday services, prayer meetings, and general fellowship among the members. Bible reading and family worship were neglected by much of the church. These conditions greatly concerned many of the leaders of the Welsh churches, and most saw a great need for a spiritual revival through a special outpouring of the Holy Spirit.[2]

F. B. Meyer was a friend of D. L. Moody and one of several of Moody's American and British preaching associates such as Reuben A. Torrey, J. Wilbur Chapman, and Henry Varley during Moody's ministry in the latter part of the nineteenth century.[3] Meyer had become the spokesman for the "Keswick" movement in 1887, succeeding Andrew Murray, the leader of the South African revival of 1860. In 1875, the small resort town of Keswick in which the meetings were held became known as the Keswick Convention for the Deepening of the Spiritual life. The movement gained a worldwide influence and was supported in America by men such as Moody and R. A. Torrey, but its ecumenical nature was not generally well received in America due to the schisms between the holiness and liberal wings of the Protestant church.[4]

Meyer had taught many young Welsh ministers who eventually sought a Keswick-style convention in Wales. The convention was held at the beautiful Welsh spa located at Llandrindod Wells where the ministers prayed much for an awakening in Wales. A second convention was held in August 1904 at which Meyer and Dr. A. T. Pierson ministered. A number of these ministers began conducting meetings in support of the message of deepening the spiritual life of the church. Although Seth

Joshua participated in these meetings, he was not an advocate of the Keswick teachings but appreciated the Keswick efforts to promote holiness. He considered the Keswick approach as one of many. Fearing the Keswick's prevailing emphasis on spiritual qualifications would dampen the spiritual side, Joshua began praying that God would send revival to Wales through the efforts of a lowly young man from the mines or perhaps the fields. Not only would God grant Joshua's prayer, this young man would be called from one of Joshua's own meetings.[5]

But the seeds of the Welsh revival were planted months before Seth Joshua's yet unknown young miner or ploughman arrived on the scene. It was at the chapel at New Quay, Cardiganshire, in February 1904 that marked the lowly beginnings of the Welsh revival which along with other revivals would have a worldwide impact during the remainder of first decade of the twentieth century and thereafter. Rev. Joseph Jenkins was appointed to the New Quay pulpit in 1892. Over the years of his pastorate, Jenkins became greatly burdened by the spiritual indifference among Christians generally and especially among the young people of his church. He began preaching to the young people about the necessity of obeying the Holy Spirit. In the late winter of early 1904 at a young people's prayer meeting Rev. Jenkins asked for testimonies of their spiritual experience. The testimonies tended to drift to other topics, but the minister persisted in seeking to keep the young people focused on their spiritual experiences. Florrie Evans, a timid young girl, rose to speak. With a tremor in her voice, she said, "I love Jesus Christ, with all my heart." The gathered young people were greatly moved and blessed by her sincere declaration. News of the Holy Spirit's power and blessings that had begun with Flossie Evans' eight words spoken at a New Quay young people's prayer meeting soon spread throughout the area and opened the door for revival.[6]

Evan Roberts

By September 1904, the move of the Holy Spirit in New Quay had been sustained for six months. When Seth Joshua arrived he found a wonderful revival spirit prevailing. His meetings lasted far into the night, and on Sunday, September 18th, Joshua said he had "never seen the power of the Holy Spirit so powerfully manifested among the people as at this place just now." After a week of unparalleled services, he traveled to Newcastle Emlyn to conduct meetings. Several ministry students from the Academy attended and were stirred by the services. Two of the students were Sidney Evans and Evan Roberts, roommates who had arrived at the Academy that same month. The two traveled with other students the next night to Seth Joshua's meeting at Blaenannerch. On Thursday morning Joshua closed the meeting with a prayer in which he cried out in Welsh, "Lord...bend us." Evan Roberts went to the front, kneeled at the altar, and cried out in agony, "Lord...bend me." A wave of peace passed over his soul which was followed by a concern for others. Joshua took note of the young man, but other leaders were disturbed by the young man's intensity. They were concerned that such free expression would lead to a spiritual uproar as opposed to a quiet, Keswick-style meeting.[7]

Evan Roberts was twenty-six at the time of his life-altering encounter with God. He was the product of a devout home centered on Bible reading, family worship, and Sunday school at the Moriah Church in Loughor which was associated with the Welsh Calvinistic Methodist denomination. Roberts was obsessed with revival from his early youth. After his father was injured in the mines, the young Roberts went to work in the mines before he reached his twelfth birthday. After twelve years in the mines he became a blacksmith for a short while, but in 1903 he committed himself to the ministry, took denominational examinations, and entered the Newcastle Emlyn Academy in September 1904.[8]

Immediately following his experience at the altar, Roberts knew that an extraordinary work of God was about to occur in his life. He began praying for his associates that would comprise his first ministry team, withdrew his savings for their support, and shared his vision with Sidney Evans, his college roommate and future brother-in-law.[9]

> I have a vision of all Wales being lifted up to heaven. We are going to see the mightiest revival that Wales has ever known—and the Holy Spirit is coming soon, so we must get ready. We must have a little band and go all over the country preaching.[10]

Roberts immediately asked Evans, "Do you believe that God can give us a hundred thousand souls now?" Before launching out with his team, Roberts returned home on October 31st to convince his family and the members of his home church in Loughor of his mission. He asked the ministers at the Moriah Church and its daughter church in Gorseinon if he would be allowed to speak. With permission, Roberts conducted a youth meeting on the evening of October 31st, 1904. Seventeen people were in attendance. Roberts shared his vision with the people and encouraged them to declare their Christian faith. Overcoming their initial reserve or shyness, all would give testimony of their faith that evening including three of Roberts' sisters.[11]

Over the next twelve days, Roberts continued to hold nightly meetings alternating between the Pisgah Chapel near the Roberts' home, the Libanus Church in Gorseinon, and at Moriah, the mother church in Loughor. On November 13th he was driven to Sunday services in Swansea where the results were disappointing as there was open criticism of the girl singers that accompanied Roberts' ministry. But on Monday the 14th Roberts spoke at the Ebenezer Chapel in Aberdare which was crowded by a thousand people eager to hear the young preacher. The next day at the early morning prayer meeting, Roberts made a prophetic announcement that a great awakening was soon to occur in Wales.[12] It had been less than forty-five days since the unknown ministry student had knelt at an altar and cried out to God, "Lord...bend me!"

And so it was that the young ex-miner would become God's chief instrument in initiating a great awakening in Wales and which would spread to many other parts of the world. Roberts began to receive invitations to speak from churches throughout Wales. Within six weeks, one hundred thousand Welsh men, women, and children came into the Kingdom of God (out of a population of one million at the time). Within eight months, one hundred fifty thousand had applied for church membership. Dr. Orr estimated that as many as a quarter of a million people could have been converted during the revival. Unfortunately, many Christians and churches in Wales rejected the message of revival and as a result many villages and towns were entirely bypassed as the outpouring of the Holy Spirit flowed across the land.[13]

The magnitude of the conversions had a profound effect on almost all daily life in Wales. A brief account of the remarkable transformation of the spiritual climate in Wales is found in Mathew Backholer's *Revival Fires and Awakenings*.

> The daily shifts at the coal mines soon started with a word of prayer...Mineshafts resonated with the hymns of the converted...pit ponies which were used to being commanded by the unconverted foul mouths refused to work as they could not recognize the sanctified tongues!...magistrates were given white gloves (a symbol of purity) as there were so few cases to hear— God's spirit brought conviction of sin, brought about changed lives, sobriety and restraint. Aberdare on

Christmas Eve was almost entirely free from drunkenness and on Christmas Day there were no prisoners at all in the cells...Whole football and rugby teams were converted and praying became more important than playing! Games were either cancelled or put off until a more convenient time, whilst other teams disbanded. Theatre attendance dropped, dance halls were deserted and pubs (drinking establishments) were emptied and closed; the proprietors were furious! Talented actors and actresses failed to draw the crowds...[14]

The magnitude of the worldwide impact of the news of the Welsh awakening in 1905 is almost incomprehensible. The following list of revivals that were birthed almost simultaneously with the Welsh revival is not meant to be exhaustive: New Zealand, Scotland, North Africa, South Africa, Algeria, South Seas, India (six different revivals across the large nation), North America (including the Azusa Street Revival of 1906-1909), Mexico City, Sweden, France, Denmark, Germany, Hungary, Bulgaria, China (Shanghai and Canton - 1906), and Korea (1907-1910).[15] Some of the revivals were sporadic such as in France while others blanketed entire nations such as North America and India.

Revival stirrings in America at the beginning of the twentieth century

Between 1900 and 1904, there were reports by the press of scattered revivals in many areas of America. However, these were generally considered to be local evangelistic meetings and were not comparable to the spontaneous outpouring of the Holy Spirit such as occurred in 1858. As early as 1900, an increasing number of conversions were occurring as a result of various Methodist evangelistic campaigns conducted throughout the United States. There was a growing optimism and expectancy that a twentieth century awakening would occur. The Baptists both in the north and south were united in prayer for revival. Although the Presbyterians were "theoretically" opposed to revival in favor of steady growth of their churches, that attitude changed in 1901. The Presbyterian Church (U.S.A.) under the leadership of J. Wilbur Chapman organized an Evangelistic Commission which fielded fifty-six evangelists in 1902 and twelve hundred pastors united in prayer in 1903.[16]

At the turn of the century, the central and western valleys of Pennsylvania had become home to many thousands of immigrants from Wales. The majority of the immigrants had become members of Welsh-speaking or bi-lingual churches. It was only natural that many of the immigrants were in frequent contact with family and friends that were left behind in Wales. One of those was Rev. J. D. Roberts whose heart had been touched by the first-hand accounts of revival received by him and many other Welsh Pennsylvanians. As a result of the various reports, a sudden awakening arose in Rev. Roberts' Wilkes-Barre church in which 123 converts were reported in one month. The revival spread to churches in many other towns and districts in Pennsylvania including New Castle and Pittsburgh.[17]

In 1905, news of the revival in Wales spread through all religious journals and newspapers of various denominations. Even the Anglo-Catholic Episcopalians in the United States had friendly opinions of the Welsh Revival brought about "by the strong breath of God's Holy Spirit." The Baptists, Lutherans, Presbyterians, and Methodists were all talking about the revival in Wales and praying for revival in America. Revival prayer meetings were held by the thousands throughout the nation.[18] By the end of 1905, the revival had spread throughout the United States—from the Atlantic to the Pacific, and from the Canadian border to the Mexican border and all points in between. Churches in Canada were similarly affected from coast to coast.[19]

But the Revival of 1905 in America was more than a revival of the church but an awakening of the larger culture to the faith and principles of the Christian life. One report from Portland, Oregon, described the deep incursions of "religious enthusiasm" (revival) not only into the church and hearts of individual Christians but into the very fabric of the everyday life of the culture.

> ...for three hours a day, business was practically suspended, and from the crowds in the great department stores to the humblest clerk, from bank presidents to bootblacks, all abandoned money making for soul saving.[20]

Such was the spirit of cooperation in the revival that two hundred major stores agreed in writing to close between 11 a.m. and 2 p.m. to allow customers and employees to attend prayer meetings. Similar actions were taken by Seattle merchants.[21]

Characteristics of the worldwide awakenings and revivals of 1900-1910

The awakenings and revivals of 1900-1910 spread across the globe and was the most evangelical of all of its predecessors. In his comprehensive *The Flaming Tongue – The Impact of Twentieth Century Revivals*, Orr wrote of the origins and characteristics of the worldwide awakening that occurred in the first decade of the twentieth century.

> The early twentieth century Evangelical Awakening was a worldwide movement. It did not begin with the phenomenal Welsh Revival of 1904-1905. Rather its sources were in the springs of little prayer meetings which seemed to arise spontaneously all over the world, combining into the streams of expectation which became a river of blessing in which the Welsh Revival became the greatest cataract.

> The first manifestations of phenomenal revival occurred simultaneously among Boer prisoners of war in places ten thousand miles apart, as far away as Bermuda and Ceylon. The work was marked by extraordinary praying, by faithful preaching, conviction of sin, confession and repentance with lasting conversions and hundreds of enlistments for missionary service.[22]

The awakenings of 1900-1910 were widely interdenominational and included many instances of various congregations sharing in the revival including Anglican, Baptist, Brethren, Congregational, Disciple, Lutheran, Methodist, Presbyterian, and Reformed churches, but there was no evidence of revival involvement among Roman Catholic and the Greek Orthodox churches.[23]

There existed similarities between the Revivals of 1857-1858 and 1900-1910: their beginnings were found in prayer meetings, repentance occurred first within the church followed by an awakening of those outside the faith, there was evidence of great conviction of sin, and public confession of sin was common in both revivals. The 1900-1910 revival exhibited many similarities with the evangelical revivals recorded in the Acts of the Apostles: awakenings began in prayer meetings; reports of a mighty rushing wind; many outpourings of the Holy Spirit; infilling of believers with the Holy Spirit; some glossolalic utterances (unknown tongue); prophesying of young men and women; reports of unusual dreams and visions; the hearts of many hearers were pierced upon hearing the message of Christ preached; under great conviction of sin, many cried out for help which was followed by repentance; fellowship and prayer were often spontaneous and guided by the Spirit; a great sense of the presence of God in meetings; and very little hostility or opposition from those outside the revival movement.[24]

Impact of the worldwide awakening of the early twentieth century

The nineteenth century was a period of massive evangelical renewal and advance in which the light of the Gospel of Christ spread across the globe.[25] The best method of gauging the impact of a revival of Christianity was to determine the number of people "revived" for Christianity and the extent to which a culture is awakened. A review of the history of the Christian church and revivals of Christianity through the centuries inevitably brings one to the conclusion that each successive evangelical awakening was more thoroughly New Testament in its emphasis and outworking than the preceding awakening. As evidence, one may point to the chain of revivals and awakenings in which each successively was more evangelical (i.e., a true reflection of New Testament Christianity): John Wycliffe's Lollards of the thirteenth century, the Reformers of the sixteenth century, the Puritans of the seventeenth century, the Revivalists of the eighteenth century, the Revivalists of the nineteenth and early twentieth centuries, and the Pentecostals of the twentieth century. Applying the same criteria to the number of people influenced and the worldwide extent of the revivals, the awakening of 1900-1910 far exceeded the Revival of 1857-1858.[26]

Recall that in an earlier chapter it was noted that the Revival of 1857-1858 caused the nation and individual men and women, in both the North and South, to be spiritually prepared for the coming Civil War (1861-1865) in which the nation would exorcize the demon of slavery and recover its national unity. In much the same manner but on a far larger scale, the unprecedented worldwide awakening of the church and spread of Christianity that occurred in the first decade of the twentieth century prepared most of mankind for the cataclysmic global conflict that would engulf much of the world with the advent of World War I (1914-1918). The Revival of 1857-1858 was a harvest before the devastation of the American nation in the Civil War. The awakenings of 1900-1910 were a harvest before the devastation of Christendom during and after World War I.[27]

The worldwide outpouring of the Holy Spirit was for the revival of the church and awakening of nations. However, the awakenings also served to build spiritual reservoirs of strength, mercy, grace, and truth to be drawn on in times of extreme wickedness, devastation, and chaos during and after World War I. May we not compare the times of revival and great spiritual blessing of the church before the War and its aftermath with Joseph's Egyptian grain bins filled to capacity during the seven good years which sustained Joseph's brethren and the Egyptians during the lean years of drought and desolation?

12

Revival in the Twentieth Century – Part II

Frank Bartleman

As noted in the previous chapter, there were reports in the press of scattered revivals in many areas of America between 1900 and 1904 that preceded the worldwide revival of 1905. To gain a broad perspective and penetrating insight into the events and outworking of the American edition of the 1905 revival and the 1906 Pentecostal revival, we can look to the life and work of a young minister who became both a participant in and historian of the great American awakening during the first decade of the twentieth century. Born in rural Pennsylvania in 1871, Frank Bartleman became a journalist and traveling evangelist for forty-three years to the time of his death in 1936. His participation in both the American Awakening of 1905 and the Pentecostal movement's embryonic stirrings in 1906 coupled with his extensive, first-hand accounts give the modern reader an unparalleled view of those momentous times in church history.

Bartleman grew up on his family's farm but left at age seventeen. He was converted in the Grace Baptist Church of Philadelphia in 1893. Within a year he felt a call to full-time ministry and was soon ordained by the Temple Baptist Church. He ended his association with the Baptists in 1897 and chose "a humble walk of poverty and suffering" which characterized his wondering lifestyle for the remainder of his life. In 1900, he married Anna Ladd who at that time was the head of a Pittsburgh home for wayward girls. Following a brief pastorate of a Wesleyan Methodist church, he left for the more emotional and expressive Holiness movement. His departure from the Wesleyans eventually led to his departure from Pennsylvania. In 1904, Bartleman, his wife, and the first of their four children arrived in California where he became the appointed director of the Peniel Mission located in Sacramento, one of several Holiness rescue missions located in California. In December 1904, the family moved to Los Angeles where his daughter died in January 1905.[1]

It was only a week after the death of his daughter that the grief-stricken father plunged himself into ministry as he began preaching twice each day at the Peniel Mission in Pasadena. His labors bore considerable fruit as several young men experienced substantial spiritual growth, some of whom were called into full-time service for the Lord. In April, Bartleman was greatly inspired by F. B. Meyer, the great English evangelist, who while visiting California gave a first-hand account of the great revival in Wales. Recall from the previous chapter that Meyer, a close friend of D. L. Moody, was greatly used by God to minister to many young Welsh ministers through the Keswick movement to deepen spiritual life. Meyer was instrumental in bringing revival to the British Isles in 1905. As a result of Meyer's influence, Bartleman was inspired to write and distribute thousands of tracts in and around Los Angeles. He prayed incessantly for revival.[2]

A great revival broke out around the first part of May at the Lake Avenue Methodist Episcopal Church in Pasadena. Young men from the Penial Mission attended this church and began praying for a revival in Pasadena and then for Los Angeles and the whole of southern California. In June Bartleman attended the First Baptist Church which was pastored by Joseph Smale who had just returned from visiting Evan Roberts in Wales. The church was seeking the same visitation of the Holy Spirit as had been experienced in Wales. Bartleman continued writing articles, preaching, visiting various churches in the Los Angeles area, and praying with "soul travail" for revival throughout the remainder of 1905. He began corresponding with Evan Roberts and asked him to pray for a revival of the church in California.[3]

Praying for a Pentecost

Bartleman was unaware that a new tributary of the 1905 revival was about to surge forth in early 1906.

> We had been for some time led to pray for a Pentecost. It seemed almost beginning. Of course we did not realize what a real Pentecost was. But the Spirit did, and led us to ask correctly. One afternoon, after a service in the New Testament Church, several of us seemed providentially led to join hands and agree in prayer to ask the Lord to pour out His Spirit speedily, with *"signs following"* (Mark 16:20)...We did not have "tongues" in mind. I think none of us had ever heard of such a thing. This was in February 1906...
>
> On March 26, I went to a cottage meeting on Bonnie Brae Street (in Los Angeles). Both white and black

believers were meeting there for prayer. I had attended another cottage meeting shortly before this, where I first met a Brother Seymour. He had just come from Texas. He was a black man, blind in one eye, very plain, spiritual, and humble. He attended the meetings at Bonnie Brae Street.[4]

Another account states that William Seymour actually lived at the cottage on North Bonnie Brae Street and was invited to also hold meetings there. At one of the meetings it was reported that a man was healed instantly after being anointed with oil. Following a second prayer, the man began to speak in tongues, but Seymour did not speak in tongues until April.[5]

On Sunday morning, April 15th, Bartleman went to Burbank Hall, the New Testament Church, where a black woman had spoken in tongues. When he learned that the Spirit had also fallen almost a week earlier on April 9th at the small cottage at Bonnie Brae Street, Bartleman went there that afternoon and found that the working of the Holy Spirit was still being manifested. The small group had been seeking for some time for an out pouring of the Holy Spirit. Many had been praying for months for a Pentecostal outpouring. Bartleman recognized that this little group that met outside of any established mission was the place where God "could have his way." The Pentecostal pioneers at Bonnie Brae Street "had broken through for the multitude to follow."[6]

On that same Sunday (April 15) when Bartleman attended the church at Burbank Hall and learned of the outpouring of the Holy Spirit at the Bonnie Brae Street cottage, he felt a great burden to begin ten days of special prayer. On Wednesday three days later, the great San Francisco earthquake (April 18) occurred and devastated the city and surrounding region. The following day Los Angeles was struck by a small earthquake. When the earthquake struck the Los Angeles area, Bartleman was attending a noon meeting at Peniel Hall, 227 Main Street. He went home and then was impressed to go to a meeting that evening at 312 Azusa Street to which the Bonnie Brae group had moved since the previous Sunday because of the increasing size of the crowds. After the message, two of those in attendance spoke in tongues, and many great blessings followed.[7] But it would be Friday, June 15th, before the Holy Spirit would "drop the 'heavenly chorus' into my soul. I found myself suddenly joining the rest who had received this supernatural gift."[8]

Bartleman wrote that the April 18th and 19th earthquakes had opened many hearts to spiritual concerns, but most of those occupying the pulpits throughout the land were vigorously attempting to dispel the fears of the people by denying the earthquakes in San Francisco and Los Angeles were a judgement of God on a wicked people. But Bartleman believed the Holy Spirit was striving to reach the hearts of the people by convicting them of their sin. By the following Wednesday Bartleman had received a message from God regarding the earthquakes in Los Angeles, had written it, had it printed, and began distributing thousands of tracts in Los Angeles. By May 11, Bartleman had finished his "Earthquake" tract distribution. In only three weeks, Bartleman had published and distributed with the help of others seventy-five thousand tracts in Los Angeles and other southern California cities. When describing the consequences of his tract distribution efforts, Bartleman wrote that, "All hell was stirred."[9]

The revival at Azusa Street lasted about three years before the power was lifted in 1909. Bartleman wrote that by then those attending had come under bondage for there was a "spirit of dictatorship." Every part of the meeting was planned and programed which did not allow for the Holy Spirit to move and work in freedom. Bartleman returned to Los Angeles from an overseas trip in late February 1911 and found that William H. Durham, a former Baptist minister from Chicago, had begun to hold meetings at the Azusa Street Mission (now called the Apostolic Faith Mission) in the absence of William Seymour. Under Durham's preaching revival had broken out once again with as many as five hundred being turned away on one Sunday. But the trustees of the church quickly summoned Seymour back from the East Coast where he had been preaching. On May 2, 1911, Seymour and his trustees padlocked the doors of the Apostolic Faith Mission to keep Durham out because they didn't like his message. But they also "locked God and the saints out from the old cradle of power."[10]

The Pentecostal movement

The Topeka Bible School in north-central Kansas was under the leadership of Charles Parham. On December 31, 1900, at 7:00 p.m., just five hours before the beginning of the twentieth century, Agnus Osman asked Parham to lay his hands on her so that she might receive the baptism of the Holy Spirit. Parham did as she requested, and "a glory fell upon her, a halo seemed to surround her head and face." As the eighteen-year-old Agnus received the baptism she began speaking in tongues. Revival historian Mathew Backholer wrote of Ozman's experience.

"This was the beginning of the first fruits of the Holy Spirit being poured out en masse at the very dawn of the twentieth century."[11]

Prior to 1900, instances of glossolalia (speaking in an unknown tongue) had been reported in Tennessee which was followed by some fanaticism. After the occurrences at Topeka, the manifestations spread to other cities such as Houston, Texas. But the real explosion of Pentecostalism began with those who ministered at and participated in the Azusa Street revival. Soon the Pentecostal revival spread to Norway, Denmark, Sweden, Finland, and the British Isles.[12]

Only a minority reached in the American revival of 1905 would become Pentecostals.[13] Dr. Orr estimated that in 1906 there were approximately ten thousand to fifteen thousand people considered to be Pentecostal, and twenty years later that number had increased ten-fold. By 1950, it was estimated that all Pentecostal denominations included more than a million adherents in the United States. The Assemblies of God established in 1914 was by far the largest of these. The Foursquare Gospel Church was another Pentecostal denomination of note and grew out of Aimee Semple McPherson's Los Angeles ministry.[14]

In describing the early Pentecostal movement in his book *The Flaming Tongue*, Dr. Orr wrote,

> There was worldwide opposition to the new manifestations and the most violent attacks came from some of the most evangelical leaders and teachers among Protestants. In "Pentecost," no John Wesley had risen to guide by wisdom or recommend by acknowledged scholarship. There were extremes and extravagances that the later Pentecostal leaders deplored...As opposition increased, Pentecostals began to withdraw membership from other denominations and form Pentecostal congregations...As early as 1907, missionaries were proceeding to far off mission fields from American Pentecostal Assemblies...[15]

The worldwide Awakening of the early 1900s and the Pentecostal revival that sprang from it were both similar and different in many respects. Of course the principal difference was that the widespread awakening of 1905, although charismatic in many ways, was not glossolalic. Early Pentecostalism also differed from the general awakening in that it stressed the spiritual gifts of tongues and healing. However, both movements rose from the common people, both were unmistakably interdenominational movements, both relied on the unplanned and sovereign ministry of the Holy Spirit, both were generally demonstrative in their worship and preaching, and both suffered from occasions of fabricated emotionalism and exploitation of feelings to achieve "religious" experiences when a genuine move of the Holy Spirit was not present.[16]

In defense of the early Pentecostal movement, it can be said that its failings in many respects were similar to the failings of the first century church which also sought to find its way without an historical pattern. Similarly, early twentieth century Pentecostals had to find their way given that the Pentecostal distinctives had generally not been operational within the body of Christ for almost two thousand years.

It was in the remainder of the twentieth century that the Pentecostal movement would span the globe and claim eight hundred million adherents by 2012.[17] By the middle of the century the Pentecostal movement had eclipsed the Awakening of 1905 to such an extent that modern historians and the church itself appear to be unaware of the magnitude and reach of the general awakening that occurred in the first decade of the twentieth century.[18]

Other American revivals in the twentieth century

There have been many revivals in America during the remainder of the twentieth century following the awakening of 1905 and the Pentecostal revival that sprang from it in 1906. However, most of these revivals occurred in the local church or community. But even local revivals have largely disappeared from the American evangelical landscape since the 1970s and 1980s as a result of the rise of the monolithic Church Growth movement which does not preach the message of Holy Spirit led revival.

In the twentieth century, district-wide and regional revivals were very rare, and it can be safely said that there has not been any true national revival or a general awakening in America since the first decade of the twentieth century. However, there have been some local revivals that have received national and even international notoriety but cannot be classified as having been truly national in character even though efforts to transplant these revivals to other parts of the country have met with very limited success. Realistically, the awakenings of the first decade of the twentieth century can be said to be the last chapter in the history of widespread American revivals and awakenings with one minor exception known as the Jesus Movement of the late 1960s and early 1970s.

The Jesus Movement contained some rudimentary but incomplete elements of revival. It started among the hippies, druggies, bikers, and others in the late 60s and early 70s who found their drug-saturated, free-love lifestyle to be empty and unfulfilling. These West Coast counter-culturalists were drawn to Jesus' teachings of love and peace. The movement was somewhat Pentecostal in its nature due to the emphasis on healing, signs, and miracles. Their new-found Christian faith included certain aspects of their old lifestyle such as communal living and modern music. A byproduct of the Jesus Movement was the development of Calvary Chapel and Vineyard churches, but the Jesus Movement as a separate recognizable entity largely died out in the 1980s.[19]

A unique occurrence in the twentieth century was the rise of several errant revivals that stand in fundamental opposition to the biblical nature and character of revivals from the first century through the worldwide awakening of the first decade of the twentieth century. These revivals, some of which are examined in Book I, have been deemed counterfeit when measured against biblical standards and the historical record of other evangelical revivals and awakenings in America.

It must be remembered that there are always those in every revival that come under the influence of self or demonic forces who knowingly or unknowingly attempt to inject the false or counterfeit into a revival. The influence of the counterfeit in revivals grew considerably in the last half of the twentieth century as the church entered the great end-time apostasy prophesied in the Bible. Apostate leaders, those who are merely deceived, and even those who lack a measure of discernment have made it possible for Satan to place false teachers and/or demonic leaders in positions of power and influence in the church to initiate, promote, and conduct counterfeit revivals that are unparalleled in church history.

The general decline of American revivals in the twentieth century

The general decline of American revivals in the twentieth century has occurred in both quantity and quality. There has been a dramatic decline in the number of local revivals coupled with a significant decline in the sustainability of the results of revival in churches and the lives of individuals. The quality of revival has been marred by increasing numbers and magnitude of counterfeit revivals based on false teachings and aberrant manifestations purported to be the work of the Holy Spirit.

265

The church has failed to distinguish between true revival and the counterfeit. True revival is measured by its impact on the individual, the church, and the community. Is Christ the center of revival? Is sin exposed and conviction present? Are believers revived? What is the depth of the spiritual renewal in the individual heart and church body? Is there a general spiritual and moral uplift of the individual, church, community, and beyond?

By contrast, counterfeit revivals are leader-centered; identified with bazaar manifestations that are not consistent with the history of authentic, biblically sound revivals and awakenings; are not Christ-centered; have brought widespread reproach upon the church; have little positive impact on the community; and substantially ignore sin, conviction, repentance, and living a holy lifestyle.

There are several elements that have greatly contributed to the decline of revivals in the twentieth century and include:

- The Protestant split between the liberals and fundamentalists during the early twentieth century
- Two world wars and the Great Depression over the brief span of thirty years
- The cultural suicide of Western civilization as it embraced and became dominated by humanism and its anti-God worldview that invaded the culture, the state, and much of the church
- The substitution of mass evangelism for revival, the essential prerequisite for evangelism
- The late twentieth century domination of the evangelical church by the Church Growth movement, its philosophies, and seeker-sensitive methods of doing church which stand in opposition to the message of revival

These and other causes are discussed in the chapter on hindrances to revival in Book I.

For those contrite and lowly Christians who yearn for and seek revival of the church, it is difficult to close this section about the history of revivals on such a low note. However, we must remember the words of John, "Truly, truly, I say to you, that you will weep and lament, but the world will rejoice; you will grieve, but your grief will be turned into joy." [John 16:20. KJV] We must also remember that it is when the hour is the darkest and the situation the bleakest that Christians must pray with "soul travail" for revival. Heartfelt prayer has been the precursor for

266

every revival in the history of the church, and it is no different for us today.

I close by repeating the words of comfort from Isaiah that I gave in the first chapter of Book I, "I live in a high and holy place, but also with him who is contrite and lowly in spirit, to *revive* the spirit of the lowly and to *revive* the heart of the contrite." [Isaiah 57:15. NIV] [emphasis added]

NOTES

Book I – Chapter 1 - The Only Hope for the Church and America

[1] Martyn Lloyd-Jones, *Revival*, (Wheaton, Illinois: Crossway Books, 1987), pp. iv-v.

[2] Ibid., p. 13.

[3] Rev. Pierre Bynum, Family Research Council Prayer Team, April 19, 2017. http://www.frc.org/prayerteam/prayer-targets-rev-ro-roberts-the-solemn-assembly-national-day-of-prayer-may-4-2017 (accessed April 20, 2017).

[4] Lloyd-Jones, *Revival*, p. vi.

[5] A. W. Tozer. *The Waning Authority of Christ in the Churches*, (Nyack, New York: Christian and Missionary Alliance, 1963), pp. 4-5.

[6] Richard M. Weaver, *Visions of Order – The Cultural Crisis of Our Time*, (Wilmington, Delaware: Intercollegiate Studies Institute, 1964), p. 3.

[7] Aleksandr Solzhenitsyn, "Men have forgotten God" – The Templeton Address, May 1983, *The Voice Crying in the Wilderness*, July 5, 2011. http://orthodoxnet.com/blog/2011/07/men-have-forgotten-god-alexander-solzhenitsyn/ (accessed October 13, 2017).

[8] Francis A. Schaeffer, *The Great Evangelical Disaster*, (Arcadia, California: Focus on the Family, 1984), p. 37.

[9] Robert H. Bork, *Slouching Towards Gomorrah*, (New York: Regan Books, 1996), pp. 280-281.

[10] Os Guinness, *Prophetic Untimeliness-A Challenge to the Idol of Relevance*, (Grand Rapids, Michigan: Baker Books, 2003), p. 12.

[11] Kevin Swanson, *Apostate – The Men who Destroyed the Christian West*, (Parker, Colorado: Generations with Vision, 2013), pp. 13, 19.

[12] Bynum, Family Research Council Prayer Team, April 19, 2017.

[13] Ibid.

Book I – Chapter 2 – The General Nature and Purpose of Revivals and Awakenings

[1] Edwin Orr, *The Light of the Nations – Evangelical Renewal and Advance in the Nineteenth Century*, (Eugene, Oregon: Wipf & Stock Publishers, 1965), p. 265.

[2] Donald C. Stamps, Commentary on Romans 8:10-11, *Fire Bible: Global Study Edition*, New International Version, ed. Donald C. Stamps, (Springfield, Missouri: Life Publishers International, 2009), p. 2109.

[3] Stamps, "Baptism in the Holy Spirit," *Fire Bible: Global Study Edition*, p. 1988.

[4] Orr, *The Light of the Nations – Evangelical Renewal and Advance in the Nineteenth Century*, p. 265.

[5] Ibid.

[6] A. W. Tozer, *The Root of the Righteous*, (Camp Hill, Pennsylvania:

WingSpread Publishers, 1955, 1986), p. 39.

[7] R. C. Sproul, "What does it mean to fear God?" *Ligonier Ministries*, January 12, 2018.

[8] Lloyd-Jones, *Revival*, p. 119.

[9] Ibid., p. 122.

[10] Ibid., pp. 126-127.

[11] Ibid., p. 128.

[12] Mathew Backholer, *Revival Fires and Awakenings-Thirty Six Visitations of the Holy Spirit*, (ByFaith Media, 2009, 2012), p. 19.

[13] Stamps, "The Spirit in the Old Testament," *Fire Bible: Global Study Edition*, pp. 1540-1541.

[14] Backholer, *Revival Fires and Awakenings*, pp. 20-24.

[15] Lloyd-Jones, *Revival*, p. 24.

[16] Backholer, *Revival First and Awakenings*, p. 7.

Book I – Chapter 3 – What is True Revival?

[1] Noah Webster, "revival," Noah Webster, *American Dictionary of the English Language 1828*, Facsimile Edition, (San Francisco, California: Foundation for American Christian Education, 1967, 1995 by Rosalie J. Slater).

[2] Jim Cymbala, *Storm-Hearing Jesus for the Times We Live In*, (Grand Rapids, Michigan: Zondervan, 2014), pp. 26-28, 79.

[3] Backholer, *Revival Fires and Awakenings,* p. 15.

[4] Lloyd-Jones, *Revival*, p. 213.

[5] Ibid., p. 306.

[6] Backholer, *Revival Fires and Awakenings*, p. 11.

[7] Lloyd-Jones, *Revival*, p. 149.

[8] J. Edwin Orr, "Revival and Prayer." http://www.jedwinorr.com/resources/articles/prayandrevival.pdf (accessed April 11, 2017)

[9] Andrew Strom, *True & False Revival*, (www.revivalschool.com: Revival School, 2008), p. 45.

[10] Ibid., p. 46.

[11] Backholer, *Revival Fires and Awakenings*, pp. 126, 148-149.

[12] Charles G. Finney, "What a Revival of Religion Is," *Lectures on Revivals of Religion*, Lecture I, 1835, *TeachingAmericanHistory.org*. http://teachingamericanhistory.org/library/document/what-a-revival-of-religion-is/ (accessed January 13, 2018).

[13] Charles E. Hambrick-Stowe, *Charles G. Finney and the Spirit of American Evangelicalism*, (Grand Rapids, Michigan: William B. Eerdmans Publishing Company, 1996), pp. 36-37.

[14] Orr, *The Light of the Nations,* p. 60.

[15] Backholer, *Revival Fires and Awakenings*, p. 17.

[16] Ibid.

Book I – Chapter 4 – The General Course of Events in Revival

[1] Lloyd-Jones, *Revival,* p. 306.

[2] Ibid., p. 199.

[3] Ibid., p. 204.

[4] Ibid., pp. 204-205.

[5] Ibid., pp. 206-207.

[6] Ibid., pp. 207-208.

[7] Eric Metaxas with Christine M. Anderson, *Study Guide - Bonhoeffer, The Life and Writings of Dietrich Bonhoeffer*, (Nashville, Tennessee: Thomas Nelson, 2014), p. 59.

[8] Lloyd-Jones, Revival, pp. 208-209.

[9] Ibid., p. 209.

[10] Ibid., p. 210.

[11] Backholer, *Revival Fires and Awakenings*, p. 171.

[12] Ibid.

[13] Ibid.

Book I – Chapter 5 – Vibrancy and Compelling Nature of Holy Spirit Led Revival

[1] Lloyd-Jones, *Revival*, pp. 161, 163.

[2] Frank Bartleman, *Azusa Street*, (New Kensington, Pennsylvania: Whitaker House, 1982), p. 8.

[3] Lloyd-Jones, *Revival*, pp. 165-167.

[4] Ibid., p. 169.

[5] Ibid.

[6] Ibid., p. 171.

[7] Ibid., p. 175.

[8] Ibid., pp. 177-178.

[9] Ibid., pp. 180-182.

[10] Ibid., pp. 182-183.

[11] Stamps, "The Glory of God," *The Fire Bible*, Global Study Edition, New International Version, p. 1406.

[12] David Wilkerson, "The effects of Seeing The Glory of God!" *World Challenge Pulpit Series*, June 21,1999, (Lindale, Texas: World Challenge, Inc., 1999). http://www.tscpulpitseries.org/english/1990s/ts990621.html (accessed April 17, 2018).

Book I – Chapter 6 – Characteristics of Revivals and Awakenings

[1] Backholer, *Revival Fires and Awakenings*, pp. 9, 13.

[2] Ibid., p. 171.

[3] Lloyd-Jones, *Revival*, pp. 105-106.

[4] Ibid., p. 107.

[5] Backholer, *Revival Fires and Awakenings*, p. 227.

[6] Ibid.

[7] Ibid., p. 234.

[8] Udo W. Middelmann, *The Market Driven Church*, (Wheaton, Illinois: Crossway Books, 2004), p. 15

[9] Thomas S. Kidd, *The Great Awakening-The Roots of Evangelical Christianity in colonial America*, (New Haven, Connecticut: Yale University Press, 2007), p. 13.

[10] Thomas A. Schafer, "Jonathan Edwards-American Theologian," *Encyclopedia Britannica*, https://www.britannica.com/biography/Jonathan-Edwards (accessed May 45, 2018).

[11] Kidd, *The Great Awakening*, pp. 25-27.

[12] J. Edwin Orr, *The Flaming Tongue-The Impact of 20th Century Revivals*, (Chicago, Illinois: Moody Press, 1973), pp. 4-6, 8-13, 28.

[13] Ibid., pp. 2-3.

[14] Lloyd-Jones, *Revival*, pp. 108-109.

[15] Orr, *The Flaming Tongue*, p. 97.

[16] Ibid.

[17] Lloyd-Jones, Revival, pp. 107-108.

[18] Backholer, *Revival Fires and Awakenings*, pp. 126-127.

[19] Ibid., pp.127-128.

[20] Ibid., pp. 128-129, 131.

Book I – Chapter 7 – Physical Phenomena that Accompany Revival

[1] Orr, *The Light of the Nations*, p. 265.

[2] Kidd, *The Great Awakening*, pp. 19-20.

[3] Ibid., p. 20.

[4] Backholer, *Revival Fires and Awakenings,* 34-35.

[5] John Pollock, *George Whitefield – The Evangelist*, (Fearn, Ross-shire, Great Britain: Christian Focus, 1973), pp. 153-154.

[6] Strom, *True & False Revival*, p. 47.

[7] Ibid.

[8] Ibid.

[9] Statement of the General Presbytery, "End-Time Revival – Spirit-Led and Spirit-Controlled," General Council of the Assemblies of God, August 11, 2000. https://ag.org/Beliefs/Topics-Index/Revival-Endtime-Revival--Spirit-Led-and-Spirit-Controlled (accessed June 19, 2018).

[10] Orr, *The Flaming Tongue*, p. ix

[11] Paul Johnson, *A History of the American People*, (New York: HarperCollins Publishers, 1997), p. 839.

[12] Ross Douthat, *Bad Religion – How We Became a Nation of Heretics*, (New York: Free Press, 2012), p. 32.

[13] Johnson, *A History of the American People*, p. 839.

[14] Orr, *The Flaming Tongue*, p. ix.

[15] Lloyd-Jones, *Revival*, pp. 108-109.

[16] Backholer, *Revival Fires and Awakenings*, p. 227.

Book I – Chapter 8 – Manifestations – The Distinguishing Marks of a Work of the Spirit of God

[1] Jonathan Edwards, "Introduction," *The Distinguishing Marks of a Work of the Spirit of God*, 1741. The Revival Library. http://revival-library.org/index.php/catalogues-menu/revival-miscellanies/theology-dynamics/the-distinguishing-marks-of-a-work-of-the-spirit-of-god (accessed June 21, 2018).

[2] Ibid.

[3] Edwards, "Section 2. "What are distinguishing scripture evidences of a work of the Spirit of God," *The Distinguishing Marks of a Work of the Spirit of God.*

[4] Ibid.

[5] Ibid.

[6] Ibid.

[7] Ibid.

[8] Ibid.

[9] Ibid.

[10] Ibid.

[11] Ibid.

[12] Ibid.

[13] Ibid.

[14] Edwards, "Section 1. Negative Signs; or, What are no signs by which we are to judge of a work - and especially, What are no evidences that a work is not from the Spirit of God," *The Distinguishing Marks of a Work of the Spirit of God.*

[15] Ibid.

[16] Ibid.

[17] Ibid.

[18] Ibid.

[19] Ibid.

[20] Ibid.

[21] Ibid.

[22] Ibid.

[23] Ibid.

[24] Ibid.

[25] Ibid.

[26] Ibid.

[27] Ibid.

[28] Ibid.

[29] Ibid.

[30] Ibid.

[31] Ibid.

[32] Ibid.

[33] Ibid.

[34] Ibid.

[35] Edwards, "Section 3. Practical inferences and application," *The Distinguishing Marks of a Work of the Spirit of God.*

Book I – Chapter 9 – Hindrances to True Revival

[1] Larry G. Johnson, *Evangelical Winter – Restoring New Testament Christianity*, (Owasso, Oklahoma: Anvil House Publishers, 2016).

[2] Stamps, Commentary – Revelation 1:1-4, *The Fire Bible*, Global Study Edition, p. 2513.

[3] Matthew Henry, *Commentary on the Whole Bible*, (Grand Rapids, Michigan: Zondervan Publishing House, 1961), pp. 1970-1974.

[4] Johnson, *Evangelical Winter – Restoring New Testament Christianity*, p. 273.

[5] Erwin W. Lutzer, *When a Nation Forgets God*, (Chicago, Illinois: Moody Publishers, 2010), pp. 117-118.

[6] Os Guinness, *Prophetic Untimeliness-A Challenge to the Idol of Relevance,"* (Grand Rapids, Michigan: Baker Books, 2003), p. 98.

[7] Peter F. Jensen, "A Vision for Preachers," *Doing Theology for the People of God*, (Eds., Donald Lewis and Alister McGrath, (Downers Grove, Illinois: InterVarsity Press, 1996), p. 219.

[8] E. M. Bounds, *The Necessity of Prayer*, from *The Complete Works of E. M. Bounds on Prayer*, (Grand Rapids, Michigan: Baker Books, 1990), p. 78.

[9] Dr. Richard J. Krejcir, "Statistics on Why Churches Fail," *ChurchLeadership.org*. Institute of Church Leadership, 1994-2004, revised 2007. http://www.churchleadership.org/apps/articles/default.asp?articleid =42338&columnid=4545 (accessed July 25, 2018).

[10] Lloyd-Jones, *Revival*, pp. 31-32.

[11] Henry, *Commentary on the Whole Bible*, p. 1832.

[12] Lloyd-Jones, *Revival*, p. 35.

[13] Statement of the General Presbytery, "End-Time Revival – Spirit-Led and Spirit-Controlled," General Council of the Assemblies of God, August 11, 2000. https://ag.org/Beliefs/Topics-Index/Revival-Endtime-Revival-- Spirit-Led-and-Spirit-Controlled (accessed June 19, 2018).

[14] Strom, *True & False Revival*, P. 62.

[15] Statement of the General Presbytery, "End-Time Revival – Spirit-Led and Spirit-Controlled," General Council of the Assemblies of God, August 11, 2000.

[16] Ibid.

[17] Ibid.

[18] Strom, *True & False Revival*, pp. 61-63.

[19] Lloyd-Jones, *Revival*, p. 24.

[20] Christian Smith, "Introduction," *The Secular Revolution*, Ed. Christian Smith, (Berkeley, California: University of California Press, 2003), p. 54.

[21] Lloyd-Jones, *Revival*, pp. 25-26.

Book I – Chapter 10 – Test the Spirits in Revivals and Manifestations

[1] Strom, *True & False Revival*, pp. 75-76.

[2] Gary E. Gilley, "The Toronto Blessing and the Laughing Revival," rapidnet.com, adapted from an article by the same name in October 1999,

Think on These Things, Southern View Chapel, Springfield, IL. http://www.rapidnet.com/%7Ejbeard/bdm/Psychology/char/more/bless.htm (accessed July 24, 2017).

[3] Strom, *True and False Revival*, p. 63.

[4] David Dombrowski, *Signs & Wonders! Five Things You Should Consider*, (Eureka, Montana: Lighthouse Trails Publishing, 2016), p. 5.

[5] Ibid., pp. 6, 8.

[6] Ibid., p. 6.

[7] Strom, *True & False Revival*, p. 62.

[8] Ibid., p. 66-67.

[9] Thomas S. Kidd, *The Great Awakening – The Roots of Evangelical Christianity in Colonial America*, (New Haven, Connecticut: Yale University Press, 2007), pp. 138, 140, 154-155.

[10] Strom, *True & False Revival*, p. 66.

[11] Kidd, *The Great Awakening – The Roots of Evangelical Christianity in Colonial America*, p. 148.

[12] Ibid., p. 268.

[13] J. Edwin Orr, "Prayer brought Revival," *oChristian.com*. http://articles.ochristian.com/article8330.shtml (accessed December 28, 2017).

[14] Strom, *True & False Revival*, p. 67.

[15] Ellen Eslinger, "Cane Ridge Revival," *Encyclopedia of Religious Revivals in America*, Volume 1, A-Z, ed. Michael McClymond, (Westport, Connecticut: Greenwood Press, 2007), p. 89.

[16] Strom, *Ture & False Revival*, p. 67.

[17] Ibid., p. 68.

[18] Ibid.

[19] Orr, *The Light of the Nations*, pp. 4-5.

[20] Backholer, *Revival Fires and Awakenings*, pp. 75-76, 78.

[21] Strom, *True & False Revival*, p. 69.

Book I – Chapter 11 – False Prophets, False Revivals, and False Manifestations

[1] Stamps, Commentary – Matthew 24-11, *The Fire Bible*, Global Study Edition, p. 1741.

[2] Orr, *The Light of the Nations*, pp. 60-61, 99-100.

[3] "An Examination of Kingdom Theology" – Part I – Kingdom Theology Defined, *ApologeticsIndex*. http://www.apologeticsindex.org/l04.html (accessed July 24, 2018).

[4] Alexis de Tocqueville, *Democracy in America*, Trans. Gerald E. Bevan, (London, England: Penguin Books, 2003), pp. 343, 345.

[5] *Gary B. McGee and Darrin J. Rodgers*, "The Assemblies of God – Our Heritage in Perspective," Flower Pentecostal Heritage Center. https://ifphc.org/index.cfm?fuseaction=history.main (accessed March 9, 2018).

[6] "An Examination of Kingdom Theology" – Part I – The Latter Rain Movement, *ApologeticsIndex*. http://www.apologeticsindex.org/l05.html (accessed July 24, 2018).

[7] "An Examination of Kingdom Theology" – Part I – The Latter Rain Continues, *ApologeticsIndex*. http://www.apologeticsindex.org/l10.html (accessed July 24, 2018).

[8] Mary Danielsen, *The Perfect Storm of Apostasy – An Introduction to the Kansas City Prophets and Other Latter-Day Prognosticators*, (Eureka, Montana: Lighthouse Trails Publication, 2015), pp.3-5.

[9] Ibid., pp.5-8.

[10] Ibid., pp. 8-11.

[11] Ibid.,

[12] Ibid., pp. 8-11.

[13] Ibid., pp. 5-6.

[14] Kevin Reeves and Editors at Lighthouse Trails, *D is for Deception*, (Eureka, Montana: Lighthouse Trails Publication, 2016), p. 13.

[15] Danielsen, *The Perfect Storm of Apostasy*, pp. 5-7.

[16] Gilley, "The Toronto Blessing and the Laughing Revival," rapidnet.com.

[17] Ibid.

[18] Warren B. Smith, *False Revival Coming? – Part 1 – Holy Laughter or Strong Delusion?* (Eureka, Montana: Lighthouse Trails Publishing, 2015), pp. 9-10.

[19] Strom, *True & False Revival*, pp. 30-31.

[20] Ibid., p. 31.

[21] Ibid., p. 32.

[22] Ibid., p34.

[23] John Lanagan, *The New Age Propensities of Bethel Church's Bill Johnson*, (Eureka, Montana: Lighthouse Trails Publishing, 2014), p. 3.

[24] Ibid., p. 4.

[25] *Amazon.com*, Excerpt from website description of *The Physics of Heaven* by Judy Franklin and Ellyn Davis.

[26] Andrew Strom, "Second Warning – Bill Johnson and Bethel Church," *RevivalSchool.com*. http://www.revivalschool.com/second-warning-bill-johnson-and-bethel-church/ (accessed August 28, 2018).

[27] Lanagan, *The New Age Propensities of Bethel Church's Bill Johnson*, p. 9.

[28] Bill Randles, *Beware of Bethel – A brief Summary of Bill Johnson's Unbiblical Teachings*, (Eureka, Montana: Lighthouse Trails Publishing, 2016), pp. 5-6.

[29] Lanagan, *The New Age Propensities of Bethel Church's Bill Johnson*, p. 9.

[30] Randles, *Beware of Bethel*, p. 11-12.

[31] "What is grave sucking, grave soaking, mantle grabbing?" *God Questions*. https://www.gotquestions.org/grave-sucking.html

Book I – Chapter 12 – New Age Spirituality and Man's Fascination With the Mystical

[1] Stamps, Commentary – 2 Corinthians 11:34, *The Fire Bible*, Global Study Edition, pp. 2216-2217.

[2] Dr. David R. Reagan, "The Church in Prophecy – Past, Present and Future," *Lamplighter*, Vol. XXXIX, No. 3 (May-June 2018), 4-5.

[3] Larry G. Johnson, "Growing Apostasy in the Last Days – Part I," *culturewarrior.net*, May 23, 2016. https://www.culturewarrior.net/2016/05/13/growing-apostasy-of-the-last-days-part-i/ (accessed August 7, 2018).

[4] Stamps, Commentary – 2 Corinthians 11:34, *The Fire Bible*, Global Study Edition, pp. 2216-2217.

[5] Charles Colson and Nancy Pearcey, *How Now Shall We Live?* (Wheaton, Illinois: Tyndale House Publishers, Inc., 1999), p. 263.

[6] Kevin Reeves and the Editors of Lighthouse Trails, *D is for Deception*, (Eureka, Montana: Lighthouse Trails Publishing, 2016), p. 13.

[7] Ibid., pp. 4-19.

[8] *Is Your Church Doing Spiritual Reformation?* (Eureka, Montana: Lighthouse Trails Publishing, 2014), p. 3.

[9] Editors of Lighthouse Trails, *An Epidemic of Apostasy*, (Eureka, Montana: Lighthouse Trails Publishing, 2013), pp. 3-4, 11-14.

[10] Roger Oakland, *Faith Undone*, (Eureka, Montana: Lighthouse Trails Publishing, 2007), p. 91.

[11] Reeves, *D is for Deception*, p. 16.

[12] Ibid., pp. 6, 12, 13.

[13] Ibid. pp. 12, 13.

[14] Ibid., p. 8.

[15] Ibid., pp. 4, 5,6, 10, 16, 17.

[16] Ibid., pp. 6, 7.

[17] Ibid., pp. 11, 14.

[18] Ibid., p. 19.

[19] Ibid., pp. 9, 11.

[20] Ibid., pp. 10, 13.

Book I – Chapter 13 – The Emergent Church – Mystical Experiences Replace the Holy Spirit

[1] Carol V. R. George, *God's Salesman – Norman Vincent Peale and The Power of Positive Thinking*, (New York: Oxford University Press, 1993), pp. 56-57.

[2] "Works of Florence Scovel Shinn," *Internet Sacred Text Archive*. http://www.sacred-texts.com/nth/shinn/index.htm (accessed October 13, 2015).

[3] Douthat, *Bad Religion – How We Became a Nation of Heretics*, p. 184.

[4] Kenneth E. Hagin, *How To Write Your Own Ticket With God*, Kindle Cloud Reader, (Tulsa, Oklahoma: Rhema Bible Church aka Kenneth Hagin

Ministries, 1979).

[5] "The Believer and Positive Confession," The General Council of the Assemblies of God, August 19, 1980, p. 2. http://ag.org/top/Beliefs/ Position_Papers/pp_downloads/pp_4183_confession.pdf (accessed October 6, 2015).

[6] Robert H. Schuller, *My Journey*, (New York: HarperSanFrancisco, 2001), pp. 127-128.

[7] Marshall Davis, *More than a Purpose*, (Enumclaw, Washington: Pleasant Word, 2006), p. 155.

[8] Ray Yungen, *A Time of Departing*, 2nd Edition, (Eureka, Montana: Lighthouse Trails Publishing, 2002, 2006), p. 155.

[9] Ibid., pp. 155-156.

[10] Rick Warren, *The Purpose Driven Church*, (Grand Rapids, Michigan: Zondervan Publishing House, 1995), pp. 334, 348.

[11] Yungen, *A Time of Departing*, p. 145.

[12] Roger Oakland, *Emerging Church*, (Eureka, Montana: Lighthouse Trails Publishing, 2013), p. 3.

[13] Roger Oakland, *Faith Undone*, (Eureka, Montana: Lighthouse Trails Publishing, 2007), pp. 23, 28-30.

[14] Oakland, *Emerging Church*, pp. 10-11.

[15] Oakland, *Faith Undone*, p. 28.

[16] Ibid., p. 40.

[17] Yungen, *A Time of Departing*, p. 10.

[18] Oakland, *Faith Undone*, p. 45.

[19] Yungen, *A Time of Departing*, p. 144.

[20] Oakland, *Faith Undone*, p. 11.

[21] Ibid., p. 199.

Book I – Chapter 14 – The American Church – R.I.P. or Revival?

[1] A. W. Tozer, *Man – The Dwelling Place of God*, (Camp Hill, Pennsylvania: WingSpread Publishers, 1966, rev.1997), p. 152.

[2] Ibid., p. 155.

[3] Ibid., p. 152.

[4] Stamps, "The Last Days of History," *Fire Bible: Global Study Edition,* p. 2501.

[5] Stamps, Commentary, 2 Chronicles 7:14, *Fire Bible: Global Study Edition*, p. 723.

[6] Lloyd-Jones, *Revival*, p. 162.

[7] Ibid., p. 169.

[8] Ibid.

[9] Reagan, "The Church in Prophecy – Past, Present and Future," *Lamplighter*, Vol. XXXIX, 4.

[10] Larry G. Johnson, "Seduction of the American Church," *culturewarrior.net*, September 12, 2014. https://www.culturewarrior.net/2014/09/05/seduction -of-the-american-church/ (accessed August 25, 2018).

[11] Larry Osborne, *Thriving in Babylon – Why Hope, Humility, and Wisdom matter in a godless culture*," (Colorado Springs, Colorado: David C. Cook, 2015), pp. 150-151.

[12] Ibid., p.149.

[13] "humility," Noah Webster, *American Dictionary of the English Language 1828*, Facsimile Edition, (San Francisco, California: Foundation for American Christian Education, 1967, 1995 by Rosalie J. Slater).

[14] "humble, humility," *Webster's Seventh New Collegiate Dictionary*, (Springfield, Massachusetts: G. & C. Merriam Company, Publishers, 1963), pp. 404-405.

[15] Tozer, *The Root of the Righteous*, p. 60.

[16] "Prayer and Intercession Quotes, Tentmaker. https://www.tentmaker.org /Quotes/prayerquotes5.htm (accessed August 28, 2018).

[17] Stamps, Commentary, Revelation 3:17-18, *Fire Bible: Global Study Edition*, p. 2524.

[18] David Wilkerson, "The Dangers of the Gospel of Accommodation," *Assemblies of God Enrichment Journal*. http://enrichmentjournal.ag.org /199901/078_accommodation.cfm (accessed August 31, 2018).

Book II – Chapter 1 – Purifying the Reformation – England and America

[1] Larry G. Johnson, *Evangelical Winter – Restoring New Testament Christianity*, (Owasso, Oklahoma: Anvil House Publishers, 2016).

[2] Paul Johnson, *A History of Christianity*, (New York: HarperCollins Publishers, 1997) p. 288.

[3] B. K. Kuiper, *The Church in History*, (Grand Rapids, Michigan: Wm. B. Eerdmans Publishing Co., 1950, 1964, p. 157.

[4] Ibid., p. 244-245.

[5] Ibid., pp. 233-234.

[6] Ibid., pp. 244-245.

[7] J. M. Roberts, *The New History of the World*, (New York: Oxford University Press, 2003), pp. 579-580; "Henry VIII," *Encyclopedia Britannica*. http://www.britannica.com/biography/Henry-VIII-king-of-England (accessed August 10, 2015).

[8] Kuiper, *The Church in History*, pp. 223, 229.

[9] Ibid., pp. 253-257.

[10] Ibid., pp. 249-251.

[11] Johnson, *A History of the American People*, pp. 28-29.

[12] Evans, pp. 186-188.

[13] Kuiper, *The Church in History*, pp. 327-328.

[14] Sherwood Eddy, *The Kingdom of God and the American Dream*, (New York: Harper & Brothers Publishers, 1941), pp. 40-41.

[15] Ibid., pp. 48, 56.

[16] Kuiper, *The Church in History*, p. 328.

[17] Eddy, *The Kingdom of God and the American Dream*, p. 56.

Book II – Chapter 2 – The British Great Awakening

[1] Backholer, *Revival Fires and Awakenings*, pp. 29-30.
[2] Ibid., p. 30.
[3] John Pollock, *George Whitefield – The Evangelist*, (Fearn, Ross-shire, Great Britain: Christian Focus, 1973), pp.
   11-12.
[4] Ibid., pp. 15-16.
[5] Backholer, *Revival Fires and Awakenings*, pp. 30-31.
[6] Ibid., p. 31.
[7] Pollock, *George Whitefield – The Evangelist*, pp. 82, 85-86.
[8] Ibid., pp. 88-91.
[9] Ibid., p. 91.
[10] Ibid., pp. 91-92.
[11] Ibid.
[12] Ibid., p. 92.
[13] Ibid., pp. 93-98.
[14] Ibid., p. 99.
[15] Backholer, *Revival Fires and Awakenings*, pp.31-32.
[16] Ibid., pp. 29, 32.
[17] Ibid., p. 37.
[18] Ibid.
[19] Ibid., pp. 37-38.

Book II – Chapter 3 – Spiritual Conditions in America 1620-1720

[1] Sherwood Eddy, *The Kingdom of God and the American Dream*, (New York: Harper & Brothers Publishers, 1941), pp. 48-49, 74.
[2] Kidd, *The Great Awakening – The Roots of Evangelical Christianity in Colonial America*, p. xvi.
[3] Joseph Tracy, *The Great Awakening – A History of the Revival of Religion in the Time of Edwards and Whitefield*, Public Domain. Facsimile edition reproduced from original documents, pp. 1-2. Originally published in Boston, Massachusetts by Tappan and Dennet, 1842.
[4] Ibid. p. 2.
[5] Ibid., p. 3.
[6] Ibid.
[7] Ibid., p. 4.
[8] Ibid.
[9] Kidd, *The Great Awakening*, p. 3.
[10] Eddy, *The Kingdom of God and the American Dream*, p. 55.
[11] Tracey, *The Great Awakening*, pp. 4-5.
[12] Ibid., pp. 5-6.
[13] Ibid.
[14] Ibid., p. 6.
[15] Kidd, *The Great Awakening*, p. 1-3.

[16] Ibid., p. 4.

[17] Ibid., pp. 4-5.

[18] Nancy Pearcey, *Total Truth*, (Wheaton, Illinois: Crossway, 2004, 2005), pp. 253, 256-257.

[19] Kidd, *The Great Awakening*, p. xvi.

[20] Ibid., p. 39.

[21] Ibid., p. 25.

Book II – Chapter 4 – The Great Awakening in America – The Early Years

[1] Kidd, *The Great Awakening – The Roots of Evangelical Christianity in Colonial America*, pp. xix, 9-10.

[2] Ibid.

[3] Backholer, *Revival Fires and Awakenings*, p. 27.

[4] Ibid.

[5] Kidd, *The Great Awakening*, pp. 9-10.

[6] Ibid., pp. 31, 35.

[7] Ibid., pp. 32-33.

[8] Ibid., p. 37

[9] Ibid., pp. 59-60.

[10] Ibid., p. 31.

[11] Ibid., pp. 13-15.

[12] Ibid., pp. 7, 9, 10, 15.

[13] Ibid., p. 15.

[14] Ibid. p. 16.

[15] Ibid., pp. 16-17.

[16] Backholer, *Revival Fires and Awakenings*, p. 26.

[17] Tracy, *The Great Awakening – A History of the Revival of Religion in the Time of Edwards and Whitefield*, p. 12.

[18] Ibid.

[19] Kidd, *The Great Awakening*, pp. 19-20.

[20] Backholer, *Revival Fires and Awakenings*, p. 26.

[21] Kidd, The *Great Awakening*, p. 18.

[22] Ibid., pp. 21-23.

[23] Tracy, *The Great Awakening*, pp. 18-21.

[24] Ibid., pp. 21-22.

[25] Kidd, *The Great Awakening*, pp. 6-7.

[26] Ibid., p. 194.

Book II – Chapter 5 – The Great Awakening in America – The Later Years

[1] Kidd, *The Great Awakening – The Roots of Evangelical Christianity in Colonial America,* pp. 1-2.

[2] Ibid., p. 3.

[3] Ibid., p. 54.

[4] "'Old Lights' vs. 'New Lights' Debating the Great Awakening 1742-1743,"

National Humanities Center Resource Toolbox.
http://nationalhumanitiescenter.org/pds/becomingamer/ideas/text2/
clergymendebate.pdf (accessed December 13, 2017).

[5] Ibid.

[6] Kidd, *The Great Awakening*, p. 116.

[7] "An Assemblies of God Response to Reformed Theology," (Position Paper – Adopted by the General Presbytery in Session August 1 & 3, 2015), General Council of the Assemblies of God. https://ag.org/Beliefs/Topics-Index/Reformed-Theology-Response-of-the-AG-Position-Paper (accessed December 2, 2017).

[8] B. K. Kuiper, *The Church in History*, (Grand Rapids, Michigan: Wm. B. Eerdmans Publishing Co., 1951, 1964), p. 294.

[9] Pollock, *George Whitefield – The Evangelist*, pp. 173-175.

[10] Backholer, *Revival Fires and Awakenings*, pp. 33-34.

[11] Pollock, *George Whitefield – The Evangelist*, pp. 192-193.

[12] Tracy, *The Great Awakening – A History of the Revival of Religion in the Time of Edwards and Whitefield*, pp. 302-304, 307-309.

[13] Kidd, *The Great Awakening*, pp. 138-141.

[14] Ibid., pp. 138, 140, 154-155.

[15] Strom, *True & False Revival*, p. 66.

[16] Kidd, *The Great Awakening – The Roots of Evangelical Christianity in Colonial America*, p. 162.

[17] Ibid., p. 155.

[18] Ibid., p. 174.

[19] Ibid., p. 188.

[20] Ibid., p. 187.

[21] Ibid., p. 268.

[22] Ibid., pp. 319, 323.

[23] Johnson, *A History of the American People*, p. 116.

[24] Eddy, *The Kingdom of God and the American Dream*, p. 77.

[25] Ibid, p. 115.

[26] Johnson, *A History of the American People*, pp. 110, 116-117.

Book II – Chapter 6 – Spiritual Conditions in America 1760-1790

[1] Richard B. Morris, *Encyclopedia of American History*, (New York: Harper & Brothers Publishers, 1953), pp. 67-73.

[2] Ibid., pp. 85, 109.

[3] Kidd, *The Great Awakening – The Roots of Evangelical Christianity in Colonial America,* p. 313.

[4] Ibid., pp. 319-320.

[5] Gordon S. Wood, "Religion and the American Revolution," *New Directions in American Religious History*, ed. Harry S. Stout and D. G. Hart, (New York: Oxford University Press, 1997), pp. 174-175.

[6] Larry G. Johnson, *Ye shall be as gods: Humanism and Christianity – The Battle for Supremacy in the American Cultural Vision*, (Owasso, Oklahoma:

Anvil House Publishers, 2011), p. 131.

[7] Wood, "Religion and the American Revolution," *New Directions in American Religious History*, pp. 185-188.

[8] Orr, "Prayer brought Revival," *ochristian.com.*

[9] Ibid.

[10] Ibid.

[11] Backholer, *Revival Fires and Awakenings*, pp. 29, 32.

[12] Kidd, *The Great Awakening*, pp. 22, 44.

[13] Jonathan Edwards, "An Humble Attempt to Promote Prayer for Revival," Revival Library. http://www.revival-library.org/index.php/catalogues-menu/revival-miscellanies/revival-prayer/an-humble-attempt-to-promote-prayer-for-revival (accessed December 22, 2017).

[14] Michael A. G. Haykin, "John Sutcliffe and the Concert of Prayer," *Reformation & Revival*, Volume 1, Number 3, Summer, 1992, pp. 66, 68, 73-74, 82-83. https://biblicalstudies.org.uk/pdf/ref-rev/01-3/1-3_haykin.pdf (accessed December 22, 2017).

[15] Thomas J. Nettles, "Backus, Isaac (1724-1806)," *Encyclopedia of Religious Revivals in America* Volume 1, A-Z, ed. Michael McClymond, (Westport, Connecticut: Greenwood Press, 2007), p. 43.

[16] Kidd, *The Great Awakening*, p. 182.

[17] Nettles, *Encyclopedia of Religious Revivals in America* Volume 1, A-Z, p. 43.

[18] Kidd, The Great Awakening, pp. 184-186.

[19] Nettles, *Encyclopedia of Religious Revivals in America* Volume 1, A-Z, pp. 43-44.

[20] Ibid.

[21] Rick Ostrander, *Encyclopedia of Religious Revivals in America* Volume 1, A-Z, ed. Michael McClymond, (Westport, Connecticut: Greenwood Press, 2007), p. 334.

Book II – Chapter 7 – The Second Great Awakening in America – The Early Years – 1794-1812

[1] Orr, "Prayer brought Revival," *oChristian.com.*

[2] Orr, *The Light of the Nations*, p. 54.

[3] Wood, "Religion and the American Revolution," *New Directions in American Religious History*, , pp.185-188.

[4] Kidd, *The Great Awakening – The Roots of Evangelical Christianity in Colonial America*, pp.286-287.

[5] Ibid., pp. 312-313, 319.

[6] Ibid., p. 323.

[7] Orr, *The Light of the Nations*, pp. 15, 17, 20.

[8] Ibid., p. 17.

[9] Arthur Skevington Wood quoted by Orr, *The Light of the Nations*, p. 14.

[10] J. Edwin Orr, "Prayer brought Revival," *oChristian.com.*

[11] Orr, *The Light of the Nations*, pp. 21-22.

[12] Ibid., p. 22.

[13] Ibid.

[14] Ibid., pp. 23-24.

[15] Ibid., p. 24.

[16] Orr, "Prayer brought Revival," *oChristian.com.*

[17] Ellen Eslinger, "Cane Ridge Revival," *Encyclopedia of Religious Revivals in America*, Volume 1, A-Z, ed. Michael McClymond, (Westport, Connecticut: Greenwood Press, 2007), p. 89.

[18] Orr, "Prayer brought Revival," *oChristian.com.*

[19] Eslinger, "Cane Ridge Revival," *Encyclopedia of Religious Revivals in America*, p. 88.

[20] Ibid., pp. 88, 90.

[21] Orr, *The Light of the Nations*, pp. 25-27.

[22] Ibid., p. 18.

Book II – Chapter 8 – The Second Great Awakening in America – The Later Years – 1822-1842

[1] Orr, *The Light of the Nations*, pp. 40-42.

[2] Ibid., p. 54.

[3] Ibid., p. 56.

[4] Ibid., p. 58.

[5] Hambrick-Stowe, *Charles G. Finney and the Spirit of American Evangelicalism*, pp. 36-37.*Evangelicalism*, pp. 36-37.

[6] Ibid., p. 39.

[7] Orr, *The Light of the Nations*, p. 19.

[8] Hambrick-Stowe, *Charles G. Finney*, p. 38.

[9] Ibid., p. 47.

[10] Ibid., pp. 73-74.

[11] Ibid., pp. 100-103.

[12] Ibid., pp. 106, 110-111, 113.

[13] Orr, *The Light of the Nations*, p. 59.

[14] Hambrick-Stowe, *Charles G. Finney*, p. 113.

[15] Orr, *The Light of the Nations*, p. 54.

[16] Ibid., pp. 59-60.

[17] Charles G. Finney, "What a Revival of Religion Is," *Lectures on Revivals of Religion*, Lecture I, 1835, *TeachingAmericanHistory.org.* http://teachingamericanhistory.org/library/document/what-a-revival-of-religion-is/ (accessed January 13, 2018).

[18] Hambrick-Stowe, *Charles G. Finney*, pp. 220-221.

[19] Orr, *The Light of the Nations*, p. 60.

[20] Hambrick-Stowe, *Charles G. Finney*, p. 39.

[21] Orr, *The Light of the Nations*, pp. 60-61.

[22] Ibid., pp. 99-100.

[23] Ibid., p. 100.

[24] Larry Schweikart and Michael Allen, *A Patriot's History of the United*

States, (New York: Sentinel, 2004), p. 219.
[25] Hambrick-Stowe, *Charles G. Finney*, pp. 173-174.

Book II – Chapter 9 – The Third Great Awakening in America 1857-1858
[1] Gerald Procee, "Revivals in North America: The Hamilton, Ontario, Canada Revival of 1857," *ReformResource.net*. http://reformedresource.net /index.php/worldviews/the-hand-of-god-in-history/124-revivals-in-north-america-the-hamilton-ontario-canada-revival-of-1857.html (accessed January 16, 2018).
[2] Ibid.
[3] Ibid.
[4] Ibid.
[5] Backholer, *Revival Fires and Awakenings*, p. 61.
[6] Orr, *The Light of the*, pp. 102-103.
[7] Ibid., p. 103.
[8] Ibid., p. 100.
[9] Kathryn Teresa Long, "Revival of 1857-1858," *Encyclopedia of Religious Revivals in America*, Vol. 1, A- Z, ed. Michael McClymond, (Westport, Connecticut: Greenwood Press, 2007), p. 362.
[10] Orr, *The Light of the Nations*, p. 104.
[11] Backholer, *Revival Fires and Awakenings*, p. 62.
[12] Orr, *The Light of the nations*, pp. 107, 109.
[13] Backholer, *Revival Fires and Awakenings*, p. 63.
[14] Ibid., pp. 63-67.
[15] Darrell W. Stowell, "Civil War Revivals," *Encyclopedia of Religious Revivals in America*, Vol. 1, A-Z, ed. Michael McClymond, (Westport, Connecticut: Greenwood Press, 2007), pp. 117-118
[16] Eddy, *The Kingdom of God and the American Dream*, pp. 177, 179-180.
[17] Richard M. Weaver, *The Southern Essays of Richard M. Weaver*, Eds. George M. Curtis, III and James J. Thompson, Jr., (Indianapolis, Indiana: Liberty Fund, 1987), p. 216.
[18] Gardiner H. Shattuck, Jr., *A Shield and Hiding Place – The Religious Life of the Civil War Armies*, (Macon, Georgia: Mercer University Press, 1987), pp. 129-130.
[19] Schweikart and Allen, *A Patriot's History of the United States*, p. 497.
[20] Shattuck, *A Shield and hiding Place*, pp. 12, 125, 127-128, 130-131, 135-136.
[21] Stowell, "Civil War Revivals," *Encyclopedia of Religious Revivals in America*, pp. 120-121.
[22] Long, "Revival of 1857-1858," *Encyclopedia of Religious Revivals in America*, p. 365.
[23] Ibid., pp. 365-366.

Book II – Chapter 10 – America Embraces Babylon 1870-1930
[1] J. M. Roberts, *The New History of the World*, (New York: Oxford University

Press, 2003), pp. 708-709, 711-712.

[2] Schweikart and Allen, *A Patriot's History of the United States,* pp. 443-444. Orr, *The Faming Tongue,* p. xiv.

[3] J. Edwin Orr, *The Faming Tongue – The Impact of 20th Century Revivals,* (Chicago, Illinois: Moody Press, 1973), p. xiv.

[4] Johnson, *Evangelical Winter – Restoring New Testament Christianity,* p. 77.

[5] Eddy, *The Kingdom of God and the American Dream,* pp. 182-183.

[6] Schweikart and Allen, *A Patriot's History of the United States,* pp. 182-183.

[7] Christian Smith, "Introduction," *The Secular Revolution,* ed. Christian Smith, (Berkeley, California: The University of California Press, 2003), pp. 58, 67; Johnson, *Ye shall be as gods-Humanism and Christianity,* pp. 213-214.

[8] Kuiper, *The Church in History,* p. 389.

[9] Ibid.

[10] "Holiness Movement," *Encyclopedia Britannica.* https://www.britannica .com /event/Holiness-movement (accessed January 22, 2018).

[11] Orr, *The Light of the Nations,* pp. 190-191.

[12] Ibid., pp. 191-192.

[13] Ibid., pp. 192-195.

[14] Ibid., p. 194.

[15] Ibid., p. 191.

[16] Ibid., p. 193.

[17] Ibid., p. 194.

[18] Ibid., p. 194.

[19] Ibid., pp. 229-230.

[20] Ibid., p. 229.

[21] Ibid., pp. 275-276.

Book II – Chapter 11 – Revival in the Twentieth Century – Part I

[1] Backholer, *Revival Fires and Awakenings,* p. 74.

[2] Orr, *The Flaming Tongue,* p. 1.

[3] Orr, *The Light of the Nations,* p. 194.

[4] Ibid., pp. 204-207

[5] Orr, *The Flaming Tongue,* pp. 1-2.

[6] Ibid., pp. 2-3.

[7] Ibid., pp. 3-5.

[8] Ibid., pp. 4-5.

[9] Ibid., p. 6.

[10] Ibid.

[11] Ibid., p. 8.

[12] Ibid., pp. 8-11.

[13] Backholer, *Revival Fires and Awakenings,* pp. 75-76.

[14] Ibid., pp. 76-77.

[15] Ibid., p. 78.

[16] Orr, *The Flaming Tongue,* pp. 66-67.

[17] Ibid., p. 70.

[18] Ibid., p. 68-69.

[19] Ibid., p. 80.

[20] Ibid.

[21] Ibid.

[22] Ibid., p. 188.

[23] Ibid., pp. 195-196.

[24] Ibid., pp. 198-200.

[25] Orr, *The Light of the Nations*, p. 275.

[26] Orr, *The Flaming Tongue*, pp. 186-187.

[27] Ibid., p. 287.

Book II – Chapter 12 – Revival in the Twentieth Century – Part II

[1] Frank Bartleman, *Azusa Street*, (New Kensington, Pennsylvania: Whitaker House, 1982), pp. 169-170.

[2] Ibid., pp. 7-8.

[3] Ibid., pp. 12, 14-15.

[4] Ibid., pp. 37-38.

[5] Backholer, *Revival Fires and Awakenings*, p. 85.

[6] Bartleman, *Azusa Street*, p. 39.

[7] Ibid., pp. 44-46.

[8] Ibid., p. 53.

[9] Ibid., pp. 47-49.

[10] Ibid., pp. 117-118.

[11] Ibid., p. 84.

[12] Orr, *The Flaming Tongue*, pp. 179, 181-183.

[13] Ibid., p. 178.

[14] Ibid., p. 184.

[15] Ibid., p. 185.

[16] Ibid., p. 185.

[17] Backholer, *Revival Fires and Awakenings*, p. 83.

[18] Orr, *The Flaming Tongue*, p. 178.

[19] "Who were the Jesus freaks? What was the Jesus Movement?" *Compelling Truth.* https://www.compellingtruth.org/Jesus-freak.html (accessed March 10, 2018).

SELECTED BIBLIOGRAPHY

This bibliography is a substantial but not a complete record of all the works and sources I have consulted. It represents the substance and range of reading upon which I have formed my ideas presented in this book. I intend that these sources serve as a convenience for those who wish to pursue further research and study on the concepts and ideas presented.

Backholer, Mathew. *Revival Fires and Awakenings-Thirty Six Visitations of the Holy Spirit*. ByFaith Media, 2009, 2012.

Bartleman, Frank. *Azusa Street*. New Kensington, Pennsylvania: Whitaker House, 1982.

Bible. Scripture quotations marked CEB are taken from the Holy Bible, Common English Bible, CEB. Copyright © 2011 Common English Bible, Nashville, Tennessee.

Bible. Scripture quotations marked KJV are taken from the Holy Bible, King James Version.

Bible. Scripture quotations marked NIV are taken from the Holy Bible, New International Version, NIV. Copyright © 1973, 1978, 1984 Biblica, Inc. Used by permission of Zondervan. All rights reserved worldwide. www.zondervan.com.

Bork, Robert H. Bork. *Slouching Towards Gomorrah*. New York: Regan Books, 1996.

Bounds, E. M. *The Necessity of Prayer*, from *The Complete Works of E. M. Bounds on Prayer*. Grand Rapids, Michigan: Baker Books, 1990.

Colson, Charles, and Nancy Pearcey. *How Now Shall We Live?* Wheaton, Illinois: Tyndale House Publishers, Inc., 1999.

Cymbala, Jim. *Storm-Hearing Jesus for the Times We Live In*. Grand Rapids, Michigan: Zondervan, 2014.

Danielsen, Mary. *The Perfect Storm of Apostasy – An Introduction to the Kansas City Prophets and Other Latter-Day Prognosticators*. Eureka, Montana: Lighthouse Trails Publication, 2015.

Davis, Marshall. *More than a Purpose*. Enumclaw, Washington: Pleasant Word, 2006.

Dombrowski, David. *Signs & Wonders! Five Things You Should Consider.* Eureka, Montana: Lighthouse Trails Publishing, 2016.

Douthat, Ross. *Bad Religion – How We Became a Nation of Heretics.* New York: Free Press, 2012.

Eddy, Sherwood. *The Kingdom of God and the American Dream.* New York: Harper & Brothers Publishers, 1941.

Edwards, Jonathan. "An Humble Attempt to Promote Prayer for Revival." Revival Library. http://www.revival-library.org/index.php/catalogues-menu/revival-miscellanies/revival-prayer/an-humble-attempt-to-promote-prayer-for-revival (accessed December 22, 2017).

_____. *The Distinguishing Marks of a Work of the Spirit of God,* 1741. The Revival Library. http://revival-library.org/index.php/ catalogues-menu/revival-miscellanies/theology-dynamics/the-distinguishing-marks-of-a-work-of-the-spirit-of-god (accessed June 21, 2018).

Eslinger, Ellen. "Cane Ridge Revival." *Encyclopedia of Religious Revivals in America*, Volume 1, A-Z, ed. Michael McClymond. Westport, Connecticut: Greenwood Press, 2007.

Finney, Charles G. "What a Revival of Religion Is," *Lectures on Revivals of Religion. TeachingAmericanHistory.org.* http://teachingamericanhistory.org/library/document/what-a-revival-of-religion-is/ (accessed January 13, 2018).

George, Carol V. R. *God's Salesman – Norman Vincent Peale and The Power of Positive Thinking.* New York: Oxford University Press, 1993.

Gilley, Gary E. "The Toronto Blessing and the Laughing Revival." rapidnet.com, adapted from an article by the same name in October 1999, *Think on These Things*, Southern View Chapel, Springfield, IL. http://www.rapidnet.com/%7Ejbeard/bdm/Psychology/char/more/bless.htm (accessed July 24, 2017).

Guinness, Os. *Prophetic Untimeliness-A Challenge to the Idol of Relevance.* Grand Rapids, Michigan: Baker Books, 2003.

Hagin, Kenneth E, *How To Write Your Own Ticket With God.* Kindle Cloud Reader. Tulsa, Oklahoma: Rhema Bible Church aka Kenneth Hagin Ministries, 1979.

Hambrick-Stowe, Charles E. *Charles G. Finney and the Spirit of American Evangelicalism.* Grand Rapids, Michigan: William B. Eerdmans Publishing Company, 1996.

Haykin, Michael A. G. "John Sutcliffe and the Concert of Prayer." *Reformation & Revival*, Volume 1, Number 3, Summer, 1992. https://biblicalstudies.org.uk/pdf/ref-rev/01-3/1-3_haykin.pdf (accessed December 22, 2017).

Henry, Matthew. *Commentary on the Whole Bible* Grand Rapids, Michigan: Zondervan Publishing House, 1961.

Jensen, Peter F. "A Vision for Preachers." *Doing Theology for the People of God.* Eds., Donald Lewis and Alister McGrath. Downers Grove, Illinois: InterVarsity Press, 1996.

Johnson, Larry G. *Evangelical Winter – Restoring New Testament Christianity.* Owasso, Oklahoma: Anvil House Publishers, 2016.

_____. *Ye shall be as gods: Humanism and Christianity – The Battle for Supremacy in the American Cultural Vision.* Owasso, Oklahoma: Anvil House Publishers, 2011.

_____. "Growing Apostasy in the Last Days – Part I." *culturewarrior.net*, May 23, 2016. https://www.culturewarrior.net/2016/05/13/growing-apostasy-of-the-last-days-part-i/

_____. "Seduction of the American Church." *culturewarrior.net*, September 12, 2014. https://www.culturewarrior.net/2014/09/05/seduction-of-the-american-church/

Johnson, Paul. *A History of the American People.* New York: HarperCollins Publishers, 1997.

Kidd, Thomas S. *The Great Awakening-The Roots of Evangelical Christianity in colonial America.* New Haven, Connecticut: Yale University Press, 2007.

Krejcir, Dr. Richard J. "Statistics on Why Churches Fail." *ChurchLeadership.org.* Institute of Church Leadership, 1994-2004, revised 2007. http://www.churchleadership.org/apps/articles/default.asp?articleid=42338&columnid=4545 (accessed July 25, 2018).

Kuiper, B. K. *The Church in History.* Grand Rapids, Michigan: Wm. B. Eerdmans Publishing Co., 1950, 1964.

Lanagan, John. *The New Age Propensities of Bethel Church's Bill Johnson.* Eureka, Montana: Lighthouse Trails Publishing, 2014.

Lighthouse Trails, The Editors. *Is Your Church Doing Spiritual Reformation?* Eureka, Montana: Lighthouse Trails Publishing, 2014.

_____. *An Epidemic of Apostasy.* Eureka, Montana: Lighthouse Trails Publishing, 2013.

Lloyd-Jones, Martyn. *Revival.* Wheaton, Illinois: Crossway Books, 1987.

Long, Kathryn Teresa. "Revival of 1857-1858." *Encyclopedia of Religious Revivals in America*, Vol. 1, A- Z, ed. Michael McClymond. Westport, Connecticut: Greenwood Press, 2007.

Lutzer, Erwin W. *When a Nation Forgets God.* Chicago, Illinois: Moody Publishers, 2010.

McGee, Gary B. and Darrin J. Rodgers. "The Assemblies of God – Our Heritage in Perspective." Flower Pentecostal Heritage Center. https://ifphc.org/index.cfm?fuseaction=history.main (accessed March 9, 2018).

Metaxas, Eric, with Christine M. Anderson. *Study Guide - Bonhoeffer, The Life and Writings of Dietrich Bonhoeffer.* Nashville, Tennessee: Thomas Nelson, 2014.

Middelmann, Udo W. *The Market Driven Church.* Wheaton, Illinois: Crossway Books, 2004.

Nettles, Thomas J. "Backus, Isaac (1724-1806)." *Encyclopedia of Religious Revivals in America* Volume 1, A-Z, ed. Michael McClymond. Westport, Connecticut: Greenwood Press, 2007.

Oakland, Roger. *Emerging Church.* Eureka, Montana: Lighthouse Trails Publishing, 2013.

_____. *Faith Undone.* Eureka, Montana: Lighthouse Trails Publishing, 2007.

Orr, J. Edwin. *The Flaming Tongue – The Impact of 20th Century Revivals.* Chicago, Illinois: Moody Press, 1973.

_____. *The Light of the Nations – Evangelical Renewal and Advance in the Nineteenth Century.* Eugene, Oregon: Wipf & Stock Publishers, 1965.

_____. "Prayer brought Revival." *oChristian.com.* http://articles. ochristian.com/article8330.shtml (accessed December 28, 2017).

_____. "Revival and Prayer." http://www.jedwinorr.com/resources/ articles/prayandrevival.pdf (accessed April 11, 2017).

Osborne, Larry. *Thriving in Babylon – Why Hope, Humility, and Wisdom matter in a godless culture."* Colorado Springs, Colorado: David C. Cook, 2015.

Ostrander, Rick. *Encyclopedia of Religious Revivals in America* Volume 1, A-Z, ed. Michael McClymond. Westport, Connecticut: Greenwood Press, 2007.

Pearcey, Nancy. *Total Truth.* Wheaton, Illinois: Crossway, 2004, 2005.

Pollock, John. *George Whitefield – The Evangelist.* Fearn, Ross-shire, Great Britain: Christian Focus, 1973.

Procee, Gerald. "Revivals in North America: The Hamilton, Ontario, Canada Revival of 1857." *ReformResource.net.* http://reformedresource.net /index.php/worldviews/the-hand-of-god-in-history/124-revivals-in-north-america-the-hamilton-ontario-canada-revival-of-1857.html (accessed January 16, 2018).

Randles, Bill. *Beware of Bethel – A brief Summary of Bill Johnson's Unbiblical Teachings.* Eureka, Montana: Lighthouse Trails Publishing, 2016.

Reagan, Dr. David R. "The Church in Prophecy – Past, Present and Future." *Lamplighter*, Vol. XXXIX, No. 3 (May-June 2018).

Reeves, Kevin and Editors at Lighthouse Trails. *D is for Deception.* Eureka, Montana: Lighthouse Trails Publication, 2016.

Roberts, J. M. *The New History of the World.* New York: Oxford University Press, 2003.

Schafer, Thomas A. "Jonathan Edwards-American Theologian," *Encyclopedia Britannica.* https://www.britannica.com/biography/Jonathan-Edwards (accessed May 45, 2018).

Schaeffer, Francis A. *The Great Evangelical Disaster.* Arcadia, California: Focus on the Family, 1984.

Schuller, Robert H. *My Journey*. New York: HarperSanFrancisco, 2001.

Schweikart, Larry, and Michael Allen. *A Patriot's History of the United States*. New York: Sentinel, 2004.

Shinn, Florence Scovel. "Works of Florence Scovel Shinn." *Internet Sacred Text Archive*. http://www.sacred-texts.com/nth/shinn/index.htm (accessed October 13, 2015).

Shattuck, Jr., Gardiner H. *A Shield and Hiding Place – The Religious Life of the Civil War Armies*. Macon, Georgia: Mercer University Press, 1987.

Smith, Christian. *The Secular Revolution*, Ed. Christian Smith. Berkeley, California: University of California Press, 2003.

Smith, Warren B. *False Revival Coming? – Part 1 – Holy Laughter or Strong Delusion?* Eureka, Montana: Lighthouse Trails Publishing, 2015.

Solzhenitsyn, Aleksandr. "Men have forgotten God" – The Templeton Address, May 1983, *The Voice Crying in the Wilderness*, July 5, 2011. http://orthodoxnet.com/blog/2011/07/men-have-forgotten-god-alexander-solzhenitsyn/ (accessed October 13, 2017).

Sproul, R. C. "What does it mean to fear God?" *Ligonier Ministries*, January 12, 2018.

Stamps, Donald C. Commentary and Articles, *Fire Bible: Global Study Edition*, New International Version, Ed. Donald C. Stamps. Springfield, Missouri: Life Publishers International, 2009.

Stowell, Darrell W. "Civil War Revivals." *Encyclopedia of Religious Revivals in America*, Vol. 1, A-Z, ed. Michael McClymond. Westport, Connecticut: Greenwood Press, 2007.

Strom, Andrew. "Second Warning – Bill Johnson and Bethel Church." *RevivalSchool.com*. http://www.revivalschool.com/second-warning-bill-johnson-and-bethel-church/ (accessed August 28, 2018).

_____. *True & False Revival*. www.revivalschool.com: Revival School, 2008.

Swanson, Kevin. *Apostate – The Men who Destroyed the Christian West*. Parker, Colorado: Generations with Vision, 2013.

Tocqueville, Alexis de. *Democracy in America*, Trans. Gerald E. Bevan.

London, England: Penguin Books, 2003.

Tozer, A. W. *Man – The Dwelling Place of God*. Camp Hill, Pennsylvania: WingSpread Publishers, 1966, rev.1997.

_____. *The Root of the Righteous*. Camp Hill, Pennsylvania: WingSpread Publishers, 1955, 1986.

_____. *The Waning Authority of Christ in the Churches*. Nyack, New York: Christian and Missionary Alliance, 1963.

Tracy, Joseph. *The Great Awakening – A History of the Revival of Religion in the Time of Edwards and Whitefield*. Public Domain. Facsimile edition reproduced from original documents, pp. 1-2. Originally published in Boston, Massachusetts by Tappan and Dennet, 1842.

Warren, Rick. *The Purpose Driven Church*. Grand Rapids, Michigan: Zondervan Publishing House, 1995.

Weaver, Richard M. *The Southern Essays of Richard M. Weaver*. Eds. George M. Curtis, III and James J. Thompson, Jr. Indianapolis, Indiana: Liberty Fund, 1987.

_____. *Visions of Order – The Cultural Crisis of Our Time*. Wilmington, Delaware: Intercollegiate Studies Institute, 1964.

Webster, Noah. *American Dictionary of the English Language 1828*, Facsimile Edition. San Francisco, California: Foundation for American Christian Education, 1967, 1995 by Rosalie J. Slater.

Wilkerson, David. "The Dangers of the Gospel of Accommodation." *Assemblies of God Enrichment Journal*. http://enrichmentjournal.ag.org /199901/078_accommodation.cfm (accessed August 31, 2018).

_____. "The effects of Seeing The Glory of God!" *World Challenge Pulpit Series*, June 21,1999. Lindale, Texas: World Challenge, Inc., 1999. http://www.tscpulpitseries.org/english/1990s/ts990621.html (accessed April 17, 2018).

Wood, Gordon S. "Religion and the American Revolution." *New Directions in American Religious History*. Eds. Harry S. Stout and D. G. Hart. New York: Oxford University Press, 1997.

Yungen, Ray. *A Time of Departing*, 2nd Edition. Eureka, Montana: Lighthouse Trails Publishing, 2002, 2006.

Index

A

Arminianism, 226
altered state of consciousness, 135-136
Anderson, Leith, 149
Anglican, 169, 171, 198, 207, 215, 221, 223, 232, 255
Apostolic-Prophetic movement, 119
Assemblies of God, 119, 134, 245
Azusa Street, 46, 253, 261-263

B

Backholer, Mathew, ix,17-18,30-31,43, 69,173, 252
Backus, Isaac, 46, 205, 210-213
Baptist,75, 112, 116, 134, 170, 187, 201, 205-207, 209-211, 213-214, 216, 219-222,232, 253, -255, 259-262
Bartleman, Frank, 46, 259-262
Beecher, Lyman, 225
Bentley, Todd, 123-124
Bethel Church, 125
Bonhoeffer, Dietrich, 41
Bork, Robert H., 6
British Great Awakening, 173-176,179, 208-209
Buddhist, 134
Buford, Bob, 147-149
Businessmen's Revival (see Third Great Awakening)
Bynum, Rev. Pierre, 4

C

Cain, Paul, 120-121
Calvary Chapel, 121, 265
Calvin, John, 127, 181, 198
Calvinism, 167-168, 206, 214, 223,226
Cane Ridge revival, 112, 219-220, 225
Chauncy, Charles, 197
Christian & Missionary Alliance,
245
Church Growth movement, 59, 95, 142, 144, 146, 264, 266
Church of England, 169-171, 176, 178-179, 181, 207, 221

Church of God, Anderson, IN, 245
Church of God, Cleveland, TN, 245
Church of the Nazarene, 245
Civil War, 206, 208, 229, 232,235-237, 242-243
Clark, Randy, 122
Congregationalist, 170, 207, 211, 223, 226
contemplative prayer, 127, 133, 135-136, 139-140, 144-146
contemplative spirituality, 134-135, 138, 145
creative visualization, 135
Cymbala, 21, 27

D

Danforth, Jr., Samuel, 185
Danielsen, Mary, 120
Darwin, Charles, 242, 244
Davenport, James, 111-112, 199-200, 210
Deism, 173, 214-215, 217
devil (see: Satan)
Dewey, John, 242
Dominion theology, 119-120, 126, 138, 144, 154
Drucker, Peter, 147
Dwight, Timothy, 217

E

Eastern Orthodox Church, 7
ecumenism (ecumenicalism), 50, 99, 100, 137-140, 144, 148, 151
Eddy, Sherwood, viii, 172, 183, 202
Edwards, Jonathan, 30, 46, 60, 68, 79, 91, 111, 187, 189, 193, 195, 197, 209, 217, 219, 225
Edwards, Timothy, 189
emerging church, 139-140, 145-147, 149-151

Erskine, John, 209
Evangelicalism, vii-vii, 67, 71, 77, 98, 108, 140-141, 144, 152, 186, 192, 194-196, 200, 202, 206, 213-215, 222, 244
Evangelism, 30, 41, 54, 75-77, 219-220, 223, 227, 238, 246-247, 266
Evans, Flossie, 61, 250
Evans, Sidney, 250-251

F

Finney, Charles G., 30-31, 46, 58, 71, 77,127, 213, 223-229, 232, 245, 247
First Great Awakening, vii, 7, 46, 69, 79, 103, 111, 186, 220, 222, 225
Franklin, Judy, 125
Frelinghuysen, Theodorus, 187

G

Grant, Ulysses, 243
Guinness, Os, 6, 97

H

Hagin, Kenneth, 142-143, 146
Harris, Howell, 31, 209
heart religion, 186, 194, 215, 244
Henry VIII, 169
Hindu, 133, 150
baptism in the Holy Spirit, 12, 38-40, 142, 262
Howard-Brown, Rodney, 122
Hunt, Dave, 146
Hybels, Bill, 121, 139, 144, 146-147

I

Interspirituality, 137

J

Jampolsky, Gerald, 144
Jensen, Peter F., 98, 99
Jesus Movement, 265
Joel's Army, 120
John the apostle, 49, 79-80, 83, 140, 159

Johnson, Bill, 125
Johnson, Paul, 75, 170, 202, 203
Joshua, Seth, 60, 249-251
Joyner, Rick, 120-121

K

Kansas City Prophets, 120
Kidd, Thomas S., ix, 60, 111, 185, 188, 190, 196, 202
Kimball, Dan, 145
King James I, 171

L

Lamphier, Jeremiah, 46, 77, 232-233
Lanagan, John, 125-126
Langdell, Christopher, 242
Laodicea, 94
Laodicean, 47, 159-160, 162 -164
Latter Rain, 116-120, 138
Laughing revival, 107, 122
Lloyd-Jones, Martyn, ix, 3-4, 14-16, 23-24, 31, 42, 45, 48, 50, 103-104, 156-157
Long, Kathryn Teresa, 238
Luther, Martin, 47, 167-169, 207, 223-225
Lutheran, 167-168, 207, 223, 254-255

M

Manifest Sons of God, 119-120
Marx Karl, 242
McCready, James., 112, 218-219
McLaren, Brian, 150-151
McPherson, Amiee Semple, 263
Meditation, 127, 135, 137, 140, 144
Methodist. 112, 134, 174-176, 180, 198, 201, 206-207, 213-214, 218-222, 231-232, 244, 251, 253-255, 259-260
Meyer, F. B., 249, 260
Middelmann, Udo, 59
Miller, William, 16, 227, 228
Millerism (Millerites) 116, 118, 228
Mills, Samuel J., 217